Postwar Politics, Society and the Folk Revival in England, 1945–65

Postwar Politics, Society and the Folk Revival in England, 1945–65

Julia Mitchell

BLOOMSBURY ACADEMIC
LONDON • NEW YORK • OXFORD • NEW DELHI • SYDNEY

BLOOMSBURY ACADEMIC
Bloomsbury Publishing Plc
50 Bedford Square, London, WC1B 3DP, UK
1385 Broadway, New York, NY 10018, USA

BLOOMSBURY, BLOOMSBURY ACADEMIC and the Diana logo
are trademarks of Bloomsbury Publishing Plc

First published in Great Britain 2020

A catalogue record for this book is available from the British Library.

A catalog record for this book is available from the Library of Congress.

ISBN: HB: 978-1-3500-7121-6
        ePDF: 978-1-3500-7122-3
        eBook: 978-1-3500-7123-0

Typeset by Integra Software Services Pvt. Ltd.
Printed and bound in Great Britain

To find out more about our authors and books visit www.bloomsbury.com
and sign up for our newsletters.

For my parents, Ken and Jeanne

Contents

Preface   ix

Acknowledgements   xiii

Abbreviations   xv

Biographic Notes   xvii

'Folk Song without Folk': An Introduction to Folk Music Revivalism in
    Twentieth-Century England   1

    Introduction   1

    Historiography   3

    A grassroots movement   6

    Arts, crafts and socialism: Early folk music collection   7

    Defining folk music in a technological age   9

    Skiffle and jazz   13

    Conclusion   15

1   The Pub and the Beeb: Structural Foundations of the
    English Folk Revival   17

    Introduction   17

    The folk club   18

    The folk music press   24

    Record labels   30

    The BBC   32

    Folk festivals   39

    Conclusion   41

2   'Its Music Was Folk': Folk Revivalism and Socialist Politics   43

    Introduction   43

    A. L. Lloyd and the revival of industrial songs   44

    Art and socialism: Political culture and cultural politics   46

    Topical songwriting   52

    Conclusion   60

3   A Dialectic of Class and Region: Folk Music in an 'Affluent Society'   61

    Introduction   61

'Vicious allurements': The consumer economy,
    the teenager and the 'affluent worker'   62
Mining songs, the 'Pit Elegy' and the
    cultural response to nationalization   70
Conclusion   81

4   'Accent Speaks Louder than Words':
   Imagining Regional and National Community through Folk Music   83
   Introduction   83
   Creating a national folk canon: The legacy of early collection   84
   Regional identity and folk song in England   85
   Utopian communities in the Northeast   91
   Conclusion   95

5   Folk Music and Cultural Exchange: The 'Shiny Barbarism'
   of Americanization   97
   Introduction   97
   The Policy   105
   Conclusion   108

6   'With Bob on Our Side': Folk Music, the Culture Industry and
   Commercial Success   111
   Introduction   111
   Folk music and the culture industry   118
   Conclusion   128

Conclusions   129

Notes   135
Bibliography   163
Index   179

Preface

This book came out of the work I did for my PhD dissertation, 'Subterranean Bourgeois Blues: The Second English Folk Revival, *c.* 1945–1970'. The thesis and this book explore the folk revival phenomenon in England, through an examination of its place in the social and political history of the country after the Second World War. Although its roots stretched back to the early twentieth century, the postwar English folk revival significantly occurred in the context of the nation's deindustrialization, and exposed tensions between, on the one hand, a nostalgic lament for a fast-disappearing working-class life, and a 'forward-looking' socialist vision of working-class culture. It looks at the revival from the outside in, and contextualizes the movement in the social and political story of postwar England, while also placing it within a dynamic transnational framework, a complex cross-Atlantic cultural exchange with its more well-known American contemporary. In so doing, it contributes to the existing historiographies of folk revivalism in England, as well as the social and political historiographical discourses of the postwar period: the continued salience of class in English society; the transformation of the nation's economic infrastructures; the social and political influence of the welfare state – the folk revival tapped into all of these overlapping strands, and helped to magnify them. My hope is that this book will be a welcome addition to the historiographies of both postwar England and the folk revival, that it will be appealing, entertaining and most of all informative to students of postwar England and Britain, academics in the field and fans of folk music.

As one might expect, the process of researching and writing about such a rich and complex subject was not without its difficulties. This project started out as a comparison of two concurrent folk revivals in Britain and the United States after the Second World War. What it became is both more, and less, than that. Many, many difficult choices needed to be made. This is not a straight comparison of two postwar folk movements (for that, see Rachel Clare Donaldson and Ronald D. Cohen's *Roots of the Revival: American and British Folk Music in the 1950s*), nor is it an in-depth study of the *British* folk revival; I will not be dealing, in detail, with the accompanying folk revivalist movements in Scotland, Northern Ireland or Wales, although these were significant in their own right. There simply was not enough space in this project to do them justice.

In general, I have taken pains to focus on English singers and groups, without altogether ignoring pertinent examples or anecdotes involving Scottish, Northern Irish or Welsh singers. Throughout this book – especially in chapters 3 and 4, dealing with class and regional identities, respectively – the Northeast of England will be featured as a significant region both culturally and politically. Although folk music experienced a significant popular revival in all parts of the country, the North – and specifically the Northeast – held a special place in the hearts and minds of folk collectors and contemporary revivalists after the war, as a place where a particularly strong and previously under-appreciated musical tradition had been 'uncovered' – part of the postwar revival's attempt to rehabilitate the folk songs and culture of industrial workers. The focus on Northeast culture is as important to this study as it was to postwar folk revivalists; the exploration of the region's central importance to the political culture of the postwar period in England and the expression of that importance through folk music are what set this book apart.

This project makes use of a wide range of primary source material, including sound and video recordings, photographs, newspaper articles, bulletins and newsletters, printed ephemera (festival posters, folk club newsletters, songbooks), interviews and oral histories. My methodological approach has focused largely on an analysis of song material – taken from commercial recordings, radio programmes, unissued recordings from record companies and archived collections compiled by twentieth-century folklorists like A. L. Lloyd in England and Alan Lomax in the United States. Although I was interested in looking at the songs themselves, I was also concerned with the ways in which songs were chosen, interpreted and discussed by folk revivalists. The sound collections at the British Library house a comprehensive archive of material relating to folk music in Britain, and on the folk music revival. The A. L. Lloyd Collection, for instance, includes recordings made by Lloyd for the BBC on topics such as 'childrens' songs', 'songs of the Durham miners', 'folk song and authority', 'industrial song' and 'folk song revival', as well as live recordings Lloyd made at various folk clubs throughout the country, both for projects in the making and often for public lectures he was giving.

The Topic Records Collection comprises material both released on the label and unreleased material by people like Lloyd and MacColl, Leon Rosselson and Stan Kelly, the Seegers (Pete and Peggy) as well as interview material with groups like the Ian Campbell Folk Group, and audio recordings of concerts and life performances, including a live recording of a 1963 anti-racism concert in Birmingham. The British Library sound archive is also home to hundreds of BBC radio programmes. For the purposes of this project, some of the most useful programmes included *The Song Carriers, Folk Song Cellar* (a music performance programme broadcast between 1966– 67), as well as the *Oral History of Recorded Sound* programme and the Millennium Memory Bank collection, featuring interviews with folk singers like John Tams, Barry Renshaw and Cliff Hall. The sound archive also provided important access to commercial recordings which would otherwise have been difficult to acquire, notably the Leader Sound LP *Jack Elliott of Birtley: The Songs and Stories of a Durham Miner* (1969), as well as recordings from the Topic Records Collection.

The BBC Written Archive in Reading contains all of the broadcaster's written correspondence – including receipts, transcripts, letters, contracts, media releases and policy statements – going back to its earliest days. Particularly useful were the documents relating to 'James H. Miller' (aka Ewan MacColl), Peggy Seeger, A. L. Lloyd and Alan Lomax, covering their professional relationships with the BBC between c.1945 and 1970. These documents also shed light on the programmes these figures helped to produce, especially *Radio Ballads, A Ballad Hunter Looks at Britain*, and *Ballads and Blues*. The minutiae of payment slips, copyright claims, audience satisfaction reports – all have helped to give this project structure and focus. Further afield, the archive at the University of Newcastle Special Collections, especially in material relating to Durham writer Sid Chaplin, was particularly useful on the importance of coal and the vibrancy of culture in the Northeast during the revival period. Chaplin's writings on the cultural identity and social transformation of the region during the postwar period were particularly illuminating.

The American Folklife Center at the Library of Congress houses a vast collection of primary source material relating to American and British folk music, and provided many important details relating to the transatlantic networking of folk revivalism after the war in the Alan Lomax Collection, as well as the James Madison Carpenter Collection – holding the largest archive of British folk music in America, some of which was also collected by Alan Lomax while in Britain during the 1950s. In addition, the Richard Reuss Folk Music Ephemera Collection yielded valuable print sources (posters, pamphlets, tickets, newspaper clippings) relating to the folk revivals in both the United States and the UK.

Many of the songs discussed in this project appeared in print in various magazines, established throughout the postwar period, which were devoted entirely to folk music and its popular revival. Publications such as *Melody Maker, Sing, Ethnic, Folk Review* and *Spin* (often taking their cue from American counterparts *Sing Out!* and *Broadside*) were important in disseminating the newest and best songs of the time, but also in disseminating the central, and often discordant, political and social ideologies driving the folk revival in England. The magazines were rife with debate, which often bordered on hectoring in tone, between revival participants. From these magazines and others, it has been possible not only to get a sense of what the leaders of the revival felt regarding the movement's direction, but also what fans valued – what 'sold', essentially, in both economic and ideological terms. Reception is an important part of any project aiming to come to terms with the social and political effects of a cultural movement – what were the sociological impacts of the folk revival? Who was driving the movement? How did it respond to popular tastes and help to shape them? In attempting to consider the wide range of social, cultural and political factors determining the direction and relevance of folk music after the Second World War, I will attempt to chart the reception of the folk revival amongst fans and critics, as well as the public, through niche publications such as *Sing* and *Ethnic*, as well as through national, regional and local newspapers.

Acknowledgements

I owe a great debt of gratitude to Jeanne Shami, Adam Smith and Axel Körner, all of whom have, at one stage or another, read this entire manuscript, and provided invaluable feedback and criticism. Thank you also to Renee Wilkinson and Ken Mitchell for reading and commenting on selected chapters. I am grateful to those at Bloomsbury Academic, including Dan Hutchins and Beatriz Lopez, as well as the anonymous reviewers who have provided thoughtful, critical and essential feedback on many aspects, at various stages, of the book. I also really want to thank all the amazing librarians and archivists who were – whether they knew it or not – part of this project, and especially Ike, Yeardly, Ian and Rachel in the British Library Sound Archive, who were knowledgeable and helpful, and who 'flipped' many, many, an un-digitized folk recording for the benefit of this book.

This book started life as a PhD thesis. I spent three years in London researching and writing much of what follows here, traveling to folk clubs throughout the country and generally enjoying being a student in the best university town in the world. I could not have completed this project without the help of my wonderful supervisors, Axel Körner and Adam Smith, both of whom were incredibly generous with their time, expertise, academic support and encouragement. They helped to shape the dissertation, and ultimately this book, into the best possible product of my work and it is largely to them that I owe its publication. I also owe a great debt of gratitude to my peers, colleagues and friends both in England and here in Canada, who have been so supportive – in innumerable and sometimes (probably) unconscious ways – throughout this process. They are too numerous to name here, but I hope they know how thankful I am for their friendship, patience and encouragement. Heartfelt thanks to my parents, to whom this book is dedicated; my partner, Joel, who gamely decided to cohabitate with me during the latter stages of the writing and editing process, and who is a constant source of love, strength and distraction; my dog, Elka, who doesn't know and doesn't care about this book, but who seems to like me anyway; and finally, my siblings and extended family who have, over a lifetime, offered a refreshing mix of genuine excitement/barely concealed *ennui* when told about this project and the many other academic adventures preceding it. Thanks for always being there for me in all the ways that count.

Abbreviations

AFN	American Forces Network
AFS	American Folklore Society
EFDSS	English Folk Dance and Song Society
FSS	Folk Song Society
HUAC	House Un-American Activities Committee
PAI	People's Artists, Inc.
PSI	People's Songs, Inc.
NCB	National Coal Board
NLR	*New Left Review*
NUM	National Union of Mineworkers
ULR	*Universities and Left Review*
WMA	Workers' Music Association

Biographic Notes

Joan Baez (b. 1941) was born in Staten Island, New York. She began her recording career in 1958, and rose to fame as an unbilled performer at the 1959 Newport Folk Festival, achieving immediate success. Her first three albums, *Joan Baez, Joan Baez, Vol. 2* and *Joan Baez in Concert* all achieved gold record status, an almost-unheard-of feat, especially for a female artist, at the time. In the early years of Baez's career, the civil rights movement in the United States became a prominent issue. Her performance of 'We Shall Overcome' at the 1963 March in Washington permanently linked her with the song, which she still sings at almost every concert. Highly visible in civil rights marches and events from an early stage, Baez also became increasingly vocal about her disagreement with the Vietnam War. A lifelong Quaker, she founded the Institute for the Study of Nonviolence and encouraged draft resistance at her concerts. Famously, Baez began performing Bob Dylan's material early in her career, replacing the traditional English and Scottish ballads that had made her famous.

Sydney Carter (1915–2004) was born in Camden, London. He attended Balliol College, Oxford, graduating with a degree in history in 1936. A conscientious objector to the Second World War, he joined the Friends' Ambulance Unit and served in Egypt, Palestine and Greece. Carter was one of the most prolific songwriters of the revival movement, and often contributed written pieces for folk periodicals such as Sing and the EFDSS's *Folk Music Journal*. Perhaps Carter's most well-known work was the lullaby 'Crow in the Cradle'.

Karl (Fred) Dallas (1931–2016) was born in Bradford, West Yorkshire, but grew up in Whitley Bay, Northumberland, although he attended secondary school in Tooting, South London. Named after both Karl Marx and Friedrich Engels, Dallas was enrolled in the Independent Labour Party on the day of his birth. He became actively involved in the English folk revival from the beginning, as a journalist, musician, author, record producer and political activist. His articles could be found in such wide-ranging publications as *Melody Maker*, The *Independent* and The *Times*. He also published his own music magazines, including *Folk Music, Folk News* and *Jazz Music News*.

Bob Dylan (b. 1941) was born Robert Allen Zimmerman in Duluth, Minnesota, but grew up in the small mining town of Hibbing, near the Canadian border. His career ambition, as stated in his high school yearbook, was to 'Join Little Richard'. Despite these early rock 'n' roll ambitions, Dylan became arguably the most famous 'protest singer' of the US revival. A number of his early songs, such as 'Blowin' in the Wind' and 'The Times They Are A-Changin', became anthems for the civil rights and anti-war movements. Dylan famously 'went electric' in 1965, and very publicly left his initial base in the culture of folk music behind; his revolutionary six-minute single 'Like a Rolling Stone' not only symbolized his rejection of an erstwhile folk-hero status, but radically altered the known parameters of popular music. Although he eventually eschewed the folk movement and its political pressures, Dylan's works remain amongst the most well-known and influential associated with the causes of the American New Left.

Woody Guthrie (1912–67) was born Woodrow Wilson Guthrie in Okemah, Oklahoma. He is widely regarded as one of the most significant figures in American folk music; his songs, such as 'This Land Is Your Land' – written as an angry riposte to Irving Berlin's 'God Bless America' – were often of a social justice bent, and have inspired several generations both politically and musically. In his lifetime, he wrote hundreds of political, folk and children's songs, along with ballads and improvised works. His album of songs about the Dust Bowl period, *Dust Bowl Ballads,* is included on *Mojo's* 100 Records That Changed the World. He married at 19, but left his wife and three children to join the thousands of Okies who were migrating to California looking for work. He worked at Los Angeles radio station KVFD, achieving some fame from playing hill-billy music; made friends with Will Geer and John Steinbeck; and wrote a column for the Communist newspaper *People's World* from May 1939 to January 1940. Guthrie died from complications of Huntington's disease. During his later years, in spite of his illness, Guthrie served as a figurehead in the American folk revival, providing inspiration to a generation of new folk musicians, including mentoring Ramblin' Jack Elliott and Bob Dylan.

Albert Lancaster Lloyd (1908–81) was born to a middle-class family in Wandsworth, South London. He was a well-known member of the Communist Party of Great Britain, a political association which informed many of his artistic choices. By the early 1950s he had established himself as a professional folklorist. Lloyd recorded many albums of English folk music, most notably several albums of the Child Ballads with Ewan MacColl. He also published many books on folk music and related topics, including *The Singing Englishman, Come All Ye Bold Miners* and *Folk Song in England.* He was a founding member of Topic Records and remained as their artistic director until his death. While Lloyd is most widely known for his work with British folk music, he also had a keen interest in the music of Spain, Latin America, Southeastern Europe and Australia. Lloyd also helped establish the folk music subgenre of industrial folk music through his books, recordings, collecting and theoretical writings. His biographer Dave Arthur has noted that Lloyd was instrumental in thinking about northern industrial music differently, crucially bringing to prominence 'an area of songs generally unexplored by the bucolically-focused, middle-class folk songs collectors and scholars', and asserting 'the possibilities of industrial song in his quest for a people's music relevant to a postwar urban audience.' (Arthur 162)

Alan Lomax (1915–2002) was born in Austin, Texas, the son of folklorist John Avery Lomax. He himself became a world-renowned folklorist, ethnomusicologist, archivist, writer, scholar, political activist, oral historian and film-maker. Lomax produced recordings, concerts and radio shows in the United States and in England, which played an important role in both the American and British folk revivals. With his father, Lomax recorded thousands of songs and interviews for the Archive of American Folk Song at the Library of Congress on aluminium and acetate discs. His biography is entitled *The Man Who Recorded the World*, and this is hardly hyperbole. A pioneering oral historian, he also recorded substantial interviews with many legendary folk and jazz musicians, including Woody Guthrie, Leadbelly, Muddy Waters, Jelly Roll Morton and Big Bill Broonzy. Lomax spent the 1950s exiled in London, from where he edited the eighteen-volume *Columbia World Library of Folk and Primitive Music*. He worked extensively with the BBC and other European broadcasters during this period as well.

Ewan MacColl (1915–89) was born James H. Miller in Salford, Lancashire, to Scottish parents. His father was an iron-moulder, militant trade-unionist and communist, and both parents were active in socialist causes. MacColl grew up in a household where both political discussion and singing were emphasized as part of family life. He left school in 1930, and worked throughout the Depression as a mechanic, factory worker, construction worker and street singer. MacColl's involvement with the folk music revival developed following a meeting with Alan Lomax in the early 1950s. He was among the first to recognize the importance of the folk club as a basic unit of the revival, and in London, he founded (with Lomax, Lloyd, Seamus Ennis and others) the Ballads and Blues Club, later to become the famed Singers' Club. In addition to his singing career, MacColl wrote scripts and music for BBC films, commercial television and stage. In 1965, MacColl and Peggy Seeger founded the Critics Group, a loosely organized company of revival singers who trained in folksinging and theatre techniques. MacColl's policies were the source of much controversy throughout the revival; his famous rule stipulating that performers at the Singers' Club would only perform music of their own language and national background has often been described as nativist and exclusionary. Seeger, MacColl's wife and singing partner, has written of him: 'For sixty years he was in the cultural forefront of numerous political struggles, producing plays, songs and scripts on the subjects of apartheid, fascism, industrial strife and human rights. It has been said that he was an enormous fish in a small pond – but the ocean of traditional song and speech upon which he navigated and hunted owes him a great debt for the treasures that he returned to it.'

Peggy Seeger (b. 1935) was born in New York City, to folklorist Charles Seeger and composer Ruth Crawford Seeger. Seeger is perhaps better-known in Britain than her native United States, having lived in England more or less permanently since 1956. Following an incident in 1953, when the then-eighteen years old's US passport was revoked following a trip to 'Communist China,' Seeger sought refuge in Britain. The BBC, following an appeal from producer Peter Kennedy, sponsored Seeger's work visa through 1957. Although she and Ewan MacColl had begun their musical and romantic partnership in 1953, she married Scottish folk singer Alex Campbell in 1958 in order to remain in Britain following the expiration of her visa. She and MacColl were eventually married in 1977. Asked about the origins of her musical and political educations, Seeger acknowledged the role of her musical family – including brothers

Pete and Mike Seeger, as well as her mother – as well and later, MacColl, stating that 'I got my political education from Ewan MacColl. And he was the one that tied the world all together in one piece for me. We were very complementary. I had things that he didn't have, and he had skills that I didn't have. And we were a working team for 35 years' (Smithsonian Folkways podcast, 'Music and the Winds of Change: The Women's Movement', 2006). Although she has often been associated with MacColl, Seeger has enjoyed a long and fruitful career in her own right, performing and writing songs both traditional and contemporary about issues such as CND, apartheid and perhaps most notably women's rights and gender equality. Her album *Different Therefore Equal* is still cited as one of the most important and influential on the latter subject.

Pete Seeger (1919–2014) was born in New York City, to Charles Seeger and concert violinist Constance Edson Seeger. A fixture on nationwide radio in the 1940s with the Almanac Singers (also featuring Woody Guthrie), he also had a string of hit records during the early 1950s as a member of The Weavers, most notably their recording of Leadbelly's 'Goodnight, Irene', which topped the charts for thirteen weeks in 1950. Despite his successes, Seeger was targeted by HUAC during the McCarthy era, and was blacklisted from American television and radio for almost twenty years. To earn money during the blacklist period of the late 1950s and early 1960s, Seeger had gigs as a music teacher in schools and summer camps and travelled the college campus circuit. He was a prominent, incredibly influential figure throughout the folk revival, as a singer of protest music in support of international disarmament, civil rights and environmental causes. As a song writer, he is best known as the author or co-author of 'Where Have All the Flowers Gone?', 'If I Had a Hammer (The Hammer Song)' (composed with Lee Hays of The Weavers) and 'Turn, Turn, Turn!'. Seeger was one of the folksingers responsible for adapting the spiritual 'We Shall Overcome' for the civil rights movement, a song that ultimately became the acknowledged anthem of the movement.

Cecil Sharp (1859–1924) was born in Camberwell, London, in 1859. Sharp was educated at Uppingham, but left at 15 and was privately coached for the University of Cambridge, where he graduated with a BA in music in 1882. While at Cambridge, Sharp heard the lectures of William Morris and became a Fabian Socialist and lifelong vegetarian. He also became interested in the vocal and instrumental (dance) folk music of the British Isles, and felt that speakers of English (and the other languages spoken in Britain and Ireland) ought to become acquainted with the patrimony of melodic expression that had grown up in the various regions there. At a time when state-sponsored mass public schooling was in its infancy, Sharp published songbooks intended for use by teachers and children in the then-being-formulated music curriculum. These songbooks often included arrangements of songs he had collected, and intended for choral singing. In 1911, Sharp founded the English Folk Dance Society, which promoted the traditional dances through workshops held nationwide, and which later merged with the Folk Song Society in 1932 to form the English Folk Dance and Song Society (EFDSS). During the years of the First World War, Sharp found it difficult to support himself through his customary efforts at lecturing and writing, and decided to make an extended visit to the United States. Sharp took the opportunity to do field work on English folk songs that had survived in the more remote regions of southern Appalachia, pursuing a line of research pioneered by Olive Dame Campbell. Travelling through the mountains of Virginia, North Carolina, Kentucky and Tennessee, Sharp and his assistant Maud Karpeles recorded hundreds of folk songs, many using the pentatonic scale and many in versions quite different from those Sharp had collected in rural England.

'Folk Song without Folk': An Introduction to Folk Music Revivalism in Twentieth-Century England

Introduction

"'There's just this one nagging query," said the young man with the Sammy Davis, Jr. beard. "While we're all sitting round here listening to folk-songs, what are all the folk doing?'"[1] And with this single probe, a young folk fan revealed an elemental tension – perhaps the most significant tension – within the post-Second World War English folk song revival (*c.* 1945–65)[2]; no longer was 'folk song' necessarily 'of the folk' – or, rather, the definition of 'the folk' had become much more opaque and uncertain by the mid-twentieth century, as traditional geographical and social boundaries were blurred by industrialization, urbanization and mass communication. As the *Guardian* reported in 1961, the English folk revival was a phenomenon in which a 'relatively small section of the population' had cornered the market in 'Appalachian laments, chain-gang blues, short-haul shanties, and broad Suffolk ballads.'[3] While one faction of the folk movement, some revivalists felt, was too hungry for popular approval, 'tarting itself up to look like a pop song [through] twee little harmonics and prettified words,' true folk music – others insisted – was 'bound to remain a minority taste, a lonely art, an uncompromising discipline.'[4] It was this paradoxical desire for, and fundamental belief in, a folk revival unmolested by the modern world that drove the movement in England, counterpoising its gaudier American cousin; it is also what makes the English folk revival such a fascinating window on postwar English society. The myriad interpretations of folk music's social function and political meaning in the twentieth century came to a head after the Second World War; folk music became a key medium through which young people, mostly identifying on the Left, experienced and interpreted the world around them. Particularly in the 1950s and 1960s, folk music achieved a critical mass following as teenaged baby boomers latched on to its political messaging, instrumental accessibility and subcultural authenticity. While folk music has always made a good partner for protest, in the postwar period it provided the soundtrack for the political coming-of-age of millions.

American journalist Sam Hinton contends that '[t]here has never been a lack of interest in folk music ... the [only] difference has been in the size of its audience.'[5] Folk music has long been a part of our cultural response to the surrounding world, and has likewise, in a very material way, contributed to how we understand ourselves in relation to other people and places, fostering a shared sense of humanity, and of empathy – especially, English folk singer Karl Dallas once asserted, 'in the alienated world of the factory and the machine.'[6] Dallas stated that folk music has enabled communication 'from one generation to another, part of the great corpus of stored knowledge and custom.'[7] Folk songs were ascribed increased significance throughout the twentieth century, as traditional modes of communication gave way to newer technologies – making the world smaller, more accessible and yet somehow less personal. The English folk music revival emerged during a transitionary moment in Western culture, just as an increased availability of consumer goods was becoming a way of life for many, if not most, working- and middle-class families – obscuring the fact that the movement's origins pre-dated both the phonograph and the radio.

The postwar folk revival in England occurred alongside a similar, yet much more well-known, folk music revival in the United States, and although they were in many ways distinct cultural movements, both developed as part of a unique transnational cultural exchange with the other. The English movement offered a self-conscious response to its transatlantic counterpart, mimicking yet criticizing it in ways that have helped to illuminate the divergent paths the two nations took after the war; the movements were closely linked, yet culturally distinct, and it was this dichotomous relationship that informed the unique direction the English movement took – simultaneously born of a renewed impulse to collect 'authentic' English folk songs in previously unheralded regions of the country, but also crucially made possible in part by the influence of American musical styles, including skiffle, jazz and rock 'n' roll.

There were actually two twentieth-century English folk revivals, separated by two world wars, and, at least superficially, a profound ideological schism. The first folk revival, under the auspices of Cecil Sharp and the Folk Song Society (FSS), aspired to preserve – and sanitize – the music of the 'common people' at the outset of the twentieth century. Sharp was a Fabian socialist, part of an emergent labour movement, which, as a new century dawned – bringing significant changes in how leisure time was both organized and enjoyed – was concerned with the possible social and cultural ramifications of popular culture on the lives of working people. The Fabians were responding to, and indeed helped to underline, the tension between a new popular culture and the desire for social and political reform: folk music stood, then and subsequently, in stark contrast with the 'moral quagmire' of modern society. The surge of interest in folk song around the turn of the twentieth century was part of a common sociological impulse, in both Europe and North America, to 'discover the people,' where ordinary folk and their cultural 'products' were glorified as the last vestiges of authentic society, their communities vigorously 'rediscovered' as incubators of fast-disappearing national traditions.[8] The English postwar revival had its origins in this earlier *fin-de-siècle* movement, but it was more conflicted of purpose – more ambivalent about its own social origins and determined to distance itself from the patronizing and romanticized portrayals of working people forwarded by earlier generations of folk scholars.[9] Throughout England's 'second revival', folk music was notably performed by singers from a variety of social backgrounds, incorporating a wide range of musical and cultural influences, elucidating a complex interaction of class and class consciousness during England's post-industrial 'age of affluence'.

Although the second folk revival adds much to our understanding of postwar England, until now it has evaded academic attention. This book offers a study of a 'national' folk movement in England, as well as its transnational connections, examining a dynamic network of musicians, collectors and enthusiasts as they defined and shaped their movement in deliberate contrast with a much flashier American counterpart. It will emphasize the complex ideological connections between the first and second English folk revivals, as well as between the English and US revivals.[10] Furthermore, this book offers something important to the historiography of political culture in postwar Britain – in particular, the ways in which the folk revival illuminated burgeoning tensions between the (new) Left, the Labour Party and English society.

Historiography

The historiographies from which this book draws and to which it contributes are various, beyond the history of folk music and folk revivalism. This is both a social study of postwar England and a history of the English folk revival; it examines the significant role folk music played in that history, articulating, reflecting and ultimately contributing to the contemporary social, cultural and political currents driving the country. Recent scholarship in English and British history has stressed the need to reconstruct patterns of interconnection between politics and culture, society and economy. Ultimately, this work contributes to what historian Lawrence Black has termed the 'cultural history of the political' in postwar English history.[11]

Black's seminal works *The Political Culture of the Left in Affluent Britain* (2003) and *Redefining British Politics* (2010) have helped to frame the English folk revival, and this project, within the social and political historiographies of postwar Britain. *The Political Culture of the Left* established the central issues facing Labour and the New Left during a period of relative affluence, providing important context for a concurrent folk revival movement with many of the same concerns. The identity crisis prompted by increased affluence, amongst leftist intellectuals and politicians, was reflected in the Left's 'cultural turn'. Black has argued that 'affluence threw socialism's customary ways of thinking, its language and aspirations, into doubt'[12]; it was, he contends, a metaphor for the inability of socialism to come to terms with the social, economic and political changes of the postwar world. Black argues that his work is about how 'the left's fortunes were contingent upon how it understood and described these changes and communicated with those experiencing them'[13]; culture became an integral part of this process, and the folk revival both reflected and contributed to the Left's response. This book contributes to this historiography by placing the phenomenon of folk revivalism within the context of English socialists' attempts to come to terms with culture and its uses in the modern world.

Redefining British Politics provides an expanded definition of 'political culture', in which politics would be considered within a broader social context; this definition has been particularly useful when thinking about the English folk revival's social and cultural impact, as well as its political implications. Black asserts that the political has not merely been a *product* of social forces but a social force itself[14]; the folk revival in many ways reflected this symbiosis, bringing myriad social and political strands together in one, often conflicted, movement. Black's work has been foremost in my mind when looking at the ways in which the folk revival contributed and responded to contemporary social and political forces, and the ways in which an understanding of folk revivalism in England can help to explain how political culture was created and consumed after the Second World War – increasingly, as a popular activity, not just elite intellectual discourse.[15] The ethos of 'participatory democracy', which was popular with New Leftist movements on both sides of the Atlantic, helps to explain why folk music resonated with young people in particular, as a means of participating in politics without having to engage in elitist political dialogue. *Redefining British Politics* crucially built upon Black's earlier work on the Centre 42 project, as well as other 'Labourist' initiatives like the Festival of Labour and the Festival of Britain, providing an invaluable contextual framework for the folk revival's place in the postwar political and cultural economy – built around the uneasy relationship between the Left and the working class, driven by the fear of Americanization.[16]

Several other works have provided important chronicles of the Labour Party's postwar promise, and subsequent crises, throughout the 1950s and '60s, centring on the leftist establishment's inability to come to terms with affluence, and its increasingly fraught relationships with both workers and the New Leftist 'youth culture', to the extent that the latter group existed in England. Kenneth O. Morgan's *Labour in Power 1945–1951* (1984) and Steven Fielding's *Labour Party: Socialism since 1951* (1997) have both analysed the Labour Party's postwar crisis. This crisis occurred as the relative affluence of the population seemed to undermine the most important gains of the welfare state, and the nationalization of industry – the hinge on which Labour's socialist brand rested – was met with apathy or outright derision. These issues will form the basis for Chapters 2 and 3, dealing respectively with the political culture and politics of class during the postwar period. This book sheds light on these debates by showing how closely the folk revival and its leaders were in fact associated and perceived themselves to be a part of the contemporary socio-political milieu.

The existing histories of the English folk revival have tended to be rather insular; by contrast, this work integrates the folk revival firmly within the political culture of postwar England. In doing so, several unique aspects of the movement are emphasized in new ways: foremost among these is a focus on the Northeast – as the physical location of much Labourist ideology in the postwar period – and, simultaneously, a focus on the transnational implications of a movement influenced by American styles while also being wary of being subsumed by the American culture machine. Although this study diverges from previous efforts, it owes much to foundational texts such as A. L. Lloyd's *Folk Song in England* (1967), which have provided significant inroads into the ways in which folk songs had been interpreted during periods of revival. The main contribution of Lloyd's work was his assertion that industrial workers' songs could and should be a part of the twentieth-century English folk canon; he was also instrumental in arguing that these 'industrial songs' had given new life and vibrancy to English song tradition. Woods's *Folk Revival: The Rediscovery of a National Music* (1979) has also provided a good, though far less intellectually rich, contemporary study of the folk revival movement, while the collaborative project undertaken by revival participants and documentarians Dave Laing, Karl Dallas, Robin Denselow and Robert Shelton, *The Electric Muse: The Story of Folk into Rock* (1975), represents, I think, the first attempt to understand the English and American revivals together, as contemporary movements – albeit as a precursor of 'folk-rock'.

Newer studies have expanded upon these works, providing further insight into the political and ideological tenets underlying folk revivalism. Regina Bendix's *In Search of Authenticity: The Formation of Folklore Studies* (1997) highlights the importance of folk music and folklore in fulfilling a yearning for authentic experience in an inauthentic world, arguing that 'folklore has long served as a vehicle in the search for the authentic, satisfying a longing for an escape from modernity'.[17] Authenticity was that 'longed-for' quality in folklore and music, which Bendix claims had been part of a greater contemporary 'ethno-nationalist project' that 'transformed from an experience of individual transcendence to a symbol of the inevitability of national unity'.[18] In *Fakesong: The Manufacture of British 'Folksong' 1700 to the Present Day* (1985), Dave Harker traces the influence of collectors in shaping the meaning of folksong since the eighteenth century, and argues that 'what Fakesong wants to do is to develop ways of understanding precisely what "folksongs" and "ballads" really are. And to do that, we have to examine how they have come down to us, to establish how they have been affected by their passage through time, and through the heads and hands of collectors, antiquarians and folklorists'.[19]

Niall MacKinnon's *The British Folk Scene: Musical Performance and Social Identity* (1994) constitutes a pioneering social history of the folk revival in Britain, seeking to 'understand a musical genre, the contemporary British folk scene, in terms of identifying the social factors that give it coherence'.[20] Fundamentally, I think what MacKinnon wanted to understand was why and how people became interested in folk music and its performance, both public and private. 'What wider social meanings are embodied in specific forms of musical organisation?', MacKinnon asks; the answer to this question, I believe, is that the social (and cultural) meaning of a given form is constantly in flux – new generations understand music's meaning and resonance in their lives differently; values evolve and change. One of the greatest contributions of MacKinnon's work was to provide a socio-economic profile of the typical 'folk club audience'. Although he uses data collected in the 1980s, MacKinnon effectively draws out a convincing pattern of the socio-economic profile of the average folk club attendee, based on factors such as age, occupation, political attitudes and religion.

No work has done more to expose the paradoxes of the postwar revival than Michael Brocken's *The British Folk Revival: 1944–2002* (2003). While acknowledging the significant influence of Lloyd on the second revival, Brocken remains critical of how that influence was exerted, writing that 'what is most disturbing about the heritage of Bert Lloyd is the way in which authenticity and purity have become associated with certain types of music as a consequence of his political beliefs'.[21] Ultimately, Brocken's work has provided an important introduction to crucial revivalist tensions, politically, ideologically and culturally, such as the role of the mass media, the influence of leftist politics and the importance of class – all of which this book also grapples with. He argues, compellingly, that the folk revival channelled musical performance and reception through social, political and historical 'refractions' and that the folk revival was a visible and 'clearly identifiable social movement to which an important minority were drawn'.[22]

Although Brocken claims to take into account important contextual questions involving the social and cultural conditions in which the revival developed – what it indicated about pre- and postwar Britain – I don't think his work succeeds in covering these issues as fully as it might have. Brocken devotes much space to what he deems the hypocrisies of the revival, and its central figures, but does not get to the heart of the social, cultural and political issues driving the movement. He raises many of the interesting paradoxes of folk revivalism, but does not flesh out their full implications. He claims that his work is an attempt to locate the revival within 'broader social [and] cultural changes in British society', and argues that 'these arrangements at work in performance and participation stemmed from specific contextual responses to a given era in British social history', but does not go on to explain what that means. Therefore, while Brocken's work remains significant as the most complete study of the postwar folk revival to date, it still leaves something to be desired in contextualizing the movement within a broader social, political and cultural historiography.

J. P. Bean's *Singing from the Floor: A History of British Folk Clubs* (2014), Ronald D. Cohen and Rachel Clare Donaldson's *Roots of the Revival: American & British Folk Music in the 1950s* (2014), as well as Billy Bragg's *Roots, Radicals and Rockers: How Skiffle Changed the World* (2017) have been particularly insightful and important more recent additions to the historiography of English (and American) folk music in the latter half of the twentieth century. *Singing from the Floor* offers a more comprehensive study of the social base of the revival via oral history. It gives a 'ground-up' approach to the British folk scene. The folk club, as this book will establish, was an absolutely essential element of the English folk revival's success – and its identity. Bean's account of the folk scene in postwar Britain includes anecdotal snippets from the participants themselves, offering an invaluable resource for those wanting to understand the movement's motivations and tensions, as well as accounts of petty squabbles and rumours. However, it provides little in the way of context for these debates. Bragg's history of Skiffle, unsurprisingly – and quite reasonably – paints the music as the first musical form that was accessible to working-class youth, largely because of its emphasis on less expensive, or handmade, instruments and its lack of regard for musical training. Cohen and Donaldson's *Roots of the Revival* does a very good job of telling the story of the English and American revivals in parallel. The book identifies many of the same touchstones of connection between the American and English revivals that this book does: the importance of collectors like Francis James Child, A. L. Lloyd and Alan Lomax; the role played by earlier cousins like skiffle and jazz; the fine line between traditionalism and commercialism; but like other studies of folk revivalism in England and elsewhere, *Roots* does not delve into the crucial social and political context from which folk revival movements emerge, and to which they contribute.

A grassroots movement

As American folk historian Thomas R. Gruning has argued, waning commercial popularity in the wake of the postwar revivals in both England and the United States returned the folk 'to its status as a marginalized musical community: a position that was apparently preferred by the die-hard, "real" folk who were never quite comfortable in their association with mainstream popular music.'[23] Indeed, Ewan MacColl, one of the English revival's central figures, asserted in 1965 – at the height of the movement's popularity – that '[t]he best thing would be for the folk boom to end as quickly as possible, and that the clubs should continue their steady development, acting as opinion makers. Recent sudden increases in membership in many clubs have hampered them in their work – a packed club is not always the best club.'[24] MacColl distinguished between the grassroots and the popular folk revival, which reached its crucible moment in the early 1960s, as the folk music boom was in full swing and the protest song phenomenon began to garner attention even in the popular music magazines. When asked by fellow revivalist Karl Dallas whether he had helped to create the folk boom in England, MacColl responded: 'I didn't create it. You've got to make a distinction between the systematic development of the folk revival, and the boom, with its accent on pop, its concern for a "sound."'[25]

At the heart of this distinction are several important implications for how we understand the English folk revival: was it a bona fide grassroots movement, or did it merely benefit from an auspicious coincidence of commercial opportunism and socio-political upheaval? There is a tension between the revival's emphasis on the enduring nature of the folk and the argument that folk music mattered *more* in the 1950s and '60s because of the intersection of culture and politics. The grassroots element was such an important ideological underpinning of the English folk movement – as was evident in its stubborn emphasis on the small, the local and the amateur. But how do we hear those voices? How is the grassroots measured, if at all? Ironically, *one* of the ways is on record, through people like the miner Jack Elliott of Birtley (Durham) and his family. The Elliotts were instrumental in telling the story of coal miners' culture in Durham. Another is through the direct correspondence between the leaders of the movement and its fans. Letters to the editor in magazines like *Melody Maker* and *Sing* give a sense of what folk fans valued, and how they interpreted the debates raging throughout the folk world.[26]

Part of the debate over the grassroots status of the English revival involves, and indeed stems from, folk music's status as an antithesis to commercial culture, a position compromised by its growing popular appeal after the Second World War. As a subject of historical study, folk music is *particularly* interesting because the idea of its 'revival' necessarily involves the negotiation of several paradoxical tenets. It offers a uniquely interesting point of entry for cultural study, as a supposedly non-commercial form, which experienced a significant commercial revival during the 1950s and '60s, as postwar austerity gradually and unevenly gave way to affluence in England. But for all of the changes wrought by the war and its aftermath, the revival of folk music on both sides of the Atlantic was driven by a remarkably consistent set of socio-political anxieties, going back to the late nineteenth century.

Arts, crafts and socialism: Early folk music collection

The collection and distribution of folk music in the modern era have always involved, according to folk historian Benjamin Filene, 'a complex series of ideological decisions.'[27] The first concentrated efforts of intellectuals and an emergent cadre of folklorists to collect and understand folk music and its place in the modern world began in the late nineteenth century. This period also, significantly, saw the development of the Romantic movement in art, and Nationalist political movements as dominant ideological trends in the West, which in turn gave rise to an increased interest in folklore and song on both sides of the Atlantic Ocean. Francis James Child was the first great folk music collector in the United States and the first president of the American Folklore Society, established in 1888. Child maintained that commercial ballads and printed music had 'polluted the oral tradition', and so the majority of the songs included in his epic collection of English and Scottish ballads – which totalled more than 300, focused exclusively in the Anglo-Saxon tradition – pre-dated the printing press.[28]

Folk music scholar Georgina Boyes has argued that popular, or 'art', music was vilified by Victorian collectors as 'a challenge to the class system, a threat to morality and a perverter of art'.[29] Folk songs and folklore, by contrast, were recognized by early collectors as expressions of some primordial national identity, telling the story of a society's development. Simon Bronner describes nineteenth-century folk song collection as a pseudo-Darwinian endeavour, arguing that 'Folk was a clear label to set materials apart from modern life. Folklorists displayed tales, rituals, and artifacts equally as material specimens, which were meant to be classified in the natural history of civilization'.[30] As was the case in the United States, in Europe around the turn of the century, 'the folk' were being discovered, and as Krishan Kumar has argued, 'where necessary, invented … They were investigated and explored, their lore and language, their songs and dances, their customs and stories, collected and written down', uncovering a deep-seated impulse to get back to a pre-industrial, bucolic past.[31] This turn towards a disappearing rural 'past' could be seen in the work of Cecil Sharp and the nascent Folk Song Society, as they laid the groundwork for the first twentieth-century English folk revival.

The underlying ideological impulse in England, both at the turn of the century and after the Second World War, was to build a truly *popular* culture through the music of 'the folk' – however broadly defined – as a means of bringing socialism to the people. In the nineteenth century, William Morris pioneered this idea of politically conscious, socially restorative art in Britain. Morris placed 'common things' on a pedestal of social, and political, significance; folk music, in particular, was seen as an appropriate vehicle for this socio-political project. Although Morris's vision, of marrying art and socialism, was important for its pioneering promotion of the social and political value of workers' art, it was still governed by problematic bourgeois assumptions *about* that art. As historian Chris Waters has argued, 'The call for an "art of their own" could serve as a rallying cry for those who sought a new popular culture. But it could also be an empty rhetorical device, deployed by those who sought to "improve" workers by imposing their own cultural preferences onto them'.[32] For nineteenth-century socialists, music became a tool for both the moral reform of the individual and the nurturing of the human spirit. There was a paradoxical distrust of contemporary musical taste, coupled with a romanticized notion of popular creativity.[33] Donald Sassoon has asserted that these early socialists were wealthy idealists, intent on 'progressive bourgeois reforms', who abhorred most forms of popular culture.[34] It was from this background that Cecil Sharp and the FSS – later EFDSS (English Folk Dance and Song Society) – emerged.

In England, Sharp's reputation has more recently suffered. The bulk of the negative criticism has been based upon his censorship of the more salacious songs he collected, his nativist leanings and his class bias. Sharp's romantic impulse to rescue the bucolic folk tradition from the onslaught of urbanization and industrialization seemed, especially in light of the work done by A. L. Lloyd and others on industrial workers' songs in the postwar period, particularly outdated. Music historian Dave Harker has argued that, despite noble aims, what Sharp rather dubiously accomplished was 'to impose on to the living culture of English working people (few of whom were agricultural laborers), in some parts of some predominantly rural counties in the south-west, notions of history and of culture which owe more to romance than reality.'[35] Harker further attacked Sharp as an 'unapologetic racist', who once allegedly described Charleston, South Carolina, as a place where the air was 'impregnated with tobacco, molasses and nigger.'[36] There has been an increasing acknowledgement of Sharp's failures – along with a somewhat more muted defence of his triumphs – amongst historians and participants of the postwar English folk revival. Britta Sweers argued that Sharp was 'strongly influenced by contemporaneous late Victorian ideas ("offensive" and sociocritical material was either ignored or edited),' and that 'this written form of traditional music was fixed outside its original social context and collected for an educated urban audience that was no longer close to the traditional structures. On a sociocultural level, this additional layer of reinterpretation is embodied in the EFDSS.'[37] Although he offered far from a complete vision of what the English folk could contribute in the twentieth century, under Sharp's guidance, the Folk Song Society was founded in London in 1898. It was the precursor to the EFDSS, which took over as the society's moniker in 1933.

In many ways, the postwar folk revival offered an antithetical interpretation of Sharp's folk music – promoting folk tradition as something that was vital, and still very much present in many communities throughout the country, especially in communities of industrial workers; however, the 'first' and 'second' English folk revivals were much more ideologically similar than many postwar folk scholars and singers cared to acknowledge. The conservative, nativist and often patronizing impulse propelling Sharp's study was certainly recognizable in some of the work done by postwar revivalists such as Lloyd and MacColl, in their treatment of the Durham miners, for instance – discussed in Chapter 3 – or in MacColl's folk club policy, discussed in Chapter 5.

Defining folk music in a technological age

The ambiguity surrounding the definition of 'folk music' has been the source of heated debate throughout the twentieth century, as collectors and performers have fought to promote their particular vision of 'the folk'. Folk music has often been defined in terms of class: Lloyd called it 'the peak cultural achievement of the English lower classes'; implicit in all folk songs, of any place and period, he argued, was 'a deep longing for a better life.'[38] In a somewhat more encompassing statement – one that acknowledged the collector's crucial role in creating and shaping folk traditions – American folk singer Pete Seeger argued that the term 'folk music' was 'invented by nineteenth-century scholars to describe the music of peasantry, age-old and anonymous. To me, it means homemade-type music, played mainly by ear, arising out of older traditions, but with a meaning for today. I use it only for lack of a better word.'[39] These two definitions echo the often paradoxical and hotly contested interpretations of folk music and its purpose in a modern, technological, world – as it was increasingly shared across local, regional and international boundaries. The difficult, if not impossible, task of defining 'folk' and 'folk music' lies at the heart of many studies of folk revivalism.

For many, what distinguished folk song from popular song was simply how long it had been around; traditionally, folk songs were supposed to have passed through generations of singers orally, without third-party mediation. The International Folk Music Council, which was formed in London in 1947, and was supported by UNESCO, defined folk song as:

> The product of a musical tradition that has been evolved through the process of oral transmission. The factors that shape the tradition are: (i) continuity which links the present with the past; (ii) variation which springs from the creative impulse of the individual or group; and (iii) selection by the community which determines the form or forms in which the music survives. The term can be applied to music that has been evolved from rudimentary beginnings by a community uninfluenced by popular and art music and it can likewise be applied to music which has originated with an individual composer and has subsequently been absorbed into the unwritten living tradition of a community.[40]

This emphasis on apparently un-mediated transmission was still remarkably potent amongst many revivalists and scholars after the Second World War, even as vinyl recording and the radio had effectively made it a moot point.[41] This ideal persisted – along with the somewhat narrow definition of 'folk music' it necessitated – amongst the more doctrinaire traditionalists of the revival. Others, however, recognized the expansive possibilities of a more broadly defined folk music.

Richard Peterson contends that the term 'folk' was a desirable categorization for the music as it developed in the twentieth century because it 'could be used elastically to include diverse varieties of music from bluegrass to movie western songs, and from honky-tonk to country gospel. It also had the clear advantage of implying a connection between current product and innumerable works that had come before, and, above all, it suggested authenticity.'[42] The yearning for 'authentic experience' was an increasingly desired quality to be found in folk songs. Folk music in the twentieth century was both trusted as an authentic expression of reality, of everyday life, work and protest, and also presenting an idealized vision of that reality; it has been hailed as part of both nationalistic and proletarian traditions, exploited by politicians and collectors alike.

Although it had its origins in the old ballad form, the postwar revival was in part defined by the concurrent emergence of topical and more personal songwriting, eventually spawning the popular sub-genre of 'singer-songwriter'. This ultimately necessitated a distinction between folk songs and 'songs in the folk idiom', as a means of dealing with writers who used folk melodies, instruments and themes to talk about contemporary issues. This distinction became a way to incorporate contemporary compositions into centuries-old traditions, to imbue them with the same kind of authority, and to maintain the idea of 'living tradition'. This was a pattern followed by many postwar revivalists, causing much anxiety amongst the more doctrinaire traditionalists of the movement, who revered 'authenticity' above all other folk values.

Many folk fans got in on the debate over authenticity as well. A letter to the editor of *The Observer*, dated 22 September 1963, expressed the following in support of the work of Cecil Sharp:

> The very essence of the description folk is that these songs, no matter how they originated, have been shaped and moulded by generations of singers. Folk songs may have a style of their own, and modern song writers may well copy this style, but it is not the style that makes a song a folk song. If one must include the term folk to distinguish from pop, then perhaps folksy, folklike or folknik would be appropriate. But let us preserve the meaning of folk as defined by Cecil Sharp and others.[43]

Later, in 1980, *New York Times* columnist Neil Alan Marks remarked, about the American revival, that 'much "root" material was rediscovered and passed through a series of filters, and artists relayed their interpretations in varying degrees of authenticity in relation to the original. Thus, Peter, Paul and Mary were perhaps no more or less "folksingers" than Pete Seeger or Reverend Gary Davis; they were all simply at different points of the filtration system.'[44] 'Authenticity' was one of the central organizing ideals of folk revivalism on either side of the Atlantic; but who decided what the term meant, and where it was applied, were issues that became problematically nebulous at times. Arguments favouring 'respect for the tradition' abounded during the folk revival in England, creating the dividing line between the 'authentic' and the 'commercial', tradition and innovation.

Traditions are a way of conversing with the past, with personal as well as collective histories, but are also, significantly, key touchstones in creating present identities. MacColl, echoing the thoughts of Lloyd on 'living traditions', argued in 1962 that:

> It is a completely fallacious thing to suggest that a folk tradition is something which belongs to the past. A tradition which cannot make terms with contemporary life is a dead thing. It belongs to the museums, and to the library shelves ... Our experiences of recording, among coal miners and so on has told us, proved to us, that it is nonsense to say that tradition is dead.[45]

He and Peggy Seeger talked openly about 'creating an idiom' of folk music for the postwar generation. In 1962, Seeger claimed that 'we're creating something dramatic ... we are trying to create a folk idiom' based on particular speech, songs, rhythms, and instrumentation. Using what 'people give us', Seeger asserted that 'tradition is changeable', and fundamentally dynamic.[46] In 'creating an idiom', MacColl and Seeger – and a handful of other individuals – for many years maintained almost complete creative control over the folk revival in England. In their selective presentation of that tradition, MacColl et al. highlighted some of the ideological underpinnings of these created idioms, the problems of invented traditions and orthodoxies of authenticity, in a similar vein to the earliest days of folk collection. As folk songs were collected and re-collected, across generations, these issues came increasingly to the fore of artistic debate. Folk song collectors in the twentieth century have been guilty of sanitizing, censoring and paternalizing the sources of their material, of 'inventing tradition' while setting out to preserve it. Indeed, in this respect, the second folk revival in England was really no more enlightened than the first.

Part of this work is to try to understand why, when and how certain traditions are 'created' or emphasized over others. Eric Hobsbawm's notion of the 'invention of tradition' seems especially useful in recounting the social and cultural processes underlying the various revivals of folk music in the twentieth century. Hobsbawm describes the idea of 'invented tradition' as one that 'includes both "traditions" actually invented, constructed, and formally instituted and those emerging in a less easily traceable manner within a brief and dateable period – a matter of a few years perhaps – and establishing themselves with great rapidity.'[47] He asserts that 'inventing tradition' was a means of establishing continuity with a 'usable,' often idealized, past: 'Invented tradition is taken to mean a set of practices, normally governed by overtly or tacitly accepted rules and of a ritual or symbolic nature, which seek to inculcate certain values and norms of behavior by repetition, which automatically implies continuity with the past. In fact, where possible, they normally attempt to establish continuity with a suitable historic past.'[48]

Traditions are invented, argues Hobsbawm, in order to explain, understand and cope with rapid social and political change: 'It is the contrast between the constant change and innovation of the modern world and the attempt to structure at least some parts of social life within it as unchanging and invariant, that makes the "invention of tradition" so interesting.'[49] It is not coincidence, then, that the mid-twentieth-century push to revive folk culture in England emerged during a time of celebration, after the nation had survived almost six years of war, but also, much more intriguingly, at a time of crisis – for the Labour Left specifically, and more generally (though obliquely) for liberal progressivism. In both England and the United States, as industrialization fundamentally transformed traditional modes of living and working in the twentieth century, ideas of tradition and belonging became increasingly malleable.

Tradition and nostalgia have been closely connected by history and theory, often going hand-in-hand to explain society's relationship with the past and with memory. Fred Davis has examined the sociology of the nostalgic impulse, writing that 'nostalgia is a distinctive way ... of relating our past to our present and future ... [It] is one of the means ... we employ in the never ending work of constructing, maintaining, and reconstructing our identities.'[50] Davis argues that nostalgia, like tradition, has been a coping mechanism in dealing with rapid change and transformation in society, as it attends 'to the pleas of continuity with the past [and] thrives on transition, on the subjective discontinuities that engender our yearning for continuity.'[51] Folk music has played an important role in both creating and re-creating local and regional, as well as national traditions.[52] During the postwar folk revival period, traditions took on, as Ron Eyerman and Andrew Jamieson have argued, 'a new significance with the breakdown of national and local communities.'[53] Folk tradition also crucially contributed to leftist idealizations of community and belonging in the 1950s and '60s, as conventional social boundaries were both subverted and celebrated. Chapter 2 will deal more particularly with the idea of nostalgia and tradition through an examination of the Labour Party's attempts to tap in to a national workers' culture.

Skiffle and jazz

There is no question that folk music in England benefited enormously from the inroads made by American musical forms such as jazz, skiffle and rock 'n' roll before the war, but also succeeded in part by providing a less-commercialized (i.e. less American) alternative to these musics. Skiffle was an ad hoc style of music, often played on whatever instruments were available – including pots, pans and washer boards, as well as the more usual guitars, banjos and ukuleles. It proved popular, especially, with working-class young people, but it was equally popular in Soho with the bohemian hipsters, many of whom affected a 'working-class' style to play it. *Observer* columnist Hugh Latimer described the Soho skiffle scene in June, 1957, at its height:

> Down a dusty curve of bare board stairs in the eastern, cheaper, part of Soho … the visitor pauses to give his name, full address, and 3s. or 3s. 6d. to a bored youth in jeans. Beyond the rows of big-eyed girls and bespectacled young men in thick grey pullovers stands a little stage, from which in the semi-darkness pushes the heavy, bumpy beat of skiffle.[54]

Composed of men in 'open shirts and sometimes beards of an archducal splendour', skiffle groups – producing their signature 'rub-a-dub noise' – were defined by Latimer as 'a band to accompany the single singing guitarist, or more rarely banjoist; they give him exaggerated rhythmic support on a variety of instruments – other guitars, a bass to thump and a washboard to strum, rattles, drums, whistles, anything you like so long as it looks as if it had been assembled from the municipal rubbish-dump.'[55] Although often denigrated as 'Teddy Boy Jazz', skiffle in many ways provided the most direct path to folk music for young people wanting to develop their own traditions, and express themselves with a minimal economic commitment, without the need for a vast amount of musical talent. As Latimer so deftly described in his *Observer* piece, 'The remarkable thing is that in an age of high-fidelity sound, long-players and tape-recorders, the young should suddenly decide to make their own music. It is fantastic. What are they to do with all those guitars when the craze goes?'[56] The answer, as we now know, was folk music. Skiffle, although a short-lived cultural phenomenon in its own right, nonetheless occupies an incredibly important place in English musical history.[57]

Stephen Barnard writes of the importance of skiffle in the history of British popular music, particularly as an influence on young people: 'Skiffle's importance to the development of British popular music, the manner in which its play-it-yourself qualities introduced the nation's teenager to music-making, has been described many times, but of more relevance here is the role it played in the image of youth that the media constructed.'[58] Indeed, neither the postwar folk revival nor the explosion of rock 'n' roll on Tyneside and Merseyside would have been possible without skiffle.[59] At the height of the skiffle phenomenon, in the mid-to-late 1950s, the music encouraged young people to pick up instruments and make their own music.[60] The trend encouraged a do-it-yourself ethos, and celebrated lack of musical polish as somehow more authentic. According to Hobsbawm, skiffle was 'unquestionably the most universally popular music of our generation. It broke through all barriers except those of age.'[61] Skiffle would prove to carry a resonance well beyond its short life in the spotlight. Another American-style import, jazz, also made important inroads in English youth culture after the war – at once inclusive and exclusive.

An interesting sub-cultural parallel to the revival of folk music in England was the left's fixation on jazz, itself an unquestionably American import. George McKay argues that the popularity of jazz amongst 'white European consumers' was partly due to its 'romantic' identification 'as a culture of struggle … a reductive strategy effectively confirming the social hierarchy and black cultural practitioners' allotted place in it.'[62] Like folk, according to McKay, jazz 'seemed to blossom in Britain alongside the development of the New Left.'[63] The two musics also shared an ambivalence towards American culture, which to many was synonymous with mass culture and, therefore, the death of tradition. E. P. Thompson cautioned that 'it will be useless to try to resist the American threat if we can only replace it with a vacuum … the only lasting victories will be where – whether in scholarship, or dance-tunes, or philosophy – the American substitute is driven out by a development of the living British tradition.'[64] It is in this arena, as this book will explore, that folk music was more successful than its imported cousin, jazz.[65] As a response to this dilemma of Americanization, McKay argues that the British left began preaching 'cultural if not political conservatism', as in the work of Richard Hoggart, and echoed, within folk circles, in MacColl's infamous folk club policy.[66]

All of the themes above and many others will be explored throughout this book, which is divided into six major chapters, each addressing an important aspect of the English folk revival and its place in postwar English history. The first chapter, 'The Pub and the Beeb: The Structural Foundations of the English Folk Revival', will establish the infrastructural foundations of folk revivalism, introducing the major figures, publications, organizations, festivals, record companies and radio programmes supporting the folk movement in England. Chapter 2, '"Its Music Was Folk": Folk Revivalism and Political Culture in Postwar England', will explore the political dimensions of the folk revival. Following the war, folk music was reinvigorated within the context of a transition from 'old' to 'new' left in political culture. This chapter analyses the political contexts from which the songs emerged, and to which they contributed. Folk music came to be associated powerfully with a push towards 'topical' songwriting that dealt with those issues of greatest concern to the Left in the 1950s and '60s. However, the salience of class – and significant differences in the social makeup of the 'new left' in England as opposed to in America – meant that the lingering influence of the 'old left' could be felt as well. Whereas in the United States, labour and industrial material had been almost entirely pushed aside by the late 1950s, in England these kinds of songs in fact experienced a significant cultural renaissance.

Chapter 3, 'A Dialectic of Class and Region: Folk Music in the "Affluent Society"', looks at folk music's role in accentuating class tensions as they affected fragile and changing perceptions of national identity in the immediate aftermath of the war. In England, one of the most revealing issues of the postwar era was the plight of the coal industry and its workers; the indelible imprint of coal on the nation's history, and the very public decline of that industry, brought into focus both latent and more manifest class tensions in the country. The nationalization of the coal industry and its ripple effects became the subject of many new songs written during the revival; these songs also bring into greater focus the underlying ideological similarities between the first and second English folk revivals. This chapter, finally, will address the ambivalence expressed by coal miners towards the idea of nationalization – a policy lionized by the Labour Party – and discuss how that undermined its symbolic importance and underlined the deep fissures among and between leftist intellectuals and politicians.

Chapters 4 and 5 focus in large part on geopolitical identities. Chapter 4, '"Accent Speaks Louder than Words": Imagining Regional and National Communities through Folk Music', centres on the relationship between local, regional and national identities. Celebration of regional identity was an integral part of 'national' popular culture during the postwar revival, and this chapter will address how and why regions such as the Northeast came to be celebrated by folk revivalists as the location of a more 'authentic' folk culture after the war; indeed, in the postwar period, region became politically significant, as the songs of the 'coaly Tyne', especially, were put forward as the ultimate expression of authenticity in a movement defined by the importance of that idea. Interconnected issues of class, politics and culture were significantly represented through the symbolic importance of the Northeast. Chapter 5, 'Folk Music and Cultural Exchange: The "Shiny Barbarism" of Americanization', will look at how the English revival defined itself against its American equivalent, fighting against the perceived 'Americanization' of English culture after the war, and will discuss how the nativist policies of many of the revival's leaders, in response to this implicit crisis, in fact helped link England's second revival, ideologically, with its first.

Finally, Chapter 6, '"With Bob on Our Side": Folk Music, the Culture Industry, and the Problem of Commercial Success', will consider the relationship between folk music and mass culture in the twentieth century. During the revival, folk singers defined themselves against ideas of 'commercialization' and 'mass culture' in order to establish their own authenticity in folk circles and among fans. Debates over technological intervention, copyright and the rights of the collector were all tinged with ambivalence towards mass culture. This opposition to the mass media was tied to an implicit, and at times explicit, anti-Americanism as well, as Bob Dylan in particular became a lightning rod for revivalist discontent as the embodiment of folk music's commercialization.

Conclusion

The flourishing interest in folk music in postwar England was part of a deep-seated impulse to define new cultural and political identities in the wake of the extraordinary transformations wrought by the war and its immediate aftermath. Folk music was an important part, not only of the cultural, but significantly also of the social and political fabric of post-Second World War England; to its listeners, it was authentic, unmediated and enmeshed in the salient social and political issues of the time: the triumphs and conflicted legacy of the welfare state, the subsequent crisis of leftist politics, the fight for nuclear disarmament, the social and political fallout over nationalization, fears of Americanization, the continuing importance of class divisions. The folk revival highlighted all of these issues and provided a significant cultural voice for their articulation in the public sphere.

1

The Pub and the Beeb: Structural Foundations of the English Folk Revival

Introduction

Grassroots cultural movements rarely occur in a vacuum; they require effective organization and support at the local, regional and national levels to succeed. The English folk revival was no exception; it was driven and supported by a vast framework of 'folk institutions'. These were the primary social structures of a locally and regionally vibrant movement, but they also, significantly, provided the essential means of connection between the English revival and its American counterpart – as artists, critics and fans shared music, news and debates back and forth across the Atlantic. Through dedicated networks of individuals, societies and media outlets, a folk community was created and nurtured in England, self-consciously conceived separately from the corruptive cultural influence of mainstream popular music.[67] Clubs, festivals, record labels, radio programmes, magazines and periodicals, local folk centres and societies – all provided an important foundation for the English folk movement during the postwar period. American journalist Robert Shelton remarked on a visit to Britain in 1966 that the country had seen 'a great increase in total audience as well as a concomitant rise in the number of recordings, periodicals, clubs and radio-television shows devoted to the shades of folk song. British folk fans are disputatious on how the music is to be performed and enjoyed, and their debates about traditional versus pop-style range freely but with a stronger base in philosophy than generally encountered in the United States'.[68]

This chapter will examine how the English revival created its own pseudo-socialist 'public sphere', focused on amalgamated ideologies of cultural community, left-wing politics and 'working-class values', no longer located in the bourgeois *Salons* of Jürgen Habermas's famous study, but in the local pub, working men's clubs and the converted music halls more closely associated with Richard Hoggart's.[69] It will establish the organizational and infrastructural elements of the English folk revival, introducing and analysing many of the underlying ideological and philosophical tenets of the movement as it grew and developed.

The folk club

The English folk revival was heavily dependent on, and strongly identified with, a vast system of folk clubs and societies, located in communities large and small throughout the country; these provided the foundation, the literal building blocks, of the movement. English folk clubs were often located in the back or upstairs rooms of a local pub, which helped to maintain the revival's small-scale, communal character, even as an ascendant commercial interest in folk music threatened to squash the grassroots feel. Historians and folk singers Frankie Armstrong and Brian Pearson have emphasized the fundamental importance of these clubs to the success – and unique atmosphere – of the revival in England:

> For its physical base [the revival] developed the folk club, an institution unique to these islands, housed almost without exception in the back room of a pub. Run by enthusiasts with no thought of commercial profit, the folk club concept has proved very durable, filling an empty niche in what is traditionally a key social meeting place for the community. The pub room has given the revival a secure base from which to operate, available at minimal cost and located just where people customarily go to relax. It is impossible to over-emphasize the importance of the pub, for good or ill, in shaping the British revival. The absence of a comparable institution in the USA, for example, accounts for many of the differences in the history of the folksong movement in the two countries.[70]

As Armstrong and Pearson have suggested here, there was no real equivalent in the American case to the English pub-based folk club, a fact often noted by English folk revivalists in an attempt to distinguish the movement from its American cousin. Singer Joe Boyd noted that '[t]he clubs in England were completely different to folk venues in America – pub assembly rooms rather than coffee houses. They were not run on a professional basis, there was no PA at all and no stages in most of the rooms.'[71]

In the United States, the postwar folk movement had been born in the 'coffee shops' of Greenwich Village, and spread eventually to Boston's Cambridge Square before moving on to the West Coast.[72] Like the folk clubs in England, these establishments provided a local framework for a national movement, but the coffee shop phenomenon, as it related to folk music, was more of an ephemeral development than the English clubs – which were housed in established local pubs, places which had existed long before and which would likely remain long *after*, the folk boom. In the United States, businesses grew around the popularity of folk music, in locations that were not necessarily already part of the local community, and – many English revivalists suspected – were far more focused on profiteering than providing a showcase for song traditions.

At the time, and subsequently, folk musicians in England have emphasized the fundamental importance of the public-housed folk club to the uniqueness and longevity of their revival, stressing the significance of maintaining a true community spirit – implicitly differentiated from the commercially enterprising American folk club-coffee houses. English folk singer and *Melody Maker* contributor Steve Benbow argued in 1964, 'The strength (or weakness) of the British folk song movement is that it doesn't care if there is a commercial boom or not. Its roots are local rather than national; its strength is in the folk song clubs, not the hit parade.'[73] Meanwhile, Shelton noted how the pub-based folk club contributed to the strength of the English revival despite the movement's relatively small size, writing,

> The extent of the British folk-music revival may seem minuscule in comparison with the American boom because of the country's smaller population and area. But there are other actors which make the British revival seem even deeper than the American ... The clubs meet weekly, often in a room adjoining a pub and the meetings have an atmosphere of sociability and mutual learning that few American folk cabarets or coffeehouses enjoy.[74]

Because pubs were already integral to communities large and small throughout England, they were the natural focal points for a burgeoning grassroots movement.

Many primary incarnations of later folk clubs had pre-dated large-scale interest in folk music, often previously housing skiffle or jazz clubs; the growth of new folk clubs within public houses came out of necessity – economically, spatially and ideologically. The folk clubs offered the opportunity for audience members to sing alongside other amateur singers and professionals. Here we have a telling detail which illuminates a significant distinction between the concurrent revivals in England and the United States, not least in the minds of the English revivalists: the English revivalists were much more interested in – and were even at times quite militant about – maintaining a local, amateur, grassroots quality to their movement.

Despite underlying anxieties about the size and scope of the movement, from the late 1950s onwards, the folk club scene in England developed exponentially. By the early 1960s, it was an undeniable phenomenon. *Melody Maker* noted the recent, sharp increase in folk clubs in a March 1963 issue: 'This is getting to be serious. New clubs at Hull (Folk Studio One), Matlock Training College, the Club Baltica, Manor Park, Kirkcaldy, Aberdeen, St. Andrews, Twickenham – where the Singers' have opened up on Wednesdays.'[75] Louis Killen, a member of the folk group the High Level Ranters, and founder of the Newcastle Folk Club, also commented on the meteoric rise of folk clubs in the late 1950s and early '60s: 'When I started Folk Song and Ballad in Newcastle in 1958 there weren't twenty folk clubs in the whole country, and when I left for the States [in 1966] there were maybe three hundred.'[76] By 1962, A. L. Lloyd was observing with satisfaction that there had been a 'huge growth of evening folk song clubs, several with memberships running into the thousands'; he noted further that these clubs were often committed to promoting traditional folk styles, where '[a]uthentic folk singers (let's avoid such patronizing labels as "ethnic" or "field" singers)' could be introduced to audiences throughout the country.[77]

The January 1962 issue of *Sing* magazine featured an evocative illustration of the burgeoning folk club scene in one particular region, Tyneside, with the Ranters' Folksong and Ballad club front and centre: 'Newcastle-Upon-Tyne's folksong club, which meets every Thursday night in the city's Liberal Club – Folksong and Ballad – is unique among clubs which form the backbone of the folksong scene in this country. It is a club formed and run by revivalists in a part of the country where the tradition is still very much alive.'[78] Singer Anthea Joseph argued that the richness of the tradition on Tyneside had given the Folksong and Ballad club 'a pretty wide scope, for not only is the native Northumbrian tradition around them but there are large numbers of Irish and Scots, and even a sprinkling of Southerners, who have settled in the industrial belt along the "coaly Tyne."'[79] Joseph also emphasized the club's commitment to presenting local talent, noting that guests had recently included the Elliott family of Birtley (a mining village located approximately 10 km Southeast of Newcastle), 'who took over the club for half an evening with their songs, games, and stories'; they were joined by Foster Charlton and Colin Caisley, two Northumbrian pipers. She described these guests as 'all local people', claiming that 'there are plenty more around to draw upon, though the club hopes to bring to Newcastle some of the best singers from outside the area.'[80] In fact, many of the key groups and figures within the revival established their own clubs: apart from Ewan MacColl's Ballads and Blues Club, for instance, the Spinners of Liverpool had also established their own, very successful, folk club at Gregson's Well; from the biggest centres and groups to the most humble, this pattern was repeated throughout the country.

A tiny advertisement in the September 1962 issue of *Sing* promoted the Elliott family's new club in Birtley, highlighting its very local flavour: 'the Elliott family ... have set up the Birtley Folk Song and Ballad Club, at the Red Lion Inn on Wednesdays. Anyone who has heard the record and read [Ewan] MacColl and [Peggy] Seeger's account of collecting in that area will not be surprised to hear that the whole membership is the "talent" and the "residents." Folk fans are invited to spend an evening with the Elliotts and their friends. The club's secretary is Doreen Henderson (nee Elliott) who lives at 1 The Avenue, Birtley.'[81] The previous April, an excellent account of the founding of another regional folk club, this time in Southampton, appeared in *Sing*, written by local journalist John Mann: 'A few friends and their friends turned up to constitute the public supporting the local folk song revival. As for performers, those interested numbered two: one a middle-aged housewife who knew the name Burl Ives and had sung Greensleeves in the local Women's Institute Choir, the other a girl with a guitar who didn't like singing on licenced premises.'[82] After this fairly inauspicious start, then, these two ex-skifflers – Dave Williams and Vic Wilton – returned home to 'a remote inn called the Bold Forester, where the septuagenarian landlord kept his change in his waistcoat pockets (he thought tills were new-fangled) and could sing, if asked, The Unfortunate Young Rake. Dave and Vic also appeared at another rustic retreat, the Traveller's Rest, and gradually their fame began to spread.'[83] Finally, the club grew to the point where Mann observed, 'Shoe-horns were soon routine equipment for a trip to hear the singers at the Bold and the Travellers and comparisons with sardines were often made.'[84] The first guest was Bob Davenport, and from then came the likes of Stan Kelly, Cyril Tawney, Alex Campbell, Cyril Davies – and eventually Ewan MacColl and Peggy Seeger, signalling the club's firm establishment on both the local entertainment scene and the national folk scene.

Pubs offered the ideal locations for folk clubs because of their relaxed atmosphere, and licensing laws that allowed underage folk fans to enter and participate with their of-age compatriots.[85] Admission costs were kept low, ranging usually between 40 and 70p, although the amount fluctuated depending on the performer or performers –

sometimes entry was even free.[86] A club with an audience of fifty, each paying 50p, could gross £25 on an average folk night. If the room had to be paid for, and if there were publicity charges, then these would have to be met before the artist could be paid.[87] Woods likened the postwar folk clubs to the music halls or working men's clubs of the early twentieth century, in terms of their function in fostering a community spirit around songs and singing. He wrote that the 'self-organised, participatory, community activity of a folk club is extremely close to the original working men's clubs in both atmosphere and achievement. Both can be classed as sub-cultural activities, closely related to the community, but not of official status; and both protect and foster a popular art form.'[88] As an institution, the folk club aspired to be a progressive and broadly egalitarian enterprise, unconcerned with profit; Michael Pickering and Tony Green have argued that the 'semi-professional' performers were paid through 'break-even collections staffed by volunteers'.[89] Indeed, at their most earnest, English folk clubs aspired and adhered to this pseudo-socialist artistic practice, where local and itinerant professionals and semi-professionals were gathered together along with amateur 'worker-performers' – the 'true folk'; 'authentic' singers. However, in many ways this was no more than an ideal; in reality the cooperative coexistence of amateur and professional performers throughout the revival was fraught with financial and creative tension, as the ideal of a folk community at times gave way to ideological difference over the nature and function of folk music.

Although Dallas described the growth of folk clubs as part of 'a hydra-headed undirectable community which resisted all attempts to dragoon it into federations, ideologies or mutually-warring factions,' the halcyon early years of the folk club movement, by the early 1960s, threatened to give way to a kind of 'cultural claustrophobia,' as American folk songs, especially, were increasingly squeezed out in favour of the determined preservation of English, and more broadly British, tradition.[90] Different clubs started to take on specific characteristics. Some became exclusively traditionalist, approving only of hand-on-the-ear unaccompanied singers, performing eighteenth- and nineteenth-century ballads. Others welcomed American Delta blues and the work of contemporary singer-songwriters; Dallas conceded that the traditionalists eventually created 'a ghetto' around themselves.[91]

Eric Winter, the editor of *Sing* magazine, described the united front put up by London folk club organizers on the occasion of a Pete Seeger concert at the Royal Albert Hall in 1961 – a decidedly august affair, given the revival's disdain for the trappings of celebrity – stating: 'This united act was founded on a loose, undefined unity that already existed among the clubs.'[92] However, Winter also hinted at the underlying tension in the scene, surrounding Ewan MacColl's recent establishment of a new folk club: 'In the middle of the Seeger tour there was an isolated incident that may, at first glance, appear to have nothing to do with the case. The Singers' Club claimed in an advertisement to be "the only genuine folk club" in London. The claim in itself is nothing new. Ewan MacColl has said similar things on several occasions during the past few months.'[93]

MacColl was no stranger to controversy, and as the operator of the Singers' Club in Soho Square, he often seemed to court it. Shelton, in introducing the English revival to American readers, described MacColl as the 'Charles de Gaulle of the British folk revival, with all the positive and negative elements implicit in the comparison'; he stated that, '[o]ne cannot go far here without encountering strong followers or opponents of MacColl's rigorous musical and theatrical creativity or his steel-grip esthetic.'[94] This 'steel-grip esthetic' was a conspicuous and ubiquitous feature of the English folk revival, and was the focus of a *Sing* piece from August 1961 entitled simply 'Why I Am Opening a New Club,' in which MacColl laid down the gauntlet on folk club performance policy which would underpin many of the tense interactions – debates over 'authenticity' and 'respect' for material – between clubs in London and throughout the country. MacColl's reasoning for the necessity of the new club is worth quoting in its entirety, for it provides significant insight into later revivalist debates, and a telling sketch of MacColl's own character. He began his piece with this statement: 'At a time when there are a great many folk clubs on the London scene, people may wonder why I have plunged in at the centre, in a season when attendances tend to fall off,' and addressed this presumed curiosity with the following manifesto:

1. It is necessary to rescue a large number of young people, all of whom have the right instincts, from those influences that have appeared on the folk scene during the past two or three years – influences that are doing their best to debase the meaning of folk song. The only notes that some people care about are banknotes.
2. Some top-liners of the folk song world – Bert Lloyd, Dominic Behan, for instance – have done little public singing in the past two or three years. Peggy and I have sung to live audiences more in the States and Canada than in Britain. Our new club will provide a platform for singers of this calibre who, like all folk singers, draw strength from live audiences.
3. Our experience during our US tour and at the Newport Festival have shown us the danger of singing down to an audience. It is the danger that the folk song revival can get so far away from its traditional basis that in the end it is impossible to distinguish it from pop music and cabaret. It has happened in the States at clubs like the 'Gate of Horn' in San Francisco where the cover charge and a meal are likely to run about 5 a head for an evening. True bawdiness is reduced to mere suggestiveness. The songs, sapped of their vigour, become 'quaint'. It's happening here too in the 'Tonight' programme. I was scared when I saw what's going on in some of the clubs. But it's not too late to retrieve the position.
4. The position in Britain is relatively healthy. It's easy to bring Harry Cox and Sam Larner to London and other centres and to bring fine Gaelic singers to Edinburgh, for instance. There's no tendency for them to be snapped up and commercialised. But we are determined to give top traditional singers a platform where they will be protected from the ravages of the commercial machine.
5. Finally, we need standards. Already the race for the quick pound note is on in the folk song world. 'Quaint' songs, risqué songs, poor instrumentation and no-better-than-average voices – coupled with a lack of respect for the material: against these we will fight.[95]

This piece reveals much about the cultural politics driving the revival, as well as MacColl's own – rather domineering and patronizing – character. His main concerns clearly emerged from his experience observing the American revival first-hand. His warnings against commercialization, dilution and borderline-talent performers all seem to stem from observations he made while touring the United States in the late 1950s and early 1960s. MacColl's need to differentiate the English from the American revival found an outlet in the foundation of this new club, which, just as the folk club scene was exploding, was an attempt to incubate his vision of folk culture against the perceived threat of commercialization (and implicitly, Americanization). In effect, it was an attempt to establish a universal idea of acceptable club practice, and drew a line in the sand regarding policy at English folk clubs.

From 1959, *Sing* magazine had supplied a regularly updated directory of Britain's folk clubs as the revival continued to warrant their expansion. In the May 1962 issue, the magazine reported that 'the folk club scene is bursting at the seams.'[96] It advertised on its front cover that there were 'NOW OVER 80 CLUBS ... Last September there were 45 clubs. Now there are 80, listed in the directory published as a free supplement to this issue. Several towns now boast more than one club. Many clubs are playing to large audiences. Places like the Troubadour, London, and the Howff in Dunfermline are packed to capacity every week.'[97] Along with a listing of the clubs, *Sing* provided important information to its readers, such as weekly times and featured performers for each establishment. In London, for example, the 1962 list included: the Ballads and Blues Club (2 Soho Sq. W1) on Saturdays at 7:30, featuring Stan Kelly and others; the Blues and Barrelhouse, at the Roundhouse (Wardour St. W1), Thursdays at 8:00, featuring Cyril Davies, Alexis Korner, Rory McEwen and Bob Davenport; The Cellar, at Cecil Sharp House (Regents Park Road, NW1) Mondays at 7:30 – with guitar classes at 8:30 – and a song-swap, Thursdays at 7:30; The Singers' Club (2 Soho Sq. W1) gathered on alternate Sundays at 7:30, featuring Ewan MacColl, Peggy Seeger, Bert Lloyd and Dominic Behan; The Troubadour (Old Brompton Road, SW5) had their folk club on Saturdays at 10:30, with no resident performers but often including Dominic Behan, the Spinners, the Thames-side Four and Enoch Kent; the Topical and Traditional met at the York and Albany (Parkway, NW1, near Cecil Sharp House), Sundays at 7:30, featuring John Brune, Moire Magee and Shirley Hart.[98] Those were just the clubs in central London, in 1962. In Greater London, there were several more folk clubs located in areas such as Battersea, Dulwich, New Cross, Putney, Wandsworth, Brentford, Bromley, Chigwell, Croydon, Hatfield, Hoddesdon, Richmond and Surbiton. Folk clubs also flourished in other urban centres such as Birmingham, Liverpool and Manchester, as well as in the 'provinces' (see Appendix I).[99] By the mid-1970s, the number of estimated folk clubs in Britain had quadrupled, from around 300 a decade earlier.[100] These clubs, together with local folk societies, also provided a physical base for the revival in different parts of the country.

The EFDSS was the oldest, and largest, folk society in England, and was instrumental in organizing folk music events not only throughout London but also in the provinces as well.[101] Cecil Sharp House, the society's London headquarters, was, Armstrong and Pearson wrote, a 'veritable hive of activity' during the revival, attracting folk singers and dancers from across the city and the country, with nightly activities, including ceilidhs and song swaps.[102] The EFDSS actively encouraged amateur participation in the folk revival, through various workshops they ran. A pamphlet from the early 1960s expressed this quite clearly: 'Interest in folk music is sweeping the country ... you can join in too. Dancing – singing – listening – playing – There's room for you.'[103] The society worked further to promote folk music nationally through its booking service, launched in 1965. The service booked performers for local folk clubs and societies, as well as schools and universities, television and radio stations throughout the country. The advertisement noted that 'if there are any artists whom your club would like to hear, however inaccessible geographically, please let us know ... The booking service is not a commercial agency in that our aim is to help the folk song scene as a whole rather than to push the careers of any individual artists.'[104] The EFDSS had chapters throughout the country, and similar societies existed in communities both small and large. But while folk clubs, and institutions like the EFDSS, provided a strong physical infrastructure for folk revivalism, a dedicated and increasingly varied folk music press also played a crucial role in encouraging its development, while also providing part of the revival's political voice.

The folk music press

In England, the popular music press did not tend to concern itself with folk music; it was never 'big business,' as folk became in the United States. Even at the height of the revival, only *Melody Maker*, among the major musical publications, had regular coverage of the folk music scene, with *Sounds* and *New Musical Express* chipping in very occasionally.[105] *Melody Maker* was a weekly music magazine initially focused on jazz, but which in fact provided increasing coverage of folk music as the revival developed. Coverage of the folk scene included a regular column, 'Focus on Folk,' as well as advertisements for folk records and upcoming concerts. *Melody Maker* focused on both English and American folk material; however, Britta Sweers has argued that 'what could be read about the revival in *Melody Maker* ... remained at the "star" level.'[106] Indeed, for all the 'focus on folk' there was little focus on the grassroots element. However, one edition of 'Focus on Folk,' from 19 January 1963, featured a then-little-known singer, Bob Dylan (in England to appear in a play, *Madhouse on Castle Street*). This would be the first instance of many that English revivalists would have to see Dylan, described as a 'New York folknik' and an 'anarchist on principle' by feature writer Eric Winter. Winter offered a review of Dylan's recently released eponymous debut album, writing that it introduced him as a capable 'songwriter in the folk idiom.'[107]

 Melody Maker chronicled the emergence and development of the folk revival, in both England and the United States. A 'special report' from New York, dated 24 August 1963, proclaimed 'Suddenly – It's Folk!' and asserted:

> You can throw out the bossa nova, the twist, the hully gully, surf music and a flock of other dance-based music fads. Forget them. The 'in' words in the United States this summer included 'Hootenanny', five-string banjo, 12-string guitar and most of

all, 'Folkniks' because the folkniks have given the record and music business here its biggest boost in as many years.[108]

Describing the key players, the article mentioned 'Miss Baez, an intense-looking brunette,' together with Dylan, 'a pensive, raggedy looking youngster from the Midwest'.[109] The following week, Winter's 'Focus on Folk' tempered hopes for a similar boom in England, as he wrote:

> Folk has been bigtime in the USA for a lot of years now. You could always fill the Carnegie Hall and similar places if you put on the Weavers or Pete Seeger. Recently Bob Dylan and others have moved up into the sell-out bracket. Every once in a while, somebody predicts a folk boom in Britain. There are signs, of course. But we have yet to see our top folk singers – even the less ethnic among them – becoming so 'acceptable'.[110]

Even Dusty Springfield – at the time, one of the most successful singers in Britain – weighed in on the possibility of a folk boom in England during this period:

> Folk boom? I don't see it happening in Britain … Just because it's happening in America … it doesn't necessarily mean that British kids will follow suit. There's a lot of important differences between the popular music scene in Britain and America. In America it's not the kids who are buying folk records, it's the university students. These people make up a huge audience in the States, and folk singers can get five thousand dollars a concert singing on the college campus. There's nothing like that in Britain. You won't be able to talk about a folk boom in Britain until there's folk music at one, two, and three in the hit parade – and I can't see that happening, now or ever … I'll tell you what I've got against a lot of folk singers, and this goes for some of the successful Americans, too, they're so terribly mournful. I like music to have a happy, joyous sound.[111]

And a 'folk revival', as it had developed in the United States, was not to be in Britain. In her comments, Springfield addressed many of the most important differences between the American and English revivals, including the former's emphasis on its small scale, amateur status. And yet, almost exactly one year later, to the day, *Melody Maker* reported that the Spinners of Liverpool were 'going pro', proving that money could be made from folk music, and marking the definite presence of a 'folk boom' in England.[112]

Specialized folk music magazines and periodicals sprang up as the revival grew, and were important as communicators not only of the ideological debates raging within the movement, but as distributors of the newest songs being written; they acted as the modern-day broadsides.[113] Although the EFDSS published its own folk music journal – first under the title *English Dance and Song*, and then, from 1965, as the *Folk Music Journal* (to secure 'a more attractive and readable product')[114] – the corresponding publication to the enterprising American folk magazine *Sing Out!*, in England, was in fact *Sing*. Founded in May 1954, and produced by the London Youth

Choir – which had links with the Communist Party – *Sing*'s mission statement claimed that '[t]oday there is a need for the distribution of such songs of immediate and topical interest, as widely as possible, particularly among young people. This is the task which this magazine sets itself.'[115] *Sing* was produced bi-monthly (or as funding allowed), and sold for 1 shilling. A typical issue was 15–20 pages long, and included book and record reviews, as well as printed songs on a certain theme – often surrounding a major figure such as Robbie Burns, or a topic of contemporary importance such as the Campaign for Nuclear Disarmament; there were advertisements for record companies or even other magazines, including *Sing Out!*, as well as *Ethnic* and *Spin* from Britain. Regular columns included 'What's On and Who's Singing', 'For the Record' and 'A Singer's Notebook', which featured a guest columnist in each issue who wrote about an aspect of the local scene in one area of the country.

Winter established *Sing*'s political stance in the first issue, stating that 'SING can play an important role in the struggles of the British people for peace and socialism.'[116] Alan Bush, the president of the Workers' Music Association also asserted *Sing*'s importance to a broader socialist movement: 'It is excellent that a regular song magazine has been started. This will enable topical songs to become quickly available to the movement and will supplement in an invaluable way the publications of the [WMA] and Topic Records.'[117] *Sing* included a fairly balanced mix of traditional and contemporary compositions, by artists from both sides of the Atlantic, and beyond. By 1956, it was presenting both British and American folk songs to its growing readership, often reprinting items from *Sing Out!*. In fact, in both *Sing* and *Sing Out!*, records from the opposite side of the Atlantic were promoted, introducing their respective reading audiences to a new act or group, and strengthening the connection between the two contemporary revivals. In the April 1965 issue of *Sing* alone this cooperative spirit could be felt. That issue not only included a full page ad for the new Phil Ochs record, *All the News That's Fit to Sing*, but also featured an ad emphasizing British label Fontana's promotion of American artists in LPs such as *Newport Folk Festival Evening Concert*, 1 and 2 (TFL 6041–2); Buffy Sainte Marie, *It's My Way* (TFL 6040); *Blues at Newport* (TFL 6037); and *Newport Broadside* (TFL 6038), as well as an eponymous disc by Mike Seeger (TFL 6039).[118] *Sing*'s coverage of the major figures of the US revival reflected the magazine's cooperation with *Sing Out!*, and also underlined the close relationship between the English and American folk revivals.

Through its coverage of the American movement and many of its leading figures, *Sing* proved its ideological ties with *Sing Out!*, and revivalists in the United States. However, from its first issue, the 'national' character of the English, and more broadly British, revival was also emphasized. Winter stated that '[t]he music we print has not grown without roots. The traditions of English, Welsh, Scottish and Irish folksongs, together with those of other countries, form the tap roots … From time to time we shall print examples of these traditions, so that performers can ground themselves in their heritage.'[119] While *Sing* was undoubtedly concerned with presenting a progressive political voice for the folk movement – which included printing a variety of songs, both traditional and contemporary, British and American – other publications, such as *Ethnic*, were much more militant in their avowed politics.

Ethnic, established in 1959, was touted as the antithesis to synthetic music and culture in Britain. It sold for 7/6d per year, quarterly. Editor Reg Hall stated that the magazine's ideological and epistemological origins came from the Greek – *ethnos* meaning 'that, which pertains to a nation'.[120] In terms of cultural impact, *Ethnic* had a much smaller circulation than more mainstream contemporaries – throughout 1959, it had around 150 subscribers – but it was important in defining the debate between tradition and innovation at the heart of the revival. Hall noted that amongst folklorists the term 'ethnic' had 'special significance in that it connotes a traditional performance which is virtually unconditioned by commercial considerations – which is in fact a direct expression of traditional culture'.[121] *Ethnic* pointedly did not feature any printed notation with its songs – only the words were included. Hall explained this fact by saying that the magazine wanted 'to encourage all would-be traditional singers to learn their songs directly from the live sources, because of the tendency of revivalist singers to seize upon a printed tune and to standardize it as the only tune for a particular song and because we believe that songs can still be disseminated in the form of words only'.[122]

Responding to contemporary claims that *Ethnic* represented a negatively 'purist' strand of folk revivalism, Hall countered, 'Our concern is with traditional music, dance and drama, and since by definition this is the music, dance and drama which is handed from generation to generation orally we must, if we are in our right minds, be concerned with those individuals and communities which retain the traditional habit – or, as we say, "have the tradition."'[123] The magazine took a critical stance of most 'urban' revivalists, and sought to distance itself from any associations with them, with Hall stating, 'We understand that since we started publication the word "ethnic" has become very fashionable in certain metropolitan folk song circles as a term for any performance which is not genteel. The tradition is not based in London however, and there are many singers in the Revival whose style is not genteel and is synthetic rather than ethnic'.[124] While *Ethnic* did not have the same popular readership as *Sing*, it was still an important voice for the unflinching traditionalist faction within the revival.

Some other publications, such as *Folk Review*, founded in 1963, understood the power of the mass media in promoting and distributing folk music – both traditional and contemporary – to British audiences. *Folk Review* was published out of the Isle of Man, edited by John Kaneen and David Callister. On its front cover for the first issue was Birmingham folk singer Ian Campbell, of the Ian Campbell Folk Group. The cover also featured a faceless black man in a cowboy hat, clearly evoking two classic American folk images. *Folk Review* appealed directly to organizations like the BBC in collaborating with and encouraging folk music in Britain. The editors sent a free copy of the first issue to BBC Features producer D. G. Bridson, with the following note attached:

Dear Mr. Bridson, We are pleased to enclose a complimentary copy of our new folk record review magazine. We have noted your radio folk music productions in the past. In particular the short Pete Seeger series on the Third Programme. We would be glad to receive from you, advance information on any such productions in future to include in the item called 'Folk on Sound'.[125]

In the inaugural editorial, the ethos of the magazine was explained. It was an ethos based on an avid dedication to forwarding both traditional and contemporary material to their reading audience:

This is the first of what we hope to be a long series of magazines devoted to recorded folk music. We decided to produce this magazine to help you to choose the best from the ever-increasing numbers of folk record releases. It is not intended for financial gain, nor for political reasons, but only because of our love of the music.[126]

A good deal of the magazine was taken up with reviews of new folk LPs – something which would not have been possible even five years previously – and the editors stated that readers were 'invited to praise, curse, swear at, pull to pieces, or enthuse over our efforts via the mail. The more we hear from you, the better we will like it!'[127] Also included was a 'Folk News' page with 'bits and pieces concerning the folk scene' as well as advance information of radio and TV programmes featuring folk music. The editors also vowed to 'include, from time to time, coverage of Country and Western music and certain "commercial" elements,' which they acknowledged 'may upset the purists among you'[128]; in the end, however, *Folk Review* was determined that 'all the records we review – good, bad, or indifferent – are essential ingredients of the current folk song revival. In our experience the appreciation of true traditional music is usually evolved through a process which begins with the "pop" versions dispensed by tin-pan alley.'[129] The first issue featured reviews of both British and American material, including: *This IS the Ian Campbell Folk Group* (Transatlantic TRA110); *Lost Love by Isla Cameron* (Transatlantic TRA EP 109); *Country Style, Ancient and Modern by Clinton Ford* (Oriole PS 40025); *Joan Baez in Concert* (Fontana TFL 6033); *The Spinners* (Fontana TFL 5201); *Walkin' The Strings by Merle Travis* (Capitol EAP4 1391); *Ernest V. Stoneman and the Stoneman Family* (London HA-B 8089); and *The Bluegrass Hall of Fame* (Stateside LP SL10021).[130] The magazine advertised, in 'Folk on Sound', the BBC Home Service broadcast of A. L. Lloyd's Folk Songs of Australia; 'Folk on Vision', meanwhile, announced a new Robin Hall and Jimmie MacGregor show, *White Heather Club*, as well as a programme for Border TV, *Make Mine Country Style*.

Spin was published out of Cheshire, under the auspices of the Liverpool Spinners and the Spinners Club. It sold for 1 shilling, and was edited by Beryl Davis, wife of Spinners singer Tony Davis. The magazine was described by Winter as 'anything but parochial in outlook, even if it does carry a lot of Northern material.'[131] In a supplementary publication of material, *Folk Songs from Spin*, Davis described the genesis of the magazine:

In the early days of The Spinners Club, weekly song sheets were duplicated and sold at 3d per copy, containing the words of some of the most popular songs sung in the club. These 'broadsides' were often bought by the dozen and used by members who were in other organizations to spread the songs around. As membership grew, it was felt that a magazine would be a good idea, to carry both songs and some information about songs and singers – so 'Spin' was born.[132]

The first issue was printed in October 1961, according to Davis, as a 'duplicated, 300 copy 12 page magazine devoted to songs, news and articles on the broad subject of "folk". Its aim has been to provide some background information about the traditional songs which have come down to us through the years as "folk" and to help introduce some of the many good songs written for and about today to the singing world.'[133]

By the sixth issue, there were so many inquiries and orders from all over Britain that, wrote Davis, 'it was impossible to turn the duplicator handle fast enough, and crossing their fingers the editors went into photo-offset and printed a thousand copies.'[134] The focus of the magazine was mostly on British tradition, and featured regular columns by Stan Hugill on sea shanties, Leslie Haworth on ballads and Johnny Handle on the particularities of the Northeast scene. In 1965, according to Davis, *Spin* had 5,000 readers, many of these, apparently, in the United States.[135]

There were several other magazines and pamphlets produced and available throughout England during the revival, including but not limited to *Folk Unlimited* and *Blues Unlimited* (Bexhill-on-Sea), *Folk Guide* and *Folk Music* (London) and *Folk Musician and Singer* (Manchester).[136] The growth and success of the folk press were arguably indicative of the trajectory of the revival itself. While these magazines struggled in the early days, circulation generally rose steadily from the early 1960s onwards.[137] Like the early struggles of *Sing Out!*, *Sing* was beset by financial difficulty before the folk revival took off in the early 1960s. In 1955, for instance, the following statement appeared:

> We have decided to launch a 'Sing' fund … increased circulation is, of course, the answer to our financial problems. Meanwhile we need money to buy much needed equipment and supplies and to pay our running expenses. Our target is £150 in the next three months. How about it readers? … Ours is the only magazine of people's songs in Britain. Will you help us keep our head just a little bit above the water? IF PEACE IS WORTH HAVING IT'S WORTH SINGING FOR AND WORTH PAYING FOR![138]

Despite its initial struggles, *Sing* published semi-regularly until 1969 – its last issue was published in March of that year, reflecting the declining public interest in acoustic forms of folk music.

The folk and music periodicals had an important function within the folk movement. They elucidated not only the key ideological debates and principles of the English folk revival – and its transatlantic counterpart – but were also forums for regular people and performers alike to participate in the movement. While the readership of the folk magazines might have been small, relative to more mainstream publications, they still contained the core of the movement within their pages. The songs printed and explained, the essays and op-ed pieces written by folk scholars and singers alike, the letters to the editors – these parts of the publications served an important social function, adding to a public conversation over the nature and direction of folk revivalism in postwar England. These magazines, in other words, have been the single-most important gauge for how the folk revival was publicly received and debated. They helped to create a culture of participation within the revival movement, in many ways the best forums for public opinion and reception, while also providing the means of collaboration and comparison between the two folk movements on either side of the Atlantic. While the folk music press was important in disseminating the political and aesthetic ideologies at work during the revivals, and informing a growing base of committed followers, the revivals would have been impossible without the support of the record industry and the radio.

Record labels

During the revival period, folk music on both sides of the Atlantic was recorded and distributed through a number of small record labels, alongside – in the US case – the conspicuous participation of at least one major label, Columbia Records. Major label interest in English folk music was conversely negligible. *Sing* contributor Ken Phine, in his regular 'For the Record' column, expressed frustration with the lack of support folk music received from the major record labels in England, who were timid about supporting a genre which would, he admitted, never sell a million copies: '[BBC producer] Peter Kennedy's foot is still holding the door at HMV, but I'm giving very favourable odds that [they] will do nothing about Peter's huge collaboration with [Alan] Lomax – an anthology of British material to which they have rights.'[139] Phine noted that the big companies, like HMV, 'might be persuaded to reissue the Carnegie Hall Weavers disc if someone with enough patience would explain to them that, although no folk disc will sell a million here, neither will most of the other stuff they issue. Beltona, Decca's Celtic-fringe, is issuing a lot of Scots and Irish material, but the million-sale fallacy spoils it all.'[140] However, while major label support might have been unforthcoming, the English folk revival was supported through a number of smaller labels. Of these, Topic Records became very clearly, from the beginning, the folk label.

The relationship between Topic – the self-dubbed 'little red label', and the oldest independent record company in Britain – and the Worker's Music Association (WMA) was one of the most important ideological and political partnerships of the postwar folk movement in England. The WMA's relationship with Topic was mutually beneficial, especially as Topic developed into the dominant recording company for folk music in postwar England; it quickly became, according to Colin Harper, the 'plaything' of the WMA, churning out a considerable volume of both traditional and contemporary material representing performers from all parts of Britain.[141] When the record company started in 1939, it was mostly occupied with distributing Soviet and other 'political' music via mail order, but expanded its reaches in tandem with the increasing scope and popularity of folk music after the war. Topic was the first label in England to consistently promote and record folk music; for a long time, it was the only label interested in producing and distributing folk songs.[142] A. L. Lloyd became its artistic director in 1957, and, in accordance with his lifelong championing of workers' music, released several records of 'industrial' folk songs under the Topic label at the height of the revival, including *The Iron Muse* (1963), which were then successfully sold and raffled in folk clubs throughout the country.[143] Although Topic and the

WMA formally parted company in 1958, they retained informal links throughout the revival period, mainly through their mutual relationship with producer Bill Leader and Lloyd.

Despite its monopoly on the folk market, especially in the early days of the revival, Topic struggled financially; Harker wrote that the label 'limped' through 1962.[144] Meanwhile, Lloyd biographer Dave Arthur noted that, even in the mid-1960s – at the height of the revival – Topic fell short of solvency. Sales figures for 1965–66, of 23,590 albums, fell to 16,761 in 1966–67, and hit a low of 14,461 in 1967–68.[145] Despite its financial hardships, however, Topic was crucially important to the English folk revival, and continues to make folk albums to this day. The variety and breadth of the records it issued reflected the broad range of interest and participation in the revival movement, and although it was not the only record label to distribute folk music, it was the largest and most successful. Producer Bill Leader left Topic in the late 1960s to start his own eponymous label. A contemporary advertisement for Leader Sound claimed that the company's aim was 'to represent all the outstanding tradition singers and musicians of the British Isles,' and promoted records by The High Level Ranters, Jack Elliott of Birtley, Seamus Ennis, Martin Byrnes and Seamus Tansey.[146] The label was especially keen on the music of the Northeast, and was based in Yorkshire. Leader's venture, however, proved to be unfortunately ill-timed, and it was therefore relatively short-lived.[147] Apart from Leader and Topic, other labels in England included Fontana and Transatlantic, the latter of which was also a major distributor of American Folkways LPs in Britain.

Fontana was interested in promoting American folk music in Britain, and vice versa. In the February 1966 issue of *Sing*, the following statement appeared, advertising, from the 'unexcelled Fontana catalogue … the best in British and American folk music.'[148] The ad listed LPs by Canadian duo Ian and Sylvia (*Early Morning Rain*, TFL 6053), as well as American 'Queen of Folk' Joan Baez (*Farewell Angelina*, TFL 6058) and Buffy Sainte-Marie (*Many a Mile*, TFL 6047), along with contributions from British acts such as The Spinners, Martin Carthy and the McPeake family.[149] As early as 1959, American records started to become more readily available in England, something clearly articulated in a *Sing* article reviewing new discs from December of that year: 'American LPs are more likely to be readily available now that currency restrictions have eased. Against the day, make a note now of "Nonesuch" – Pete Seeger and Frank Hamilton exploring the resources of harmonica, flute, recorder, mandolin, banjo and two kinds of guitar, as accompanying instruments, and getting a lot of fun out of it.'[150] Another review article, also from 1959, observed that 'Folkways has re-issued "Hootenanny Tonight," originally on Hootenanny label and still fifty minutes of star-studded joy from the people closest to SING OUT!', and revealed that Topic had produced an EP from that Folkways recording, featuring the tracks 'Mule Skinner', 'Talking Union', 'Dark as a Dungeon', 'California Blues' and 'Wimoweh', which Winter nominated 'as my recommended Christmas gift from anybody to anybody,' along with Pete Seeger's 5-String Banjo tutorial.[151] Then, in February 1962, *Sing* noted the sudden plethora of Pete Seeger records in Britain: 'The abundance of Pete Seeger records (nearly 50 LPs) gets confusing in Britain … after years of scarcity, zingo! 50! And they all seem to have wimoweh on them.'[152] *Melody Maker* also commented on this phenomenon in March of 1963, explaining the reasons for the delay: 'Previous efforts to arrange for the distribution here of the famous Folkways Records catalogue have come to nought for two good reasons. The trading arrangements were not viable and the price of the discs was too high for the average folk collector.'[153] The magazine elaborated that Transatlantic would distribute Folkways albums in Britain, to the benefit of both companies: 'Starting May 1, there will be selected releases each month at a price below 40s a record – which is quite something. Special orders from the 800-strong Folkways list will still cost a little over 40s but there is even hope that this price may be adjusted. Downwards. This is, of course, really splendid news.'[154]

Small record labels such as these were crucial to the success of the folk revival, both through their promotion of English and British folk music, and in their role as redistributors and re-packagers of American material in England.[155] In England, both American and British record companies depended on places like Collet's Record Shop to distribute their material. Collet's, located on New Oxford St., was the London outlet for *Sing Out!* and for many other American folk products. The shop also published a monthly review journal of folk recordings, entitled *Recorded Folk Music*; it was important in encouraging cultural exchange between the English and American revivals. An ad in the September 1961 issue of *Sing* proclaimed, 'Seekers after the truth should get themselves on the mailing list of Collet's record shop … As a direct result of Moses Asch's consumer research in London, Folkways are issuing a lot of British material, both studio and field.'[156] Collet's was the hub for American material in Britain, also partnering with one of the United States' most successful labels, in Moe Asch's Folkways Records.

Folkways was in many respects the most influential folk label in America during the revival, and was clearly respected in England as well, where many of the label's releases were sold. An article in the August 1961 issue of *Sing*, written by Robert Shelton, acted as an advertisement for Folkways, noting: 'Suddenly, the number of records available to folk fans in Britain has been increased by close on seven hundred. The Folkways catalogue has been released by Collets and at once dozens of discs – Seeger, Leadbelly, Guthrie, Broonzie, MacColl and many besides – previously unobtainable here are easy to buy.'[157] Shelton also provided an introduction to the American label for English readers: 'The unusual experiment, the off-the-beaten track recording, these are the commonplaces of Folkways, which regards records as a great device for intercommunication between peoples and societies, an easily disseminated artifact or preserving man's culture.'[158] British record labels were able to disseminate a considerable volume and variety of folk music during the revival, and after. Often, too, they helped to distribute American folk albums, many of which were sold at places like Collet's. Especially in England, however, the radio played an equally important role in the mass distribution of folk song after the war.

The BBC

In England, contrasting the American case, the importance of public radio in promoting folk music to a national audience cannot be overstated.[159] The BBC was an essential partner in the folk music revival, despite occasional claims of censorship.[160]

Woods credited the efforts of the BBC collectors and producers during the revival period as 'herculean'.[161] As early as 1942, the programme *Country Magazine* had proven the broadcaster's interest in England's folk traditions. The success of folk music at the BBC was due in no small part to the vision of its Directors-General both during the war, and immediately afterwards. The war had proven the power of radio in creating and maintaining a sense of national unity, and as Stephen Barnard has asserted, 'It was a period in which the ideological uses of entertainment – its uses in binding people together in a common cause, its identification with and portrayal of national values, however contrived or self-regarding – were appreciated in very direct ways.'[162] The BBC developed a clear policy on music from its earliest days. As Barnard argues, 'The formulation of a policy on music became one of the BBC's first priorities, giving shape and expression to the notion of cultural responsibility enshrined in the BBC Charter.'[163] Because it was publicly funded, the BBC could afford to pursue what Barnard has termed the broadcaster's 'high-minded dedication to intellectual betterment,'[164] based on a three-tiered approach to programming.

Producer D. G. Bridson was one of several BBC executives who saw the promise of folk music during the war, as feelings of nationalism and nostalgia reached new heights. Bridson was inspired, at least in part, by the gains of the pre-war American folk movement to broadcast folk music on the BBC's Third Programme:

> When I first heard modern American folk-singing during the war, I realized how truly it stemmed from the sung poetry of the past. Not merely was it reviving the proper performance of the ballads collected by Child but it was producing its own songs and ballads in exactly the same tradition. To hear Leadbelly singing John Henry or Josh White singing Hard Time Blues was to … hear poetry which had been conceived of as song in the moment of composition.[165]

Bridson expressed his belief in the continued vitality of the folk tradition, offering unique insight into the BBC's broadcasting policies on folk music after the war: 'The men who were actually writing and singing such songs in my time – Woody Guthrie, John Jacob Niles, Pete Seeger, Ewan MacColl, Bob Dylan and the rest – have given back to poetry something it should never have lost. They have re-created for us what I believe will prove to be the poetry of the future.'[166] Not only was Bridson convinced of the power of folk song in the contemporary world, he was equally confident that radio – and specifically the BBC – would play an indispensable role in conveying it to an ever-increasing segment of the population. In his inimitable style, he wrote:

> What we have seen in the last twenty years is no more than the tip of the iceberg. The seas will be seen to thrash around when the hidden bulk rears up and reveals itself for all that now lies hidden … I am happy to think that when that day arrives, radio will be known to have played its vital part in the quiet revolution.[167]

Bridson was a pioneering force at the BBC, when it came to folk music policy and programming in the postwar period.

Throughout the revival, the BBC produced a number of landmark folk programmes. *As I Roved Out* is often cited as one of the first to be exclusively devoted to folk music and its contemporary collection in Britain. *Ethnic* editor Reg Hall has asserted that *As I Roved Out* 'exposed for the first time the extent and the richness of the traditional music still alive in these islands, and was a great inspiration to many of us.'[168] The programme presented the findings of various collectors working all over Britain, especially the work of Peter Kennedy, Seamus Ennis and Bob Copper, and emphatically proved, according to Woods, 'the continuance of the English tradition'.[169] Broadcast on the Light Programme on Sunday mornings beginning in September 1953, *As I Roved Out* was conceived as an educational programme for people unfamiliar with, or even hostile to, folk music. The trailer running before the first episode asked listeners, 'Do you dislike folk music? Do you turn the radio off whenever a folk-music programme is announced? Do you believe that all folk singers are old and out of tune? If you do, then join us tomorrow morning at 1030 for "As I Roved Out," when you'll hear some songs from the sea, and will meet our own "Country Maids."'[170] Before the programme was broadcast, BBC correspondent Brian George wrote about its potential cultural value:

> In a new weekly series of programmes beginning on Sunday, September 29th, (light 10.30–11.00), listeners will be able to hear some of the results of a special piece of investigation undertaken by the BBC in the last few years, an investigation to discover the truth about the survival of living folk music in Britain. We have been told so many times that in our industrialised country there is no longer any such thing as real folk music, music inherited from the past by oral tradition and performed for the love of it by country people.[171]

As I Roved Out showed the depth, breadth and crucially the continued vitality of English folk traditions from every part of the country, in episodes on London-Bristol (West Country), Bristol-Cardiff-Fishguard (South Wales), Rosslare-Dundalk (Eire), Dundalk-Armagh-Belfast (Northern Ireland), Holyhead-Denbigh-Chester (North Wales), Liverpool-Carlisle (North West of England), Western Coast of Scotland (Including the Hebrides), Eastern Coast of Scotland (Including Orkney Islands to Berwick), Berwick-Hull (North East Coast of England), Grimsby-Harwick (East Coast) and Essex-Kent-Sussex-Surrey (Home Counties).[172]

In terms of audience appeal, *As I Roved Out* was reasonably successful. Sweers argued that it had succeeded in racking up 'remarkable audience figures'.[173] The BBC's Audience Research Department kept careful track of audience response for most BBC programmes, and a 1955 memo from the Head of Audience Research noted that the average 'appreciation index' – returned from an algorithm comprising general comments and specific questions, and taking into account the number of listeners – for *As I Roved Out* was 62, which was deemed 'Healthy'.[174] The programme had unquestionably grown in popularity since its 1953 debut, leading the Controller of the Light Programme to send a note of congratulations to the producers in February 1954: 'It is a matter for congratulation to your hardworking team and of mutual satisfaction that the audience for *As I Roved Out*, which began as 1%, has risen to 5%. You have not allowed the programme to lapse in any way from its authentic standards, in order to court popularity, and the figure, therefore, is a very good one.'[175] However, by 1955, audience numbers were again in decline.

Although *As I Roved Out* was successful in reviving an interest in the contemporary collection of folk music, Reg Hall laid out the BBC's motivation in presenting the programme: 'The BBC's motivation was not primarily to record and document the nation's traditional music but to accumulate dialect and music reference, in its sound library for its actors and for commissioned composers. *As I Roved Out* was ditched as soon as "folk" could be represented in the broadcasting schedules by the likes of Robin Hall and Jimmie MacGregor.'[176] Indeed, the broadcaster at times conformed to more popular, or commercial tastes, when it came to its programming choices; despite Hall's criticisms, however, it remained a champion for folk music after the war, working with many of the most influential figures of the movement to present the vast spectrum of British folk music traditions.

A. L. Lloyd was by far the most active folk revival figure at the BBC. He produced countless programmes over an approximately forty-year span from the mid-1930s, whether it was 'world music' for Network III, or more particular programming for the Home Service, showing his interest in very localized folk cultures in Britain and internationally. At the BBC, he produced programmes – and this is just a sampling – on 'A Village in Provence'; 'In a North American Lumber Camp'; 'A Corn Village in Kansas'; 'Cattle Country of North-Eastern Brazil'; 'Harvest in New South Wales'; 'A Village in Anatolia'; 'A Cattle Ranch in Texas'; 'Buenos Aires'; 'Australia: A Sheep Station'; 'Sofia, a Balkan City'; 'A Wayfarer in Andalusia'; 'The Mississippi River'; 'The Danube Delta'; 'On the Great Plains of Hungary'; 'In the Forests of Southern Poland'; 'Marseilles: A Mediterranean Port'; and many, many more.[177] Lloyd also produced several dozen programmes from oral histories and musical material he collected throughout Britain, including groundbreaking shows like 'Coaldust Minstrel (Life of Tommy Armstrong, the Miner-Poet)'; 'Cecil Sharp and the Music of the Appalachian Mountains'; 'Folk Music Festival at Keele University', and 'Songs of the Durham Miners', showing his adaptable interests in both traditional and contemporary folk styles.[178] Lloyd's work at the BBC was vitally important in outlining the scope and depth of folk music traditions being created and maintained at home and abroad. He was one of the first, and certainly one of the most prolific, users of the radio medium for the promotion of folk songs, both traditional and contemporary, in Britain. The American folklorist Alan Lomax was another important folk scholar and collector, whose relationship with the BBC not only affirmed the vitality of folk music in England and Britain, but also strengthened the connection between the English and American folk revivals.

Although Lomax was a brilliant folklorist and collector, his relationship with the BBC was often strained, mostly over financial issues – he was constantly asking for money for different projects, and the vast majority of his correspondence with the BBC over the years was taken up with this issue. However, he did produce, throughout his time in England in the 1950s, several landmark programmes, which were hugely influential in creating a national awareness of folk music in Britain, and in providing British audiences with an introduction to American folk traditions. Among the programmes Lomax created and narrated for the BBC were *Adventure in Folksong* (a series of three programmes for the Home Service, first broadcast on the 13th of February, 1951); *I Heard Scotland Sing* (Home Service 4.12.51); and, perhaps most significantly, a series he produced with Ewan MacColl, Seamus Ennis, Peter Kennedy and Lloyd called *A Ballad Hunter Looks at Britain*, spanning eight programmes for the Home Service, beginning on the 1st of November, 1957.

Ballad Hunter included, in order, episodes entitled 'Come Listen to My Song' (an introduction); 'From Devon to Dover' (8.11.57); 'From Cornwall to Yorkshire' (15.11.57); 'East Anglia to the Borders' (22.11.57); 'Folk Songs from the Lowlands' (29.11.57); 'Songs from the Highlands and Islands of Scotland' (6.12.57); 'A Ballad Hunter Looks at Ireland' (19.12.57); and 'Music of Ireland' (26.12.57). The first programme in the series expressed Lomax's views on the state of British listeners' understanding of their own folk traditions: 'Nowadays such music is confined within the minds and hands of a half dozen players, but once it was common to all Britain, and it can easily spring into life again if only a few people would realise how important it can be for this country.'[179] Lomax further observed, 'In the last half dozen years we found more varied and more beautiful tunes here than in any other country west of the Balkans. This is in spite of the competing roar of the factories and the radio and the cinema.'[180] A bit of the script, which was eventually edited out for the broadcast version – but which was telling of Lomax's motivation in presenting the programme – stated that his purpose was 'to show that the songs and the singers are at hand for a native music re-awakening. Like all art, British folk song waits only for appreciation and encouragement.'[181] This was the primary role Lomax carved for himself while in Britain, along with Lloyd and Ewan MacColl – he became a champion of education through broadcasting, in hopes of reviving an appreciation for native folk traditions in Britain.

MacColl had a prolonged and fruitful collaboration with the BBC, working on many programmes, as actor, playwright, singer and collector. He compiled songs for a programme on *Living Ballads* (Third Programme 3.9.53) and *Come All Ye Good People* (Third Programme 7.9.53), and helped produce programmes on characters like *The Spinner of Bolton* (North East Home Service 3.12.54) and *Scouse* (North East Home Service and Northern Ireland Home Service 9.12.52). He worked on the *Ballads and Blues* programme with Alan Lomax and Lloyd for the episode 'Song of the Iron Road', but most importantly, his *Radio Ballads* series proved to be a game changer for folk music broadcasting in the postwar period. Although he had long been singing folk songs, MacColl had become interested in collecting folk music through his association with Alan Lomax, beginning in the early 1950s.[182] MacColl had been particularly impressed with Lomax's ability to 'get the best' out of his recording subjects, and was inspired by this to set out and record 'field' singers from all over Britain.[183] His first project for the BBC was *Pleasant Journey*. He later recalled having recorded 50–60 singers for this programme, at the same time as working for the Features Department, ultimately leading to employment as host of the Radio Ballads series.[184] According to MacColl, *Radio Ballads* was conceived in hopes of righting past mistakes, where programmes about working people had focused on the occupation, rather than the human subjects. MacColl consciously sought to incorporate folk music, or the 'folk idiom' into the programme, explaining that the genius of folk music was that it subtly imposed its will on the listener.[185]

Radio Ballads was broadcast on the BBC Home Service for the Midlands, and juxtaposed folk songs, both collected and composed, with recordings of working people centred on various themes. It was a truly revolutionary endeavour; Alan Sinfield argued that, previously, the real sounds of working people had 'hardly [been] heard before on BBC radio'.[186] *Radio Ballads* emphasized the voices of the workers, in fact somewhat in conflict with the broadcaster, whose leadership felt that the points of view of employers should have been heard as well. The show introduced a completely new concept for a radio feature. At the time, tape recorders were being used, but not tape recordings. That is, tapes of 'dialect' material were transcribed and read by actors – MacColl later remembered that a recording of a Durham miner was feared indecipherable to the general public, and so was read by actors that the BBC thought could better be understood.[187] Stuart Laing has noted that this established a pattern of programmes 'built round specific occupational subcultures. The particular significance of this in the late 1950s was in the emphasis on work as the primary determinant both of lifestyle and ways of seeing the world – a contradiction of the conventional wisdom concerning the changes wrought by affluence'.[188] P. J. Waller argued, 'The BBC's committee was not a conspiracy of Home Counties or Oxbridge linguistic Tories, designing to overthrow the People's English and to establish a class dialect. Its members did not assert that there was only one right way of speaking … Their primary aim was to identify the winning side and join it'.[189] In joining that 'winning side', the BBC tapped into a sociological trend already in progress – of wanting to understand the working class in a world of relative affluence (see Chapter 3) – and also contributed to the unique culture of the English folk revival.

The first episode of *Radio Ballads*, on train driver John Axon – which produced the song 'The Ballad of John Axon', a John Henry or Casey Jones-type story – did not feature actors and was, according to MacColl, a 'tour de force, unique and full of imperfections'.[190] Writer Bill Holdsworth, in his article 'Songs of the People' in the first issue of the *New Left Review*, wrote, 'It was not until I heard the Ballad of John Axon, broadcast by the BBC Home Service in April, 1958, that I felt the great excitement and thrill of hearing a rendering of a contemporary event breaking through the thick mud of mass pop culture on the mass media itself'.[191] 'John Axon' was also hailed by *Sing* editor Eric Winter, who described it as a show 'which finds obvious favour with the audiences' because of its 'striking lack of a commercial flavour'; he argued that '[n]obody now writes new songs in the music-hall tradition, but the death of John Axon' and others like it would prove to be the 'raw material from which folk-songs of the next generation will be refined'.[192]

Another show, 'Song of a Road', focused on the construction of the M1. Other episodes included 'Singing the Fishing', about herring fishing in East Anglia, featuring singing by fisherman Sam Larner; while a show on coal mining, 'The Big Hewer', presented 'a legend, told by the men of the coal-fields of South Wales, the Midlands, Northumberland and Durham' – set into song by MacColl.[193] It featured recordings from the pit, as well as pitmen's songs by people like the Elliott family and members of the High Level Ranters.[194] *Folk Review* later praised *Radio Ballads* as 'a breakthrough in feature entertainment', having included many contemporary folk singers, but more importantly for having introduced singers like the Elliotts of Birtley to a wide audience.[195] The show had proven that folk music could tell compelling stories about previously unheralded people and places, helping to create modern-day legends out of provincial characters throughout Britain.

The BBC produced a show called *The Song Carriers* in 1965, which was meant to show the long continuity of British folk tradition. It was produced by Charles Parker for the Midlands Home Service, and was hosted by Ewan MacColl. MacColl offered this introduction before the first episode, drawing the listeners' attention to the process of reviving folk cultures:

> Little more than 15 years ago, one might with some justification have subscribed to the commonly-held point of view that folk music, in Britain, anyway, had ceased to have any future, and that its decease was not only imminent but long overdue. Today, the picture is a totally different one. The entire English-speaking world is experiencing a folk-music revival in which hundreds of thousands of people are involved. A revival so far-reaching in its influence that it now begins to occupy increasingly the attention of those who own and run the mass entertainment industry.[196]

Episodes in the series included: 'Comparison: Traditional Songs and Those Who Sing Them' (with Ewan MacColl comparing British traditions with other folk traditions throughout the world, including Azerbaijan and Syria); 'Spirit and Feeling'; 'Style and Vocal Agility'; 'Humour'; 'Ceremonial Songs' (featuring other folk traditions such as Wassailing, and the hunting of the wren on St. Stephen's Day); 'Ornaments' (featuring singers' ornamentations of songs, in which MacColl talked about voice tone and inflection and how these affected a song's effectiveness); 'The Folk Process' (in which MacColl talked about how songs could evolve and change across temporal and geographical boundaries, explaining how one could encounter songs of Scottish origin in the Appalachians or Nova Scotia, for instance); 'Work Songs' (in which MacColl claimed that the Sea Shanty was England's 'only real work song' – that is, song accompanying work processes); 'Folk Songs and Realism' (in which MacColl explained the importance of realism or believability in conveying the message of a folk song); and 'The Way Forward' (in which MacColl explained that tradition was 'like a garden run to seed', in need of tending by the right gardeners).

The final episodes of *The Song Carriers* focused on the contemporary revival: 'The British Folk Song Revival 1 and 2'. Beginning significantly in the Birtley, Co. Durham folk club run by the Elliott family, the programme featured quotes from singers explaining why they liked folk music – and revealed a pattern of musical development shared by many young singers in the folk revival: an interest in jazz, followed by the discovery of 'negro blues' and then the dawning realization that there existed a remarkable body of English, Irish and Scots songs, ready for individual discovery. MacColl asserted that having a folk music tradition was not merely a matter of repertoire; it was also a matter of style, a symbiotic relationship between traditional songs and traditional ways of singing them. He argued that when that relationship died, the tradition became 'unhealthy', explaining that the featured songs on *The Song Carriers* revealed that traditional music could become a viable form of creative expression for 'our time'.[197]

The BBC not only produced important and innovative programmes on British, American and 'world' folk music but also collaborated with the International Folk

Music Council (IFMC) and the European Broadcasting Union (EBU) to bring European folk programming to the British public, and to broadcast British folk music in Europe. Their joint project, 'Polyphony in Folk Music', reflected the broadcasters' concerns regarding the popularity of 'authentic' versus popular folk music forms, and also perhaps a slight tension between the IFMC and the EBU. The 'notes to contributors' of the project stated that 'the material [for the programme] should consist of authentic folk music (vocal or instrumental), preferably recorded in the field, and not music "arrangements" or performances by professional artists.'[198] As the revival flourished, many of those who had heard these programmes and became interested in contemporary folk song began to establish folk festivals throughout the country. In the creation and maintenance of folk community, festivals provided crucial support and affirmation of the revivalist spirit, and have – unlike many other aspects of the postwar revival – continued to grow, beyond the temporal boundaries of the second revival in England.

Folk festivals

Folk festivals became one of the most memorable features of the postwar folk revival; the imagery of the mass gathering has since become one of the most dominant features of postwar collective memory in both England and the United States. In England, many folk festivals were modelled on the success of the Newport Folk Festival in Rhode Island, and began to appear in earnest around 1964.[199] In July 1963, following singer Bob Davenport's visit to Newport, *Melody Maker* asked its readers: 'WHEN ARE WE GOING TO HAVE A BRITISH FOLK FESTIVAL ON A COMPARABLE SCALE – TO WHICH THE DAVENPORTS AND OTHERS CAN BE INVITED?'[200] The article listed the current folk festival scene in England, and established a keen demand for more:

> Every year there is the Horsham Festival, there's the big session at Cecil Sharp House in the autumn, there's the North-East Festival … The combined audiences at these big events alone were something like 3000 at least. The combined singing and playing talent was enough to stretch over a long weekend with hours to spare. At Sheffield, for instance, they thought they were over-estimating when they provided for 400 people. Over 500 turned up and more were turned down.[201]

Winter argued that the concurrent growth in folk clubs called for a bigger forum for folk fans:

> From all over the place – including clubs I never get enough time to visit – come reports of large, enthusiastic, singing audiences. The talent is there, the audience is there. All we need now is one or two people who care passionately enough to organize a British Newport – and one or two hundred people willing to give some thought to the question of what kind of a festival it should be and how best to guarantee its success.[202]

Winter's opinion was only one of many voices on the subject of the ideal size and scope of the English revival. For instance, Lloyd, on a visit to Newport in 1965, was quoted in the *New York Times* as saying that the English revival was 'healthy, but we take it in much smaller units than Newport'; festivals in Britain are few, he said, but one he just attended at Keele University in Staffordshire drew 3,000 people.[203]

English festivals at Sidmouth, Keele, Loughborough, Reading, Norwich and Cambridge – to name a few of the biggest – soon developed along a similar model to Newport. Sweers noted the transition in the folk movement exemplified by this growth in festivals: 'In England … the location of the folk revival shifted from an oral, intimate performance situation to large festival stages with a comparatively distanced and passive performer-audience relationship.'[204] Certainly, the idea of a mass gathering ran somewhat counter to the sacred intimacy of the folk clubs. Smaller festivals had been established slightly earlier, from the late 1950s, with a two-day EFDSS event at Cecil Sharp House being one of the first. These were on such a small scale that they did not really expand the reach of the folk movement in the same way as the larger, later festivals did. Even taking into account the relatively small scale of the EFDSS festival, *Ethnic* still offered its disapproval, asserting, 'While we wish to give every assistance to those who want to sing in the traditional way, we have no desire to provide material for those who want to sing like Lonnie Donegan, Engel Lund or Ewan MacColl.'[205] Small festivals, for the hardline traditionalists, could never be small enough. *Ethnic* did not report on the larger festivals, but it is not difficult to guess what their opinion might have been.

Sidmouth and Keele, and then Cambridge, became the most successful festivals in England in the mid-to-late sixties and into the seventies. Sidmouth was advertised as the festival that 'gives you everything' for the sum of £3, providing workshops on dancing and performing, as well as featuring well-known performers. Tickets for the 1971 festival were deliberately limited to 1,000, and camping spots were provided for £1.50. Advertisers assured ticket-buyers that the 'new-look' Sidmouth of 1971 would be 'even gayer and more colourful this year. The only difference will be that after 10.30 each night, the Late Night Extra will be held on the outskirts of the town.'[206] The first Keele Festival took place over the weekend of 16–18 July 1965, and over 500 folk music enthusiasts turned up at the Keele University campus in Staffordshire.[207] A feature on Keele, appearing in the November 1965 issue of *Sing*, asserted that the festival had come along 'just at the right time': 'Not much doubt about it, the Keele Folk Festival, organised by the EFDSS, was held just at the right time … No previous festival presented such a galaxy of traditional performers and such a weekend of authoritative workshops and singalong ceilidhs.'[208] *Sing* praised the variety of folk traditions presented at Keele, contending that 'a mere catalogue cannot hope to give all the flavour of Keele, cannot capture, for instance, the great circle of topical and traditional singers, swapping songs in the Students' Union lounge.'[209]

The *Guardian*'s Victor Keegan evocatively described the scene at the first Keele festival: 'Five hundred "traditional" folk singers, some strumming guitars, others with Jew's harps in their pockets, converged this afternoon on Keele University for the biggest folk festival ever held in Britain.'[210] Keegan elaborated that there seemed to be 'a distinctly purist air about the festival, organised by the English Folk Dance and Song Society, coming as it does in the same week that a song ("Mr. Tambourine Man") written by Bob Dylan, leader of the 'commercial folkniks, slips smugly into the top of the hit parade'.[211] Keele was also the focus of an A. L. Lloyd-produced BBC programme. Although Sidmouth and Keele were both successful, the Cambridge Folk Festival has maintained a reputation as the largest and most well-known festival in England.

At the time of the first Cambridge Folk Festival, in 1964, the city was home to two folk clubs – the St. Lawrence Folk Song Society (a university club) and the Cambridge Folk Club (founded 1964), later the Crofter's Club.[212] The festival was conceived in part as an overtly socialist political expression, and yet featured performers included the Clancy Brothers, Paul Simon and Sgt. Mooney. Tickets sold for £1 each – and 1,400 were sold the first year.[213] Like Newport, Cambridge emphasized the traditional alongside the contemporary. The Shropshire farm worker, Fred Jordan, and the Suffolk-based bargemaster, Bob Roberts, appeared alongside successful groups like the Watersons and the Young Tradition.[214] Some have described the Cambridge festival as a somewhat schizophrenic exercise, for its inclusion of British traditional and contemporary folk song, as well as a good deal of American music: 'Still seemingly uncertain whether it wanted to be a Mecca of superstars like Newport … Cambridge moved falteringly into a future where contemporary American song would rub shoulders with blues (both black and white), and the cream of the English traditional revival.'[215] This indictment spoke to the nature of a folk revival closely linked with its well-known cross-Atlantic counterpart, yet wanting to assert its own unique identity. The uneasiness felt by many within the movement, as popular forms existed side by side with cherished centuries-old traditions, lingered throughout the revival, and was reflected in contemporary responses to festivals like Keele and Cambridge. By 1969, the Cambridge festival's audience had grown to about 5,000, leading contemporary observer Dave Laing to note that '[l]ike the music itself, the Festival had to become more of a business.'[216] This criticism aside, the scale of Cambridge never reached the heights experienced at Newport; as Laing argued, 'It was closer to a Woodcraft Folk camp than the enormity of America's Newport.'[217] The relatively small scale of English folk festivals, in comparison with the gargantuan US affairs, was symptomatic of the English folk scene as a whole – representing an important point of departure from their transatlantic neighbours, and source of pride for English revivalists.

Conclusion

The folk music revival in England developed alongside, and partly fostered, a vast network of folk institutions. The institutions and organizations discussed in this chapter – in the form of clubs and societies, record labels and magazines, as well as radio programmes and festivals – provided the essential infrastructure for folk revivalism in England, allowing for and in fact fostering the popular and commercial success of folk music following the Second World War. They also provided the means of collaboration between the English and the American folk music revivals, where the ideological, social and political tenets of the folk movements were shared back and forth, challenged and debated within a transatlantic network of artists, collectors, scholars and enthusiasts. Woods argued that the 'essential smallness of scale' of the English revival was paramount to the movement's unique identity: 'Individual audiences tend to be small, admission charges and artists' fees are small, the scene itself is small – festivals are more like reunions than anything else, in many cases. And it is this very intimacy that has probably preserved the Folk Revival from the depredations of the mass media and Tin Pan Alley.'[218] This deliberate 'smallness of scale' was one of the essential differences between the English and American revivals, and will be further explored in subsequent chapters.

'Its Music Was Folk': Folk Revivalism and Socialist Politics*

Introduction

Bill Holdsworth, writing about the 'songs of the people' for the very first issue of the *New Left Review* (1960), argued that folk music had the power to bring alive 'the personal drama of our own day and age ... [and to] become the bed-rock of a socialist-people's culture.'[219] It seems significant that, in the inaugural issue of this journal, which in so many ways came to encapsulate the hopes and disappointments of the postwar Left in England, there was some space devoted to the reformative potential of folk music. In the United States, the folk revival has come to be associated almost exclusively with New Leftist protest, in songs dealing with African American civil rights, nuclear war and the Vietnam War. In England, where the New Left emerged from an ideological schism within an established Marxist intellectual milieu – and its relationship with any 'youth movement' was far more tenuous – the relationship between folk music and leftist politics was more ambivalent. As a result, folk songs were not appropriated or interpreted in the same ways; English folk musicians, although often sympathetic to the concerns of the New Left, placed less emphasis on 'protest' songs and movements, often preferring subjects more 'old left' in nature.

The political movements of the first half of the twentieth century, which would eventually become known as the 'old left,' were defined by the rise of trade unions and the legitimization of the Communist Party as a national and international political actor. Alastair J. Reid describes the old left as 'referring to a range of views, shaped by the Bolshevik revolution and the inter-war economic crisis, broadly in favour of organised labour pressing for a centrally planned economy and state-administered social provision.'[220] After the Second World War, as the Communist Party's international fortunes faltered under Stalin's tenure, a 'new left' – defined by its concern with a multiplicity of social ills – emerged. The New Left has been most often identified with

---

*In the United States, by the early 1960s, the folk music movement coalesced with a keen 'new Leftist' social activism, resulting, according to *New York Times* columnist Neil Alan Marks, in 'an amorphous undefined movement later called the "counterculture." In retrospect, it might be said that a general humanism had engulfed segments of American society. Its bywords were simplicity, directness and social concern. Its music was folk' (Marks, 'Reliving the "Golden Years" of Folk Music', D23).

youthful activism in the West beginning in the late 1950s, an activism that united the Ban the Bomb and anti-Vietnam movements, as well as struggles for civil rights and free – in short, an activism defined by various 'liberation initiatives' beyond class struggle.[221]

This chapter will argue that the folk revival both responded to the contemporary political culture in England and helped to shape it in significant ways. The folk revival echoed many of the larger leftist anxieties surrounding the social and political place of the working class in a postwar 'age of affluence', and was part of a new cultural wave concerned with how Clement Attlee's Welfare State had perhaps irretrievably altered the economic circumstances of the Labour Party's traditional voting base – labourers. Although inspired by some of the same issues as in the United States, especially the CND (Campaign for Nuclear Disarmament) and the Vietnam War, the English Left and the folk revival also reflected the country's postwar struggles to come to terms with both a changing international presence and a domestic crisis of industry. The folk movement in England was immersed in the politics of class, but also produced a plethora of topical songs on a number of contemporary issues, in the process pulling the English revival from local, grassroots movement to part of a global 'counterculture'. In many ways, this chapter and the one following it can be seen as parts one and two of a story about the centrality of class in English society and politics, perhaps especially during a period of relative affluence – marked by near-full employment, higher wages and greater social security. This chapter deals with the *political* dimensions of this phenomenon, exploring notions of 'radical nostalgia' and the Labour Party's 'English problem' through a discussion of folk music.

A. L. Lloyd and the revival of industrial songs

In order to understand the importance and contribution of folk song to the political culture of postwar England, it may be helpful to preface this chapter with a discussion of how the precarious Cold War climate in the United States had affected the American folk scene. The Cold War was a constant – if not always conspicuous – actor in the story of postwar folk revivalism on both sides of the Atlantic. At times, as in songs like Ewan MacColl's 'The Ballad of Joe Stalin', it offered direct context; more often, it was part of the political scaffolding, crucial to understanding what shaped and drove the folk revival and its participants, but not necessarily visible. During the 1950s, while the activities of American folk revivalists were repeatedly and without a sense of irony deemed 'un-American' by their government – and central figures including Pete Seeger and Paul Robeson were blacklisted from network television and radio – in England, such anti-Communist hysteria did not affect the country, or its folk revival, in the same ways. According to American folk song collector and publisher Gordon Friesen, 'freedom of expression had never been curtailed in Britain to the magnitude that prevailed in America during the tragic 1950's [*sic*]; there was never a British McCarthy; there was never an Un-British Activities Committee prowling the land.'[222] In fact, there was plenty of anti-Communist feeling and rhetoric in Britain, just not on the same scale as the United States, not given the same official and overweening influence. The

English folk revival, therefore, was able to develop and thrive throughout the 1950s, in marked contrast to its American counterpart.

The development of People's Songs, Inc. (PSI) and later People's Artists, Inc. (PAI) in the United States in the immediate postwar years was part of an attempt within the folk community to build on the pre-war success of politically active folk groups like the Almanac Singers. However, rather unfortunately for PSI and PAI, they were founded during a period of growing insecurity for the American Left, and the Communist Party of the United States, during the first years of the Cold War.[223] In fact, political persecution stateside drove many folk artists and collectors, including Pete Seeger and Alan Lomax, to England during the 1950s, where the situation was considerably less dangerous for left-leaning artists, and where the development of a postwar folk revival – and political topical songwriting – therefore took an earlier, and in many ways easier, path. In fact, the revival of English folk music owes much to the diaspora of American folk singers and collectors like Seeger and Lomax.

The English equivalent to PSI and PAI was the Worker's Music Association (WMA). Founded in 1936 by the London Labour Choral Union, the WMA formed, according to Michael Brocken, 'a rather nebulous offshoot of the CPGB'.[224] During and immediately following the war, the WMA had played a crucial role in 'mobilizing tradition' in England by organizing concerts of 'national songs', which were recorded by the BBC, to send aid to China and the Soviet Union – making it possible, Brocken has argued, to 'participate in an updated imagined [Marxist] community'.[225] According to the foreword to its *Pocket Song Book* (1948), the WMA was established in order to 'co-ordinate the musical activities of working-class organisations', and to provide 'the necessary music material and professional resources' for workers' political gatherings.[226] Seeing the benefits of having a popular song book for use at union and political rallies in the United States, the WMA commissioned Lloyd to produce a book on English workers' songs before the end of the war, and he also helped to produce the *Penguin Book of English Folk Songs*, a cheap source of songs for singing in folk clubs, in 1959.[227] Lloyd's work, according to Dave Harker, represented 'something of a rapprochement between the serious study of "folksong" and that of workers' history in England'.[228] Putting aside conflicting ideas regarding the nature and direction of folk music in the twentieth century, Lloyd joined the EFDSS in 1948 and became a member of the editorial board of its journal, *Folk Dance and Song*, in 1952.

Through Lloyd, the WMA was important in making a case for folk music as an agent for social and political change in postwar England. The *Pocket Song Book* included such diverse songs as 'The Marseillaise', 'Big Rock Candy Mountain', 'The Red Flag', 'The Man That Waters the Worker's Beer' and many other songs of English and international origin – intended to unite the workers of the world behind a common revolutionary heritage. Throughout the 1950s, through the collecting and recording efforts of people like Lloyd, MacColl and producers at the BBC such as Peter Kennedy, workers' music was rediscovered and nurtured in England. Lloyd's introduction of urban, industrial songs – from the factories, mills, mines and urban tenements – into the canon of English folk music radically expanded the reach and resonance of folk songs in the postwar period, imbuing them with a more acute political and social purpose, just as the Labour Party began to worry that they were 'losing' the working class.

Art and socialism: Political culture and cultural politics

The folk revival echoed many latent tensions within and between the Labour Party, the New Left and the socialist cultural milieu. The invention of (socialist) tradition through folk music and other leftist cultural 'products' was at times subtly, at times overtly present in the political-cultural scaffolding of the postwar period. This scaffolding had its roots firmly set in the nineteenth century. Britain is paradoxically home to the oldest labour movement, and the youngest Labour party, in Europe; after the Second World War, this fact contributed to increasingly pronounced tensions between the direction of the party and the concerns of those they were meant to represent. Gareth Stedman Jones has called the period from 1945 to 1951 – the tenure of Clement Attlee's pioneering Labour government – 'the high tide of the labour movement,' – during which time a '"working-class party" committed to "socialism" gained, and for a time held the support of, the clear majority of the nation'.[229] The Labour Party was founded in 1900, based on an alliance of socialist organizations and trade unions, although it has always taken a reformist rather than revolutionary position on the role of the state – committed, according to Donald Sassoon, to maintaining 'traditional institutional arrangements'.[230] Nevertheless, by 1918, the year the party published its constitution, it had developed a clear socialist imperative and a solid working-class base, especially in the industrial North of England.

Labour won its first majority in 1945, buoyed, Sassoon and others have argued, by the experience of total war, which legitimated state intervention in social policy.[231] Despite this victory, the incoming Labour government faced, according to the liberal economist John Maynard Keynes, a 'financial Dunkirk'.[232] Hugh Armstrong Clegg has also asserted that the Labour government faced the 'Herculean' task of restoring an economy devastated by war, exacerbated by the American repeal of the Lend-Lease programme in 1945, a desperate coal shortage in the winter of 1946–47 and the Korean War, beginning in 1950.[233] Labour had built its reputation as the 'party of the people' in the first half of the twentieth century.[234] However, as Ross McKibbin has noted, with few exceptions, 'every significant member of Attlee's government was of middle or upper-middle-class origin. The decay of the autodidact tradition accompanied the process by which the leadership of the Labour Party passed from being working CLASS to the educated middle class'.[235] While the Labour Party was never completely a party of the 'working-class', its achievements during that six-year period proved transformative for the working classes, showing that a democratic socialist 'welfare' state could succeed in a modern industrialized economy. Attlee's government established social security, town-planning initiatives, housing programmes, an extension of the education infrastructure and a National Health Service, in order to ease the economic burden on the nation's most vulnerable citizens – and yet, Labour lost three successive elections starting in 1951, leaving many within the party and on the Left more broadly seeking answers. This crisis of Labour, many felt, was precipitated by its fumbling response to the growing affluence of its base.

By the late 1950s, growth in popular prosperity had become a dominant feature of the socio-economic picture in England. However, full employment, a general rise in real wages and increasing access to consumer goods now seemed to be undermining the solidarity of the Labour Party's traditionally working-class base. Many historians of the postwar Labour Party have argued that this increasing affluence among working people was the source of the party's crisis: Alan Sinfield argues that Labour had 'found its crowning achievement in the welfare state, but that very success seemed to render it redundant'[236]; Steven Fielding meanwhile asserts that '[b]y the late 1950s Labour's leaders believed that as society was increasingly affluent and individualistic, so support for state collectivism was diminishing.'[237] However, Martin Pugh has argued that the Party's fortunes were determined more by contingencies – poor leadership, internal divisions and the superior political tactics of its opponents.[238]

I would argue that each of these issues was exacerbated by a critical lack of consensus about what to do about the working class in a modernizing economy. The fraught tenure of Hugh Gaitskell, in particular, represented a crucial moment for the party as it entered the second half of the twentieth century; the seeds of 'New Labour' were sown in contemporary commentaries such as Anthony Crosland's *The Future of Socialism* (1956), which put the Gaitskellite-Bevanite debate to paper. Labour's postwar crisis was in many ways exacerbated by and reflected through troubled relationships with both the New Left and the country's young people. Indeed, the English New Left played an important role in the political culture of the postwar period, in no small part by providing an ideological foil for the Labour Party. There were essentially two phases of New Left in England: the first beginning around 1956 and the second stemming from Perry Anderson's takeover of the *New Left Review* in 1962.[239]

The English New Left emerged outside the influence of the main political parties – although its members were acutely interested in parliamentary politics – and its pre-eminent personalities included Anderson, E. P. Thompson, Stuart Hall and Raymond Williams. The broad mandate for the New Left's direction in the 1960s was established in the first issue of *New Left Review* in which editor Stuart Hall argued:

> We are convinced that politics, too narrowly conceived, has been a main cause of the decline of socialism in this country, and one of the reasons for the disaffection from socialist ideas of young people in particular. The humanist strengths of socialism – which are the foundations for a genuinely popular socialist movement – must be developed in cultural and social terms, as well as economic and political.[240]

It was partially this concern for the furtherance of a truly socialist society that prompted C. Wright Mills to pen his 'Letter to the New Left', a document often cited as one of the first manifestos of the movement. Mills urged young activists to shirk the 'sickness of complacency' which he felt had plagued the Left since the war: 'Let the old men ask, sourly, "out of Apathy – into what?" The Age of Complacency is ending. Let the old women complain wisely about "the end of ideology." We are beginning to move again.'[241]

The English New Left often expressed disappointment in the decline of populist socialism in the country, a direct result of what they perceived as the Labour Party's postwar blunders. Throughout the 1950s, Labour had increasingly been criticized for abandoning its socialist ideals in favour of a more populist stance. The first issue of

NLR reflected this clear exasperation with the current state of the Labour Party and its erstwhile socialist message, under the direction of Hugh Gaitskell (1955–63) and then Prime Minister Harold Wilson (1964–70). Ralph Miliband's scathing article, 'The Sickness of Labourism' (1960) underlined the acute anxieties, and ideological tensions, between Labourists and the New Left on the cusp of the new decade. Miliband asserted that Labour's loss in the previous election had 'shocked many more people into a recognition of the fact that the Labour Party is a sick party. And it has also helped many more people within it to realise that the sickness is not a surface ailment, a temporary indisposition, but a deep organic disorder, of which repeated electoral defeats are not the cause but the symptom.'[242] Miliband accused Gaitskell and his 'ideological friends' of betraying the socialist ideals at the heart of the party's creed, writing that 'they do not believe that the purpose of the Labour Party ought to be the creation of a socialist society on the basis of common ownership. On the contrary, they believe that common ownership, as a basic purpose of the Labour Party, is not only electorally damaging, but irrelevant and obsolete.'[243]

Similar to the tenuous position the Labour Party held with New Left ideologues, it also held a precarious position in the minds and hearts of young voters. In short, it did little to inspire young people to vote in parliamentary elections. Labour Party historian Andrew Thorpe has asserted, 'The growth of youth culture had left the party cold: there was little attempt even to understand modern movements and feelings among young people.'[244] Meanwhile, Lawrence Black notes that, in the English case, 'Labour had no national youth organization between 1955 and 1960 – the period in which the teenager and a distinctive youth culture came of age.'[245] In fact, youthful disillusionment with 'official' politics – especially on the Left – had been growing for some time, and many a frustrated refrain was put to vinyl.

The English satirist Leon Rosselson's 'Battle Hymn of the New Socialist Party' attacked the pretence of a socialist party run by Eton graduates, and ultimately spoke to the youthful disenchantment with both Gaitskell's and Wilson's leadership of the Labour Party and its modernization programme: 'Firm principles and policies are open to objections; And a streamlined party image is the way to win elections./So raise the umbrella high, the bowler hat, the college tie./We'll stand united, raise a cheer/And sing The Red Flag once a year.'[246] There was a feeling amongst many intellectuals and Left-leaning young people in England that Labour politicians – in other words, the parliamentary Labour Party – had failed in their central promise of providing a functional socialist state. Whether these opinions were justified or not, they revealed an important part of the political culture of postwar England. As the popular appeal of Labour appeared to falter in three successive elections during the 1950s, the Labour Party's identity crisis came into focus; the Party's 'cultural turn' – in which film, theatre and music began to be understood in terms of their political voice, and in which so-called 'working-class culture' came to be particularly emphasized – must be viewed in this context.

Emily Robinson's work on the postwar Labour Party has been particularly useful and illuminating when it comes to this issue of crisis. Robinson asserts that Labour had, and indeed still has, an 'English problem'; what to do with an 'everyday Englishness' that was both culturally appealing and politically problematic. She writes that the notion of this 'English problem' was inextricably linked with 'longer-standing concerns about the populist right and their challenge to Labour's connection with the White working class.[247] Labour very much wanted to capture and exude an 'everyday Englishness' that would make it politically and culturally relevant to both their aforementioned working-class base, and a new generation of young voters, in the 1950s and '60s. However, to do so meant, possibly, embracing much of the 'radical nostalgia' and Little-Britain-ness more associated with Tory sensibilities. She argues:

> Patriotism in general and Englishness in particular have long been thought to be intrinsically problematic for the left. The first because it runs against socialist commitments to internationalism; the second because Englishness is assumed to be both a particularly conservative form of national identity, based upon an imagined mono-cultural past, and (somewhat contradictorily) because it is deeply implicated in the British imperial project.[248]

The folk revival solved many of these issues for Labour, and the New Left. As I've suggested elsewhere in this book, and as will be seen in subsequent chapters, the Left's appropriation of certain nostalgic impulses and the natural conservatism of folk music collection echoes more than a little of this 'radical nostalgia' as conceptualized by Robinson. Most people think of these impulses as right-wing, but there was plenty of it on the left as well. Indeed, Robinson argues for the 'importance of the past to socialists' as a means of 'remaking the present, not as a refuge'.[249] The invention of (radical nostalgic) tradition could be seen in the Festivals of Labour and Britain, in the stories of Alan Sillitoe and Ray Gosling, and in the folk revival.

The folk revival was shaped by the country's shifting economic fortunes, and it in turn contributed to the Left's cultural response. As austerity gave way to affluence, the Left sought new ways of interpreting the socio-political landscape, often seeking to marry, in William Morris's terms, the causes of art and socialism.[250] Raymond Williams's work, and later Stuart Hall's, continued Morris's tradition, and their exploration and expansion of the cultural dimensions of social struggle ultimately provided for a much more diversified, complex and inclusive understanding of culture amongst socialist intellectuals and politicians, in which products such as film, theatre and music began to be understood in terms of their political potential. In justifying the *New Left Review*'s commitment to culture, Hall argued:

> The purpose of discussing the cinema or teen-age culture in *NLR* is not to show that, in some modish way, we are keeping up with the times. These are directly relevant to the imaginative resistances of people who have to live within capitalism – the growing points of deeply-felt needs. Our experience of life today is so extraordinarily fragmented. The task of socialism is to meet people where they are, where they are touched, bitten, moved, frustrated, nauseated – to develop discontent and at the same time, to give the socialist movement some direct sense of the times and ways in which we live.[251]

In this statement, the profoundly different approach towards culture that characterized the New Left's cultural Marxism becomes more apparent. The British cultural Marxist tradition attempted to understand mass cultural consumption on its own terms, and from the point of view of the consumers, as a means of, as Hall said, 'meeting people where they *are*'.[252]

Music sociologist Simon Frith has asked how we should distinguish between the ways in which people 'use culture to "escape," to engage in pleasures that allow them a temporary respite from the oppressive relations of daily life ... and those uses of culture which are "empowering," which bring people together to change things?'[253] In many ways, this query stands at the heart of the simultaneous leftist fascination with, and distrust of, culture: was it okay for people to use cultural products merely as an escape from everyday life and work, or should culture serve a higher purpose – of education, unification and communication? In the context of Labour's postwar disarray – which was in some measure driven by the increasing mobility and consumerism of the working class – the English New Left sought new ways of interpreting and instigating socialist activity in the cultural sphere. Black has asserted that 'culture' became the keyword for the New Left, seeking to get past the 'impasse of socialism' in the 1950s.[254]

While the 'cultural Marxists' of the New Left saw culture as potentially socially and politically transformative, they were nevertheless wary of its influence. The 'herbivores' made famous by Michael Frayn's essay on the 1951 Festival of Britain – the 'radical middle classes ... the do-gooders; the readers of the *News Chronicle*, the *Guardian*, and the *Observer*; the signers of petitions; the backbone of the B.B.C'[255] – were on the front lines of the leftist cultural response to affluence, often practising what Black termed an 'enlightened elitism', promoting 'authentic' culture to a national audience.[256] Their flagship project was the Festival of Britain. The Festival has been crucial in helping to frame the discourse surrounding constructions of national and regional culture in postwar England. Becky Conekin argues that the event was planned as a 'pat on the back' for winning the war, as well as a 'tonic to the nation' in an age of austerity.[257] Furthermore, Martin Daunton asserts that it expressed a particular view of Englishness and Britishness – consistent with Frayn's 'Herbivorous' caricature – which was 'social democratic, classless and egalitarian, achieving unity through an acceptance of diversity'.[258] It was a transitionary moment, 'a rainbow', according to Frayn, which marked the end, in effect, of Herbivore Britain, and the end of the Labourist dream:

> It marked the ending of the hungry forties, and the beginning of an altogether easier decade. But it was not, as its critics had feared, to mark the consolidation of the Herbivorous forces which had made it. To adapt Rainald Wells's verdict, it may perhaps be likened to a gay and enjoyable birthday party, but one at which the host presided from his death-bed.[259]

The Centre 42 project, established by playwright Arnold Wesker and championed by Lloyd, was another initiative seeking to '[bring] art to the workers'. It was backed initially by the trade unions, as a touring art show whose intent was to decentralize art from London while promoting left wing politics and culture amongst workers throughout the country.[260] The project established festivals in places like Nottingham, Birmingham, Hayes and Southall, Leicester, Bristol and Wellingborough. Centre 42 was meant to remedy the Labour Left's tendency to 'distribute good works from on a cultural high'; defending, according to Black, 'folksy-proletarian besides elite forms'.[261] However, Wesker and Centre 42 were often criticized for having patronizing attitudes towards working-class tastes: artist and social commentator Jeff Nuttall claimed that the project succeeded only in taking up the 'flaming torch of romantic socialism', representing in microcosm 'the pathetic errors of the Left'.[262] This indictment echoed the conflict within the folk revival over authenticity and ownership of workers' songs amongst a largely middle-class artistic community. Centre 42 was partly motivated by a distrust of mass culture, as well as a certain anti-Americanism (some of Wesker's pet hates included the 'furore around the Beatles' and intellectuals who 'pretend[ed] to like Elvis').[263] It was indicative of the 'new Left moment', according to Black, which aimed 'to recover "authentic," traditional working-class experience just as this was reckoned to have evaporated and mutated … [it] was an exercise in cultural defense establishment, but defending traditional forms and struggling to rival or penetrate mainstream commercial culture'.[264]

Folk music was popular amongst socialists – as it was among the young people they so desperately wanted to inspire – because it was 'authentic'; according to Sinfield, folk was 'regarded as an authentic music of oppressed people – of Blacks and the lower classes before they were spoilt by Hollywood, advertising, rock "n" roll and the record industry. It offered the ideal imaginary resolution of the gap between new-left and lower-class culture: it was the "good" music which the working class would have been performing if it hadn't been got at'.[265] Furthermore, the acoustic guitar became 'immensely convenient as a portable signal of commitment'.[266]

The folk revival embodied the Labourist hope of uniting a viable socialist political structure with the culture of the English working class. However, as a movement, it was beset by many of the same central contradictions as the Labour Party itself, not least resulting from its focus on 'recovering' an authentic workers' culture which, many revivalists felt, was on the brink of disappearance. Folk music, in many ways, bridged the gap between the counter-cultural movements associated with young people and the New Left, and the political-intellectual establishment. But the revival of folk music during this period also raises questions about what the New Left actually represented in an English context. The folk music that most of the public is aware of – the topical, 'protest' songs emerging in the late 1950s and early 1960s – would appear to be firmly 'new left' in nature and appeal. However, the folk revival in England – in stark contrast with its US counterpart – continued to promote industrial workers' music, as a key part of its cultural project; thus, English folk song remained fundamentally 'old left' in some key areas.

While the story of the American Left in the postwar period was very much a story of the emergence of youth as a formidable political force, the story of the postwar Left in England has been tied to both the dissolution of empire and lingering class politics. The topical songs produced by revival singers in England, and the United States, became increasingly important to young people interested in social and political change, who relied on them to provide honest and truthful commentaries on the state of the world. This ran somewhat counter to the grassroots ideals of an English folk movement built upon the local. However, in the late 1950s, beginning with the CND, politics began to pull the English folk revival out of the local, and into national – and international – politics through topical songwriting.

Topical songwriting

While the *Observer* columnist Stephen Sedley wrote that the commercial publication of topical songs in England was 'still a pipe-dream' in 1964 – thus ensuring that they never became part of the popular musical lexicon – these songs still provided important commentary on the social and political issues of the day in England.[267] Although topical material has been a feature of folk music for centuries, since people started writing songs, the 'protest' songs that began appearing in the late 1950s and in the 1960s took on an increasingly important role in highlighting the political concerns of the folk revival as it developed. By 1965, *Melody Maker* was claiming on its cover that POP PROTEST SONGS SOAR, and featured essays on the likes of American superstars Bob Dylan, Joan Baez, Manfred Mann and Donovan.[268] The year 1963 marked the real boom of commercially viable topical songs, on both sides of the Atlantic, and signalled the successful and unquestioned expansion of folk music beyond 'traditional' idiom. Although the American protest song has often been touted as the apotheosis of topical songwriting in the postwar period, the American revival actually took many of its songwriting cues from British songwriters – who had cut their teeth on the CND.

The campaign for nuclear disarmament: Marching to Aldermaston

The postwar topical song movement in the United States did not really take off until Pete Seeger travelled to England in 1958, where he was impressed with the calibre of new songs being written in the folk idiom about contemporary issues – most prominently, at the time, songs surrounding the CND. Seeger wrote a *Sing Out!* article detailing his tour experience, asserting that:

> The most striking thing about the whole English scene, and the one that filled this singer with envy, was the large number of really first-rate songs being made up – which seemed to grow naturally out of their older traditions that there was no sharp break between the newer and older songs … there the best songs, like those of Woody Guthrie, seemed to capture glints of humor in the midst of tragedy.[269]

The leaders of the American folk scene saw that English, Scottish and Irish folk singers and songwriters like Ewan MacColl, Matt McGinn, Ian Campbell, Dominic Behan and others were singing songs that significantly combined a sense of established tradition with the needs of a mass movement for new, updated material in a way that had not been done in the United States since the Depression. While topical songwriting in America had languished for a time during the McCarthy era, in England it flourished as part of the CND, sparking a renewed protest song revolution in both countries.

Historian Richard Taylor has argued that the CND was 'one of the largest extra-parliamentary movements in modern Britain, and arguably the most significant.'[270] During 1958 alone, over 250 public meetings had taken place all over Britain about CND, and 272 groups were formed.[271] Although in many ways considered the quintessential New Leftist movement in England, CND was actually quite closely aligned with the Labour Party and parliamentary politics, committed, as Taylor has argued, 'to working within the parliamentary democratic framework as a legal, "respectable" pressure group.[272] Many of the earliest protest songs in England were written during the height of the CND, which was one of the most prominent issues concerning the New Left in both England and the United States in the late 1950s and early 1960s. Leon Rosselson's 'Dear John Profumo' (addressed to the Tory Minister of War) referred to the extra two minutes afforded to citizens under a new defence plan – introduced in 1963, and costing £13 million – in order to take cover in the case of a nuclear attack: 'This new warning system called MIDAS is a satellite surfing in space,/Which when the bomb drops will provide us/With two extra minutes of grace.'[273] Rosselson asserted that the two extra minutes were a waste, as 'we who are common, dull and unpolished/In those two leisure minutes before we're abolished/Won't know what to do with our time.'[274] The CND was a watershed moment for protest movements and songs in England and throughout Britain. Nuttall argued that the CND created a culture of protest in Britain, not just against the bomb, but against 'hunger, old age pensions and the whole gamut of socialist grievances'[275]; and the Aldermaston marches, beginning in 1958, have since been credited as 'the birth of the British protest song'.[276]

The Aldermaston march of 1958 was a milestone in the development of the early folk scene in England. It was characterized by mass singing, and galvanized support for the CND while introducing a number of new songs. The idea began as a proposed silent march to Aldermaston – Britain's nuclear centre – from London. However, Pete Seeger, in England on tour, noted that plans for a 'dignified silence' were apparently 'shattered' by the arrival of a skiffle band, which broke in with an African American spiritual, 'Down by the Riverside (Study War No More),' after which time *Sing* magazine began producing song sheets and organizing singing amongst the protesters.[277] Seeger was impressed with the size and musical nature of the march, writing, 'The 1958 march ended with between 3,000 and 4,000 arriving at Aldermaston ... The next year the organizers of the Aldermaston March purposely sought out songleaders like Winter and Foreman. It became a musical parade: choruses, jazz bands, bagpipers, steel bands.'[278]

New songs from the marches included Fred (Karl) Dallas's 'The Family of Man', Ann and Marti Cleary's 'Strontium 90', Ian Campbell's 'The Sun Is Burning in the Sky' – 'Now the sun has come to earth/Shrouded in a mushroom cloud of death/Death comes in a blinding flash/Of hellish heat and leaves a smear of ash/And the sun has come to earth'[279] – and John Brunner's 'The H-Bomb's Thunder', which eventually became the movement's anthem: 'Don't you hear the H-bomb's thunder/Echo like the crack of doom?/While they rend the skies asunder/Fall-out makes the world a tomb.'[280] The CND was defined by a certain anti-American character, which was related at least partially to a desire for England to reassert itself as a moral leader on the world stage, separate from what many saw as a negative American influence.[281] A pamphlet for the 1961 Aldermaston march, published by the National Youth CND, demanded that Britain 'lead the world' in banning nuclear weapons, bases and policies.[282] Indeed, unlike many other postwar leftist initiatives in Britain, the CND had a considerable youth presence – Michael Brake cited a 1951 survey that claimed that 40 per cent of CND participants were under the age of 21, and drew parallels to the American student movement, writing that '[the CND] members were young ... mostly in full-time education, and from radical, middle-class homes. In this sense they reflected the Berkeley radicals of the 1960s.'[283]

While the CND was a focal point for the expression of leftist discontent in England, in the United States, it was, as Nuttall asserted, 'just one item amidst the violent actualities of the Negro civil rights programme.'[284] Or, rather, it came to be 'just one item' amongst the many grievances of the American New Left; it started out by being the issue concerning American topical songwriters in the late '50s and early '60s. It was not only The Bomb that concerned young activists on the Left in the United States, it was, as the Port Huron Statement suggested, the entire military-industrial-political complex – what they saw as a deep-seated socio-cultural malady – of which the bomb was seen to be a symptom. Bob Dylan has stated that, as a teenager in the late 1950s, he was struck by the 'surreally inhuman logic of the fallout shelter boom,'[285] later explaining that 'our reality was fear, that any moment this black cloud would explode and everybody would be dead.'[286] However, after the denouement of the Cuban Missile Crisis in late 1962 and the signing of the nuclear test ban treaty in 1963, the acute danger of nuclear war dissipated, in both the public consciousness and as a topic of folk protest songs, and the Vietnam War emerged as a new focal point for leftist discontent and topical songwriting in both the United States and England.

Vietnam

Folk revival songwriters from both England and the United States put forth a plethora of material on the Vietnam conflict. Ewan MacColl's 'Ballad of Ho Chi Minh,' although written before the American war began, was performed throughout the sixties in protest of that war, and forwarded a distinct Marxist message in keeping with MacColl's political ethos, in which he sang that 'Young and old workers/peasants and the toiling tenant farmers/Fight for freedom with Uncle Ho.'[287] *Sing* printed the best contemporary material on the subject as well. In their July 1965 issue, they included two new songs, 'Rain in the Forest' (written by Alex Comfort) and 'No More War' (written by Alex Campbell).[288] 'Rain in the Forest' was an indictment of the US government's actions – both in Vietnam and 'at home' – which curiously took on an American voice: 'There's cant in the Congress and pie in the sky/There's a cool rain of Liberty on the children that die/And one day the jackal will bed with the lamb/But it's our flames are falling in the fields of Vietnam.'[289] Alex Campbell's 'No More War', meanwhile, took on the persona of a working man empathizing with the Vietnamese as a disinherited people: 'I'm just a working man but I can understand/That things aren't as they should be/There's men going to a war that's not worth fighting for/'Gainst people just like you and me.'[290] 'No More Rain' was apparently written for the protest march headed by American folk singer Joan Baez when she came over to England in May 1965.[291] It was sung in Trafalgar Square in London to a large crowd on 29 May. The opposition to the war in Vietnam was one of the most recognizable and well-documented concerns of the New Left – and the folk revivals – in both England and the United States.

The CND and Vietnam were issues of common concern for the New Left and the folk revivals on either side of the Atlantic Ocean. There were, naturally, other issues, which affected one country more acutely. In the United States, for instance, the African

American civil rights campaign took precedence, becoming inextricably linked with the folk revival in the process. In England, issues of race were conspicuously subdued as part of the topical song movement; instead, one of the most defining social and political issues of the postwar era was the plight of the coal industry and its workers. This key difference between two revivals otherwise closely linked by leftist ideology was telling, arguably hinting at some of the fundamental socio-economic differences between England and the United States in the postwar period.

Race and immigration

While folk music was a highly visible and effective partner in the fight for African-American civil rights between roughly 1955 and 1965, the relationship between the English folk revival and the struggle for racial justice in England was far more tenuous. The sight of Bob Dylan and Joan Baez performing at the 1963 March on Washington, or the SNCC Freedom Singers on stage at the Newport Folk Festival, are images deeply resonant not only of the unique collaborative spirit between the two movements in America, but of the power of folk music as a tool for effecting real social and political change. In England – although issues of racial inequality clearly troubled many folk performers – the revival was on the whole far less involved in broadcasting the domestic problem of racial injustice to a wider public. In the context of a socially conscious transatlantic, and global, campaign against racial discrimination, associated with the New Left, the contrasting relationship between folk music and race in England and the United States remains a curiosity.

The extent to which 'race' or a 'colour bar' was perceived to be a problem in English society must inform, at least partially, an assessment of the folk revival's involvement in racial politics. At the same time as those famous images of police dogs and fire hoses in Birmingham, Alabama, shocked and outraged the international community, there persisted the idea that England did not have a race problem; 'race' had not traditionally been an integral part of the domestic culture in England, and was a relatively new phenomenon in the wake of a massive postwar migration of non-white Commonwealth citizens to Britain. Bill Schwarz argued that the 'colonial frontier' 'came home' to England with immigration, and that race then moved from a peripheral position in the national culture to a central one. He wrote that 'a nominally archaic vocabulary was called upon to make sense of a peculiarly modern situation – the impact of mass immigration ... the syntax of Englishness itself was profoundly re-racialised.'[292]

Issues of race and class were closely connected in England, and the massive influx of immigrants from former British colonies to the country after the war meant a significant reordering of the class system. Tom Nairn has argued that the wave of new immigrants 'amounted to a new bottom layer of the old class-structure ... The new stratum soon occupied the worst housing, concentrated in the most decaying inner-city areas: conditions which of course reinforced stereotypes about them, and added to the already massive discrimination which they experienced.'[293] In England, as elsewhere, racial tensions were inextricably linked with economics. The promise of employment soured, for many new immigrants, with a harsh reality of discrimination at work and in the search for housing. Speaking about the immigrant labour situation at a symposium on poverty in 1968, Shirley Joshi, a lecturer at Warwick University and the wife of the Secretary of the Indian Workers Association, placed the problem firmly within a post-imperialist framework:

> There is an imperialist background to this country, because of British History, with a deep under-current of racialism [*sic*] from outright discrimination to the patronising attitude which is present in the Labour Movement. It is against this background that we can view the immigrant poverty here. Because they are largely condemned to low-paid heavy manual work, the question of housing and related neighbourhood services is determined for them, and is also characterised by poverty.[294]

She further asserted:

> The immigrant is being relegated to a lumpen proletariat. Like the indigenous working class they are dependant [*sic*] on the labour market. But the latter have, through political pressure, managed to make some improvement, including the field of housing, getting out of slum areas. The immigrant is denied this. In the long run, only solidarity between both sections of the working class can provide a solution.[295]

Unlike in the United States, the idea of a 'colour bar' was a new and relatively unexplored phenomenon at the time of the folk boom in England. In a way similar to the obfuscation of class in postwar American society, the problem of race was generally seen as alien to England – it had been observed during the war with segregated American regiments, but was seen as complete anathema to the postwar ideology of a widespread and diverse Commonwealth of nations.[296] It would be unfair to say that the palpable racial tensions within England were ignored completely by folk musicians and topical songwriters. In fact, there are examples of evocative and powerful expressions of anger and dismay at injustices being perpetrated at home. However, in comparison with the United States, and in light of the serious and sometimes violent nature of the 'colour problem' in England, there was a remarkable difference in the volume and intensity of attention given to these issues by the folk movement.

The English folk revival was overwhelmingly white. Arthur noted that, 'apart from performers such as Johnny Silvo, Cliff Hall from the Spinners and Fitzroy Coleman, black faces were not to be seen in [English] folk clubs.'[297] The volume of songs written by these white performers as expressions of solidarity with victims of racial discrimination, or as condemnations of a racist social and political system in England, was also relatively limited; there were more songs written about problems elsewhere – in South Africa or the United States. Although a strong campaign against discrimination developed in the wake of racially motivated violence in Birmingham and London in 1958 – strengthened by the contributions of intellectuals like Stuart Hall, and later visits by prominent American writers and civil rights workers, such as Martin Luther King Jr. and James Baldwin – the English folk revival was notably mum on the subject, with few exceptions.

The Spinners' Cliff Hall, interviewed in 1999 for the BBC's *Millennium Memory Bank* series, related some of his personal experiences as a recent immigrant to England after the war, and as a member of the Spinners at the height of the folk revival. Hall had served during the Second World War with the RAF in an all-black unit, before returning to the West Indies. However, he came back to England on the Empire Windrush; as he recalled, 'When all those West Indians arrived ... They were coming to the Mother Country, as they called it. As far as they were concerned, and I was concerned in those days, coming to England was like coming to Heaven.'[298] Upon his return, he had problems finding housing – often having to send a white person to apply for a flat – and was even told, later in life, not to move to Kent because 'there isn't any cotton picking down there.'[299] In response to a question addressing the political nature – or lack thereof – of the Spinners' repertoire, Hall said that while the Spinners' songs were about life, few had a 'message'. He considered the group's music to be a part of the country's rich and 'diverse' folk tradition – although he admitted that all the original folk songs he'd known had come from (Anglo-Saxon) British sources.[300]

There had been notable conflicts between black and white citizens in England dating back to the late 1940s in centres like Birmingham and Liverpool, as well as Camden in August 1954. However, the most well-documented clash of the postwar period occurred at Notting Hill in 1958.[301] The Notting Hill riots in particular seemed to shatter liberal optimism about the innate tolerance of English society. Notting Hill shocked English society out of its liberal complacency, and prompted a number of studies and inquiries into the problem of race in Britain. By the late 1950s, and after Notting Hill, it was no longer possible to say that England, and Britain, did not have a 'colour bar'. As Webster has argued, 'The disturbing evidence about Britain not only threatened Britain's self-representation as a liberal and tolerant nation, but also a collapse of the construction of British tolerance against the USA and South Africa.'[302] Liberal hand-wringing about the colour bar continued even as attempts were made to distance what was happening in England from the gravity of the situation in the United States.

The social situation in the West London neighbourhood, leading up to the riots, has been described by Stuart Hall, who argued that the riots were a problem of community disintegration – based on economic hardship – rather than purely racial hatred:

> The problem of Notting Hill is not, at root, a question of race at all – though the racial situation naturally sharpened every aspect. It is primarily a product of the community itself – the shocking condition of housing, the lack of community amenities, the shifting nature of the population, the difficulties of employment, and the short-sighted and temporizing policies of the council planners and builders.[303]

He further asserted, crucially, that, 'Notting Hill had no human resources with which to combat the especial problems of a multi-racial population.'[304] Notting Hill exemplified the inextricability of the British government's immigration legislation and the growing racial tension; the riots had begun after two MPs called for 'immigration control' in response to an earlier incident in Nottingham. Crowds of white citizens – by some counts up to 400 – launched a series of attacks over two nights on the neighbourhood's black citizens, their houses and businesses. On the third night, the black population – mostly recent immigrants from the West Indies – fought back. The police finally intervened on the fourth night.[305]

In the wake of Notting Hill, some folk musicians and media outlets responded with topical material. The BBC, under direction of Bridson, produced a ballad opera in 1959 entitled *My People and Your People* for the Home Service. The programme told the story of a group of West Indian immigrants to London, centred on a Romeo and Juliet-type love story involving a young West Indian woman (played by singer Nadia Cattouse) and a Scots skiffler (played by Ewan MacColl). According to Bridson, the denouement of the programme was set during the Notting Hill riots.[306] The music was arranged by MacColl and Peggy Seeger, with Bridson asserting that the score was 'lively and magnificent, the contrast between its Scots and West Indian rhythms being no less intriguing than the contrast between the two idioms and accents'.[307] In 1959, Karl Dallas's song, 'The Notting Hill Murder', detailed the killing of Kelso Cochrane, an Antiguan immigrant. The song was accompanied by a short history of the incident in *Sing*: 'Kelso Cochrane, a coloured man who lived in the Notting Hill area of London, was stabbed and left to die on the night of 17 May, 1959. His killer still goes free. The police have affirmed that the murder was not inspired by racial prejudice.'[308] The song offered a gruesome narrative of the incident: 'His skin was black but his blood was red; I stabbed him in the breast/He gasped and fell and lay there dead and now I know no rest./Yes, I killed Kelso Cochrane and left him there to lie./For the killing of an innocent man on the gallows I must die.'[309]

On the issue of race, *Sing* also reprinted several songs from *Sing Out!*, such as the Alan Roberts and Earl Robinson composition 'Black and White', which appeared in the same 1959 issue as Dallas's song:

A child is black, a child is white,/the whole world looks upon the sight, A beautiful sight./For very well the whole world knows this is the way that freedom grows; Freedom grows!/The world is black, the world is white,/it turns by day and then by night; it turns by night./It turns so each and everyone can take his station in the sun, in the sun![310]

However, many of the songs about racism in *Sing* dealt with the increasingly volatile situation in the United States. The magazine also reprinted a Tom Paxton song about the three civil rights workers killed in Mississippi during Freedom Summer, 'Goodman, Schwerner and Chaney'.[311] Peggy Seeger and Ewan MacColl's song 'Jimmy Wilson' began as an indictment of 'Alabama in 1958', where 'the price of human life is very low [and] A man that's black is trampled down/Just like men were ten thousand years ago'.[312] The song mocked the modern liberal notion of 'progress': 'And so through all the ages we have seen/How progress marches ever on its way', and yet asserted that 'The plague still runs in nineteen fifty-eight/From Johannesburg to Notting Hill and back.'[313]

While MacColl and Seeger made reference, at the end, to Notting Hill, 'Jimmy Wilson' did not deal in detail with the situation in England. It did, however, mention South Africa – in keeping with a trend started by several other contemporary compositions dealing with race and featured in *Sing*. Among those was a composition, appearing in a 1964 issue, called 'Hanging on a Tree': 'I saw a black man hanging on a tree/Burned by the sun as black as black can be/What can I do to set you free?/I asked and his white bones answered me – /Don't send your ships to us across the sea/Don't buy our fruit or sell your cars to me.'[314] Meanwhile, Jamaican singer Nadia Cattouse contributed the song 'Sunny South Africa', which had been sent to her by a South African fan, to a 1965 issue of *Sing*: 'In the African land/Many fine houses stand/ In their wide gardens/along the mountain side/which is only right/If you' skin it white/ But if you' skin it black/Then you got apartheid.'[315] At least in the pages of *Sing*, new songs about race were relatively few – and those that were written tended to address racial injustice in other places, notably South Africa and the United States.

An 'anti-racism' concert, recorded in Birmingham on 16 April 1962 – and featuring the Ian Campbell Folk Group, the Stuarts and the Clarion Singers – was a high-profile example of solidarity between English folk musicians and the African American civil rights movement.[316] Although a link was made to the issues of racial discrimination in England, through the involvement of the Coordinating Committee Against Racial Discrimination (CCARD), none of the performed songs at the concert related directly to contemporary racial tensions in the country. The Birmingham-based Ian Campbell Folk Group sang 'We Shall Overcome', which they noted had been 'featured on television and the great demonstrations', and 'used by the Freedom Riders', as well as the African folk song 'Cho Cho Losa' and anti-war songs such as 'Peat Bog Soldiers'; and Sydney Carter's lullaby, 'Crow in the Cradle'. The Stuarts sang spirituals of African American and West Indian origin, including 'I Know the Lord Laid His Hands on Me'; 'Roll Jordan Roll'; 'Walk in Jerusalem'; 'Nobody Knows the Trouble I've Seen'; 'I'm a-gonna Walk the Streets of Glory'; 'Deep River' and 'I Couldn't Hear Nobody Pray'. The Clarion Singers sang a Peggy Seeger song, about the boycott of South African goods, called 'I Support the Boycott', which included lines like 'I support the boycott, and here's the reason why/I can smell Apartheid in my lemon pie'; they also sang 'Nkosi Sikelel'I Afrika'. The evening's entertainment was followed by a speech by Jagmohan Joshi, in which he expressed solidarity with 'another Birmingham': 'The idea of tonight's concert is to send over appreciation to the people of Birmingham, Alabama for their heroic struggles that they have been putting up in order to achieve basic human rights, to live in peace and friendship with their fellow beings.'[317] Although an implicit connection was made between issues of race abroad and at home, the choices of song – all written about or by people in other places – failed to address the acute issues in England. Although the folk revival failed in large part to join with the anti-racism movement, Hall has argued that, by the mid-1970s, 'race had finally "come home" to Britain. It had been fully indigenized'; he asserted that there was finally 'a full blown anti-racist politics, a powerful grassroots and community mobilization against racism and racial disadvantage and a fully-formed black consciousness fed by Civil Rights anti-apartheid and other global struggles.'[318] While race became 'indigenized' in Britain, according to Hall, it was still not at the forefront of issues concerning folk revivalists.

The English folk revival had been involved quite closely with the CND, and later anti-war campaigns, but race and racial discrimination never became an integral part of the folk movement. One of the reasons for this (or perhaps one of its symptoms) was the conspicuous paucity of non-white singers within the folk scene; in the English folk movement, there had not been an equivalent impulse – as was an integral part of the American folk revival – to include non-White Anglo-Saxon Protestant musical traditions within a broadening English folk canon. The folk revivals in both countries, while each associated with the social and political ethos of the New Left, had vastly different approaches to the problem of racial discrimination 'at home'. In America, the folk revival and the civil rights movement developed along parallel – and mutually enriching – lines, reaching their zenith at roughly the same time, in the mid-1960s. In England, revivalists dealt with race relatively obliquely within a national context; often, racial tension, or the existence of a 'colour bar', was presented as a problem happening elsewhere – in the United States, often, or in South Africa.

Conclusion

In broadening 'the political' as a category of social and historical study, Lawrence Black's work has helped to re-incorporate culture into politics and vice-versa. Contextually, for this political consciousness, Black has asserted the importance of relative affluence making possible the 'political salience for issues more concerned with the quality of life than the standard of living ... Politics was increasingly about rights, tastes, culture, morality, environmental, post-industrial, even anti-materialist, desires and self-expression and less about needs.'[319] Much as their socialist predecessors had been, the English Left, after the Second World War, were increasingly concerned with popular culture, as the possibility of 'leisure on an unbelievable scale' emerged in tandem with newfound affluence.[320] The folk revival in England helped to chronicle and explain the events and issues of greatest concern to the postwar Left during an era of great change. Foremost of these, in England, was the perceived failure of 'Labourism', as the Left sought to forward a socialist state based on the full participation of the working class in politics and culture. This was a fundamental difference between the New Left movements on either side of the Atlantic. In the United States, the proliferation of songs about nuclear war, Vietnam and the Civil Rights campaign coincided with the ideals of the student movement and youth culture; in England, the CND and Vietnam were also topics of concern for folk musicians, but although English folk musicians produced many songs dealing with issues concerning a broader, global New Left, their music also reflected the particularities of English society, as industry and class refused to be sidelined as issues affecting the country's political and social direction.

3

A Dialectic of Class and Region: Folk Music in an 'Affluent Society'

Introduction

Class and its cultural expression have occupied a unique space in English society; the 'peculiar resonance' of class in English life has been such that, as E. P. Thompson argued in 1965, 'everything, from their schools to their shops, their chapels to their amusements, was turned into a battle-ground of class.'[321] The confluence of class and culture was a major theme of the postwar folk revival in England – and of postwar English political culture – as the music of working people was consciously celebrated anew, taking on greater relevancy and urgency as the promises of a postwar 'age of affluence' came up against the reality of stubbornly rigid social stratification. This represented a significant difference between the revival in England and its American counterpart. In the United States, 'class' had been all but pushed aside as a category of social study in a country that continues to pride itself on a mythology of unlimited upward social mobility; but as Edward McCreary observed, in the 1960s, no such pretence was possible in the English case: 'Class lines are carefully delineated, and the broad gap between top and bottom is often marked by genuine disdain and sometimes fear.'[322]

This chapter will focus on the period Eric Hobsbawm called a 'great leap forward' for Western capitalism, between roughly 1950–70: a *belle époque* of technological revolution and consumer spending, driven by near full employment on both sides of the Atlantic, and marked by the emergence of the teenager as a formidable social and economic force. It will argue that England's complex postwar economic transition – involving the negotiation of a de-industrializing energy sector – was partially, but significantly, reflected through the concurrent popular revival of folk music. It will examine the folk revival phenomenon through the prism of class, exploring the tensions created by the rising popularity of a traditionally working-class music amongst a largely middle-class audience, and addressing accompanying questions of authority and ownership. Finally, using the 'pit elegy' – a folk form unique to the English revival – as a case study, this chapter critically examines the responses to coal mine closures amongst workers and folk singers alike, after the nationalization of the industry in 1947. This chapter, as the one previous, underlines the essential interconnectedness of class, politics and culture in postwar England, and suggests some of the reasons why the Northeast came to be particularly celebrated by the Left.

The folk revival distinguished itself in part through a promotion of industrial folk song, which focused especially – though not exclusively – on the songs and culture of the Northeast of England; this material also helped to chronicle a declining coal industry and its social fallout. A new folk form unique to the second English revival, the 'pit elegy', provided a musical narrative for the plight of coal miners and their communities as the industry was streamlined and consolidated in the 1950s and '60s – part of the modernizing initiatives of a succession of prime ministers and Labour leaders. This chapter will examine the ways in which England's postwar social and economic transitions were reflected culturally through the popular revival of folk music; it will ultimately argue that the folk revival provided an important voice for the disillusioned coal miners of the Northeast – as mines were closed and pitmen relocated – revealing in the process a politically problematic, yet deeply felt ambivalence, towards the Labour Party, the National Coal Board (NCB) and the industry's nationalization.

'Vicious allurements': The consumer economy, the teenager and the 'affluent worker'

In order to understand how class functioned within the folk revival movement, it is important to briefly establish the socio-economic conditions in England immediately after the Second World War, as previously held notions of poverty and affluence, class and class consciousness were complicated by an expanding consumer economy. By the early 1950s, the English economy had nearly fully recovered from the war, although food rationing lasted until 1954. By 1951 – at the end of six years of a Labour-sponsored welfare state – the British people had higher incomes, longer lives, fewer dependents and more opportunities for leisure; the middle class also expanded significantly as casual employment declined.[323] By the latter half of the decade, growth in popular prosperity had become a dominant feature of the socio-economic picture, so much so that in 1957, the English lower and middle classes were famously being told that they'd 'never had it so good'.[324] Incremental improvements in living conditions and wages, as well as the greater availability of household consumer products, fostered a new phenomenon, described by Anthony Sutcliffe as a 'confident, non-deferential working-class culture based on city life, full employment and high earnings'; near-full employment had seemingly provided 'a secure basis for working-class life' in England.[325] The stuttering transition from austerity to affluence and the tensions involved in negotiating new attitudes towards class were highlighted and magnified through the folk revival. As the economic situation in the country led to shifting class divisions and relationships, the folk revival had to negotiate both prevailing and nascent moral, spiritual and political underpinnings. All the concerns about the 'bourgeoisification' of the working classes – and accompanying worries over authenticity – discussed below were concerns shared by folk music performers during the revival period as well. Indeed, the anxieties driving Labour's veneration of workers' culture were deeply embedded in the folk revival as well.

The persistence of class divisions in an age of affluence

Kenneth O. Morgan has argued that, despite all the talk of affluence, class divisions and traditional class attitudes persisted in the postwar period: 'Continuity rather than departure might be seen in the question of class attitudes. In 1945, Labour pledged itself to the creation of a "classless" society. Predictably, this hope proved naïve despite the breadth of social reform.'[326] John Clarke et al. described the conventional wisdom governing contemporary discussions of class, arguing that the idea that 'affluence' and 'consensus' together promoted a myth of 'the rapid "bourgeoisification" of the working classes'[327]; it was in part the growing consumer culture that helped create and maintain this false sense of classlessness. As consumer shops and wares became more widely distributed, 'middle-class' goods – including televisions, washing machines, refrigerators and cars – began appearing increasingly in working and middle-class households.

By the late 1950s, even many working-class couples and families found themselves to be part of the 'new England', able to enjoy greater leisure time both within and outside the home. The reality of increased real wages helped to drive the new consumer economy and seemingly also blur the lines of class distinction. Items such as a television aerial, or a car in the driveway, signalled a new way of life in many communities; in fact, the television, above all else, was the symbol of middle-class status after the war, with an estimated 13 million sets gracing living rooms throughout Britain by 1964.[328] The writer and academic Malcolm Bradbury, having just returned from the United States in the early 1960s, sardonically described the new consumerism he perceived at home:

> In London, the beehive hairdo and the glasswalled office-block spoke of the new regime; shops in Marks and Spencers' International style were going up apace; espresso bars, jazz clubs and other like accommodations for deviants and delinquents … were everywhere; and the atmosphere of the new borrowing culture – Italian coffee and Swedish glass, Danish furniture and American television programs – showed that England had acceded to cultural drag.[329]

This new consumer culture marked the transition, broadly speaking, from postwar austerity to affluence; however, this transition remained incremental and uneven, and left many behind. It also caused more than a little anxious hand-wringing on the Left. Lawrence Black cites the Labour Party's contemporary statement that 'true happiness does not come from material prosperity' as evidence of this leftist anxiety surrounding increasing consumerism: 'This was a warning and vocabulary that socialists often issued against popular consumerism, hire-purchase, advertising, youth culture and suburban living – the changes it witnessed as Britain moved from postwar privation to affluence.'[330] Although workers' wages generally rose throughout the country during the 1950s, many challenged the idea of the so-called 'affluent worker' forwarded by some contemporary sociologists. Stuart Hall cautioned at the time that the growth in volume of consumer goods and the greater availability of council housing did not, in themselves, transform the working class into the bourgeoisie. He argued that the new sense of 'classlessness' resulted from a skewed value system, 'an attitude towards things and people,' in which 'new possessions ... find meaning through use.'[331]

Joanna Bourke, meanwhile, has argued that class divisions persisted despite material improvements in everyday life for many, writing that 'declining levels of absolute deprivation obscured the widening chasm in relative wealth between the rich and the poor. In the twentieth century, absolute levels of poverty fell. In part, this was the effect of improvements in real wages.'[332] However, in the 1950s, it was the middle class, and not the workers, who derived disproportionate benefit from the welfare state.[333] According to Hall, as a result of the postwar economic 'miracle,' wealth was only nominally redistributed, with the main beneficiary of the welfare state being the middle class; the general rise in living standards helped to obfuscate the fact that relative class positions remained the same.[334] Alan Sinfield likewise asserts that it was apparent, even in the 1950s, that the new affluent society only perpetuated the same economic game, on a different scale: 'The postwar world was characterized not by a new fairness and dignity for most people, but by an economic system ... [in which] people chased endlessly round self-defeating circles of production and consumption.'[335] As was the case in the United States, the hallmark of postwar consumer culture in England became the teenager, as the economy took advantage of a new, and very large, group of young people coming of age. And the music industry, by and large, was the greatest beneficiary of this generation's purchasing power.

The teenage consumer

'The teenager,' as consumer category, had shown signs of increased purchasing power even before the war, but the term itself – and its specific economic meaning – really came to the fore during the 1950s when it came to be used for this new, and economically significant, demographic. Cars and clothing began to be marketed especially for teenagers; teen magazines and teen movies started to appear at regular intervals. And, of course, the record industry early on recognized the power that music held over a youthful population with money to spare. Teenagers were afforded greater opportunities to take part in the new consumer economy in Britain; by mid-1958, there were approximately 6,450,000 young people (15–25) in the country, comprising roughly 12 per cent of the total population (which, in 1958, has been listed as being at about 51,000,000).

Mark Abrams, in his groundbreaking 1959 study of the 'teenage consumer,' concluded that the teenager had been newly enfranchised, in an economic sense; he contended that since the end of the war, 'more and more manufacturers, before embarking on production, now consider it necessary to know something of the tastes and spending habits of these young people ... this is distinctive teenage spending for distinctive teenage ends in a distinctive teenage world.'[336] However, comparatively speaking, English teenagers were nowhere near as affluent as their American counterparts. Based on the Ministry of Labour's censuses, Britain's teenagers, as wage-earners, were drawing about £1,480 million annually, or roughly 8.5 per cent of all personal income.[337] According to Abrams's figures, almost 25 per cent of all teenagers' uncommitted money went to clothing and footwear – another 14 per cent was spent on alcohol and tobacco, 12 per cent on candy, soft drinks and snacks in cafés and restaurants, with '[a] good share of the balance' spent on 'entertainment goods' – '"pop" records, gramophones, romantic magazines and fiction paperbacks, visits to the cinema and dance hall.'[338] Significantly, the teenage market for pop records was almost entirely working class, according to Abrams. More affluent teenagers were still in school or just beginning their careers, and therefore had less disposable income overall.[339] Somewhat unexpectedly – and problematically – *unlike* consumers of rock 'n' roll, many of whom were working-class teenagers, folk audiences tended to be made up of more affluent, and slightly older, young people: university students and young professionals.

Abrams' work came out of a contemporary sociological impulse aimed at tracing the effects of the welfare state on the working-class populations. The popularity of social science in England mushroomed after the Second World War, with organizations such as the Institute of Community Studies – founded in Bethnal Green by Richard Titmuss and Michael Young (both from the London School of Economics) in 1954 – emerging to look at the 'brave new world of the welfare state.'[340] As Mike Savage has argued, the postwar years constituted a 'golden age of British occupational and industrial sociology.'[341] These studies, Savage asserts, 'were informed by fascination as to how the "modernization" of British social life would affect various social and cultural features of British society … Another focus of interest, manifest in the work of Hoggart, Williams, and in Dennis and his associates, lay in considering how working-class values might offer an alternative to those offered by modern, commercial, mass, society.'[342] Most fundamentally, amongst these sociologists and leftist intellectuals, 'there was a common focus on understanding change through the prism of self-understanding of the working class'; it was part of an 'activist Marxism, which linked academic study to socialist political concerns.'[343] The ideological and political connection between these sociological studies and the English folk revival was a desire to understand social and economic change through the working class, reflecting the immersion of the folk revival in the postwar political culture. This idea of an 'activist Marxism', seeking to unite political consciousness with so-called working-class values, could certainly be seen in the work of Lloyd, MacColl and the other leaders of the revival. Perhaps the most famous study in this sociological trend was the one undertaken by Ferdynand Zweig, of the 'affluent worker'.

The 'affluent worker'

Zweig worked on his study over the period of about a year, from May 1958 to July 1959, under the auspices of the Institute of Community Studies and the National Institute of Economic and Social Research. He looked at the lives of workers at the following companies: the River Don Works of the English Steel Corporation Ltd. in Sheffield; the Workington Iron & Steel Company in Workington; Vauxhall Motors Ltd. in Luton; The Dunlop Rubber Company Ltd. in Erdington, Birmingham; and the Mullard Radio Valve Company Ltd. in Mitcham. Zweig noted the improvement in housing conditions, and the increased acquisition of household amenities amongst workers at these companies. According to his interviews, the proportion of families with TV sets was uniformly quite high, amounting to 85 per cent, while the proportion owning record players came next at 38 per cent. Washing machines were owned by 29 per cent of the families and about 15 per cent had a refrigerator.[344] In addition to providing insight into consumer spending habits amongst a certain group of workers, one of the most important contributions of Zweig's work was his discussion of workers' class consciousness, or sense of social place.

Zweig posed the basic question to his sample group 'How do you place yourself: working class or middle class or otherwise?' and remarked that most men placed themselves as working class, although a substantial minority described themselves as middle class, or gave an indefinite answer such as working class/middle class; some refused to class themselves, saying they did not believe in classes or class differences, and not all men who classed themselves as working class in fact believed that they were, but claimed they would have regarded it as an 'act of snobbery' to place themselves higher.[345] Zweig remarked that some workers did not like the term 'working class' at all, with some stating that it was old-fashioned, or dying out; these men also stated that they would prefer 'The ordinary run of people', 'People who do not stand out', or 'respectable people'.[346] Zweig further noted that most of the workers felt that class differences were in the process of being, or had already been, erased: 'All agreed that class differences have narrowed down considerably. "It's all levelled up – the army and the war were great levellers," they said, or "Classes are coming nearer – the top grades of the working class are middle class really"; "Actually I don't see any difference: I earn as much as a shopkeeper"; "There are no differences: I live in the same neighbourhood as my manager, have the same kind of house and have a car."'[347]

In his sweeping study of postwar Britain, Arthur Marwick cited a 1948 opinion poll – albeit conducted before postwar austerity measures had ceased – in which 46 per cent of respondents described themselves as working class, as evidence of a persistent class divide in Britain.[348] Janet Howarth has argued more recently that class did indeed still matter, even if self-identification as 'working-class' diminished over time: 'Social survey data confirm that a large majority of people, when asked, do still place themselves in a social class. The British Election Studies for the period 1964 to 2005 show remarkable continuity in this respect.'[349] It was not only workers' class consciousness, but how they spent their leisure time, which interested English sociologists after the Second World War. Just as their late nineteenth-century predecessors had done, they concerned themselves with the impact of increased leisure time on working people.

Richard Hoggart's seminal work in this area was affected by his own upbringing in a working-class Leeds community. He argued that, although many writers had started to deny the existence of class stratification in English society, they still exploited the idea of working-class culture to suit their own needs. Hoggart asked, 'How many major English writers are there who do not, however slightly, over-emphasize the salty features of working-class life? ... When we come to our own much more consciously manipulative times, we meet the popular novelists' patronizingly flattered little men with their flat caps and flat vowels, their well-scrubbed wives with well-scrubbed doorsteps.'[350] The folk revival was not immune to this kind of romanticization, either, and many revivalists fell under the category of 'middle-class Marxists', which Hoggart claimed had patronizingly pitied 'the betrayed and debased worker, whose faults he sees as almost entirely the result of the grinding system which controls him. He admires the remnants of the noble savage, and has nostalgia for those "best of all" kinds of art, rural folk-art or genuinely popular urban art, and a special enthusiasm for such scraps of them as he thinks he can detect today.'[351]

Like many of his contemporaries, Hoggart was particularly concerned with the effects of the 'Americanized' commercialism on working-class life and leisure – which will be discussed in detail in Chapter 5. He wrote of his disdain for the increasing consumerist impulse he saw in English society:

> Surrounded by a great quantity of material goods designed to serve and amuse and yearly increasing in umber and ingenuity ... surrounded, in fact, by more available things than any previous generation, people are almost inevitably inclined to take up these things just as they appear and use them in the manner of the child in the fairy-tale, who found toys hanging from the trees and lollipops by the roadside.[352]

Hoggart's work represented an important contribution to New Leftist sociology, from the point of view of someone who – like Raymond Williams, whose *Culture and Society* was also a landmark work in this regard – had come from a working-class background. However, it was not without faults and hypocrisies, especially with regards to his own romanticizations of the 'working-class community'.

While it was possible to speak of a gradual improvement in the living conditions of some portion of English workers after the war, it is impossible to arrive at any certain conclusions regarding the working-class as a whole. The interest in working-class life in postwar England may have begun with the social sciences, but it was brought to popular attention through the arts. The desire to understand the working-class in a new age of affluence spread, according to Sinfield, '[t]hrough every medium and discourse – novels, plays, autobiography, sociology, political analysis, film.'[353] It suddenly became vital to think about the working class, to understand how this new society was affecting them, their political and class consciousness. In the arts, a 'New Wave' of 'kitchen sink' drama emerged, aimed at representing modern working-class life. This new wave, associated with authors such as Alan Silitoe and Ray Gosling, brought together a number of common themes: a focus on the working class, as well as a suspicion of modernity and mass culture (related to a nostalgic cultural nativism).[354] It was also associated with the Centre 42 project and other leftist cultural projects like the Festival of Britain and the Festival of Labour.

The postwar folk revival, although rarely mentioned alongside such projects, was part of the sociological and artistic impulse towards understanding working-class life in postwar England. It was a movement acutely aware of its 'working-class' origins, which sought to uphold its authenticity, and forward a political message, through those origins. This was illustrated by the movement's insistence on 'industrial folk song' as the last, best, hope of a nationally vital folk tradition. However, although contemporary sociologists searched for evidence of the 'affluent worker', the industrial folk who were of so much interest to the folk revivalists sat on the precipice of economic, and social, devastation. The leaders of the folk revival insisted that there was genuine, undisturbed, authentic music still to be found – in the coalfields and factories of the North. As such, they carried out a great collecting mission throughout the 1950s and '60s, to salvage these songs before they disappeared – much in the same way that early twentieth-century collectors had sought out the music of the rural peasantry.

A contemporary *Guardian* article on the folk revival claimed that folk song was both 'the self-made music and poetry of the English lower classes, living apart from, if not in opposition to, the upper classes', and also the domain of the university campus, where new singers were 'prepared to sing their own favourite songs to whoever wanted to listen, seemingly content with that. Some of them protested that not even the arrival of a talent scout from a commercial record company could spoil the purity of their intentions.'[355] This, again, was one of the central tensions of English folk revivalism, going back to the nineteenth century. The question to what extent the movement's two halves co-existed, or were integrated, has been a concern of this project, but perhaps comes to a head here: Peggy Seeger argued that the emergence of a 'commercial' folk movement in the United States heralded 'the entrance of the middle class into working class music'; especially in the United States, she asserted, there was 'a lack of recognition of the essential working class character of folk music – and a lack of pride in the working class character of the music'.[356] Through these statements, Seeger implicitly differentiated the English and American revivals based on their presentation of class.[357]

In England, owing largely to a remarkable recovery of industrial workers' music and culture, class was a visible and significant aspect of postwar folk revivalism. Folk singer Johnny Handle, for instance, argued that 'until recently industrial folk music was looked on with suspicion (Mr. Sharp didn't mention it you see).'[358] The postwar revival's distancing from its early twentieth-century predecessor was not, however, as complete as many of its participants might have wished. One of the most vocal celebrants of workers' music during the revival was MacColl, who argued repeatedly and vehemently that folk music and workers' music were essentially synonymous, and that folk music in fact elucidated a distinct Marxist class consciousness: 'The folk music, created by the working people, is the only touchstone we have, in the whole world of sound, of what poor people everywhere produce when they create art. This is the only thing we've got which is not the music of the Establishment.'[359] In a 1959 interview with *Sing Out!* editor Irwin Silber, MacColl stated that '[f]olk song is a product of working people ... Therefore, folk songs have a class point of view. Haven't you ever noticed the element of revenge in traditional love songs, for instance? Here's your exploited farm labourer ... He gets revenge by sleeping with the farmer's wife or daughter.'[360]

For MacColl and many other revivalists, folk music became the antithetical solution to 'Establishment', commercial (American) music. He insisted that folk music was not only a fundamentally working-class music, but that the typical revival folk club audience was *also* essentially working class, despite what 'the critics' had to say:

The critic then turns his attention to the men and women who make up the typical folk club audience. 'Intellectuals', he says, with withering contempt. And one thinks of the intellectual brick-layers and existentialist Irish navvies who are to be found when the Singer's Club is in session; of the intellectuals who work down the Durham pits when they are not singing at the Birtley club.[361]

Despite MacColl's claims, it is likely that – similar to the performers – folk club audiences were drawn from a wide strata of social backgrounds.

Niall MacKinnon's social study of folk club audiences in the 1980s found that 'a very large proportion of the folk club audience either is, or has been, a performer or organiser [of a club]. The separation between performer and audience is blurred.'[362] However, he observed that the great majority of the audience derived from upwardly mobile social classes (upper-middle class, non-manual labourers), who had very high levels of formal education.[363] He remarked that the folk scene had largely attracted 'those who have benefited materially from upward social mobility, but who have not chosen to identify with and refuse to aspire to the dominant competitive individualistic ethic.'[364] Lloyd biographer Dave Arthur meanwhile argued that during the revival, 'instead of the "workers" taking the folk baton and running with it the folk club movement would appear to have been hijacked to a certain degree by white, frequently middle-class school teachers, university and college students and graduates, and ex-grammar school pupils.'[365] MacColl's desire to paint the picture of a primarily proletarian revival speaks to the significance of class to the authenticity of folk music in the postwar period. But it was also true that the definition of 'the folk' as strictly working class had already been irretrievably altered by mid-century; the folk were still there, but their social composition had changed. Coming to terms with this fact was at the heart of revivalists' minds and hearts – could 'the folk', and the folk revival, comfortably include both coal miners and university students?

There were many who questioned the legitimacy of effectively middle-class singers performing 'working-class' music. Harker directly refuted the claim that the revivalist folk singers were in any way working class, or anti-establishment, arguing that they were proletarian neither in origin nor in lifestyle and, most importantly 'were not averse to making money'.[366] It was thus that MacColl, stalwart defender of folk music's working-class origins, came under fire from Harker: 'By 1967, MacColl had produced around 100 LPs of his own and traditional material,' and fees for club performances began to top £50 and '"high grade" accommodation for himself and Peggy Seeger.'[367] As the revival grew in popularity, Harker noted the changes that making money had engendered between folk performer and audience:

> Many – particularly of the earliest converts – retained vestiges of the ideological connections with working-class industrial culture; but they found that, just as they began to move away from their class of origin, so did their audience, until the singers were effectively retailing a nostalgic and deformed version of industrial culture to members of the aspiring working class and the petty bourgeoisie.[368]

The issue of class appropriation, and of the inherent tension between 'amateur' and 'professional' within the revival, was especially highlighted in the resurgence of mining songs after the war, as the recently nationalized industry experienced swift, and significant, decline – its workers bearing the brunt of the economic burden.

Mining songs, the 'Pit Elegy' and the cultural response to nationalization

'So much depended on coal,' the journalist Peter Jenkins argued in 1963, wistfully recalling the early promise of Clement Attlee's Prime Ministerial tenure.[369] As Jenkins' post-mortem suggested, by the early sixties the coal industry in England – under direction of the NCB – had been all but dismantled, along with dreams for a British socialist state after the Second World War. As the hope of nationalization gave way to disappointment, Robert Colls argued that 'a whole generation of North East writers and artists would dwell on what had been lost.'[370] Indeed, coal had not only been crucial to Labour ideology, it was also the lifeblood of a region, central to its economy, identity and art. The pit banners, carried so proudly through the streets of Durham during the miners' gala, represented for the people living there, 'an iconography of "Labour" and "Industry" which projected a larger association of some dignity,'[371] Colls wrote. The decline of the coal industry in the Northeast of England was expressed compellingly through the folk revival; as pits closed, and pitmen relocated, the 'pit elegy' poignantly expressed the disillusionment of many in the region as a way of life gradually passed into obscurity. The revival provided an important platform for those dispossessed of both livelihood and identity, and revealed in the process a deeply rooted ambivalence towards the Labour Party, the NCB and the industry's nationalization.

In his seminal work *Folk Song in England* (1967), Lloyd argued that the actual *creation* of folk music was still only *really* happening in the industrial working-class communities throughout the country. He directly rebutted the claim, made by Sharp and others, that 'capitalism killed folk song ... enclosure stunned it, the steam engine put paid to it, the miseries of the nineteenth century industrialism blighted the culture of the working people.'[372] His argument, that in fact all of these factors had given folk song new life, elucidated one of the defining characteristics of the postwar revival in England. In a statement for his 1964 BBC programme *Songs of the Durham Miners*, Lloyd argued that industrial – particularly miners' – songs belonged

> to a rich tradition of industrial folk song that we're only just beginning to discover. Till now, the tradition has hardly been noticed. Our great folk songs collectors, such as Sharp, Bering Gould, [and] Lucy Broadwood thought of folk song as an affair of the rural past; they didn't imagine it might also be lurking in the shadow of a factory chimney or the head-gear of a mine. Yet even a superficial examination shows that not only has industry a folklore of its own, but also the creation of folk music and folk poetry has, within the last hundred years, passed almost entirely into the hands and mouths of industrial workers. The performance of country song still goes on, though rather faintly now; but the composition of new stuff in the villages had practically ceased by the 1850s. Not so in the industrial areas, however. Miners, textile-workers and others went on making their own songs. And if this do-it-yourself song creation rather dwindled in the period between the World Wars, it's lately taken a new lease of life and is flourishing quite vigorously again.

In asserting the legitimacy of industrial workers as folk singers and 'tradition-bearers' in their own right, Lloyd offered a revisionist assessment of the early collection of English folk songs, and the work of the founding members of the English Folk Dance and Song Society (EFDSS). And thus, as Harker has argued, the postwar revival was self-consciously perceived as 'a rescue operation, an attempt to win back this form of genuinely popular song for the people as a whole'.[373]

The Iron Muse (Topic 12T86, 1963) was a landmark LP in the history of the revival in England, almost single-handedly legitimizing industrial workers' music as part of the English folk canon for a new generation of collectors and listeners. Described on its sleeve as 'a panorama of industrial folk song', the album featured the likes of Nottingham's Anne Briggs, Tynesiders Bob Davenport and Louis Killen, Glaswegian 'Peoples Historian' Matt McGinn, the Celebrated Working Man's Band and Lloyd himself. Many of these performers had been previously associated with the well-meaning, if somewhat ill-fated Centre 42 project. Significantly, this 'panorama' of songs featured mostly miners' tunes – 'The Collier's Rant'; 'The Recruited Collier'; 'Pit Boots'; 'The Donibristle Moss Moran Disaster'; 'The Durham Lockout'; 'The Blackleg Miners'; 'The Collier's Daughter', with a lesser, though still deliberate, emphasis on Weavers' songs, such as 'The Weavers' March'; 'The Weaver and the Factory Maid'; and 'The Poor Cotton Weaver'. These songs were mostly adaptations of nineteenth-century material, performed by singers who, though sometimes from lower-income backgrounds, had little or no direct experience with manual labour.

Undoubtedly, *Iron Muse*'s legacy was cemented in its symbolic redefinition of English folk song. The sleeve notes reiterated Lloyd's revolt against the purely bucolic romanticism of earlier collectors, stating, 'Sharp and other great collectors ... allowed themselves only a partial view of Britain's musical folklore, for in fact the industrial community has much to show of traditional song native to itself, and indeed the "creation" of folk song has passed almost entirely into the scope of the working class of the towns within the last century or so as this record may suggest'.[374] The album affirmed the continued vitality of English folk song, owing largely to the innovation of workers in the factory towns and pit villages of the North. Lloyd argued that, while the traditional 'lyric of the countryside' crumbled away, a new lyric – born in the industrial towns and districts – arose, 'reflecting the life and aspirations of a raw class in the making'.[375]

A conspicuous participant at the 1951 Festival of Britain had been the recently formed National Coal Board, whose exhibit featured the folklore and songs of mining communities from across England and Britain. *Come All Ye Bold Miners*, which was compiled as part of the NCB's contribution to the Festival, was crucial, not only in presenting workers' songs to a wider public, but more importantly in inspiring people to seek out and promote these songs in their own communities, and to produce their own in a similar idiom.[376] As part of the NCB display, pitmen were invited to submit any songs they knew about the life, work, pastimes, disasters and union struggles of the coalfields. Lloyd, who edited the later published collection of those songs, observed that 'a number of fine songs not hitherto seen in print came to light. These, and a few songs taken directly from the singing of pitmen, formed perhaps the most valuable part of the first edition [of this book], which otherwise was compiled from printed sources ... and from miners' manuscripts'.[377]

The NCB project encouraged miners to seek out songs in their local communities and create new ones of their own – detailing their own life experiences – in the folk idiom; Lloyd asserted that 'the compilation had the effect of restoring to vigorous life many past songs, stimulating investigators to seek out lyrics dormant in cold corners of the memory of old miners or gathering dust in library cupboards, and best of all, encouraging members of colliers' families to chance their arm at making songs for themselves about their own lives.'[378] The NCB display at such a significant national event made clear that the importance of coal mining went beyond a revitalized interest in the folk culture of the industrial North; it was a significant part of the leftist hopes for postwar England, a symbolic rapprochement of labour and Labour. After the Second World War, issues related to mining – and coal mining in particular – constituted a substantial part of the public consciousness in England. More mining songs were collected in the Northeast than in any other part of the country, with Lloyd asserting that 'perhaps our north-eastern miners have been the most prolific creators and the best maintainers of this kind of song. Certainly their territory has an unusually strong tradition of local and occupational lyric.'[379]

Much of the debate raging within the Labour Party in the late 1950s surrounded the issue of nationalization, enshrined in Clause IV of the party's 1918 constitution. Clause IV stated that the party's aim was '[t]o secure for the workers by hand or brain the full fruits of their industry and the most equitable distribution thereof that may be possible upon the basis of the common ownership of the means of production, distribution and exchange, and the best obtainable system of popular administration and control of each industry or service.'[380] The nationalization of coal, especially, would prove to be central to Labour's aforementioned postwar struggles. And although it was but one part of the constitution, public opinion – for better or worse – associated the Labour Party with nationalization. As Sassoon argues, 'All the surveys pointed out that … public opinion closely identified Labour with nationalization and had a negative view of it.'[381] This would become particularly important during the later struggles of nationalized industries, particularly coal.

The landslide Labour victory of 1945 paved the way for the passage of the Coal Industry Nationalisation Act, which took effect on the 1st of January, 1947, placing Britain's collieries, including more than 200 in Durham, Northumberland and Cumberland, under the jurisdiction of a National Coal Board.[382] Jenkins described the heavily symbolic ceremony accompanying the transition from private to public ownership: 'On January 1st, 1947, Emanuel Shinwell and Lord Hyndley stood with hats raised at the gates of Murton Colliery, County Durham, before a notice board which announced jubilantly, "This colliery is now managed by the National Coal Board on behalf of the people."'[383] As W. R. Garside has noted, nationalization was celebrated in nearly every Lodge across the country, in some cases with dances and socials. Parades with band and banner took place to the pits where the blue-and-white flag of the NCB was unfurled.[384]

The immediate effects of nationalization could be described in largely positive terms for miners, as wages rose steadily; by 1950, they were earning the most of the Industrial Wages League, which stood in stark contrast to the pre-war 'starvation pay' under private ownership.[385] Indeed, the fortunes of the industry can be helpfully tracked through its performance in the Industrial Wages League. W. Hamish Fraser noted that, by the mid-1950s, 'With falling demand for labour, earnings fell as did the miners' place in the league table of earnings. Between 1945 and 1970 they fell from first to twelfth place.'[386] When the industry was first nationalized, in 1947, it was in great need of modernization, and mechanization. Garside cited 'the need for improved methods of coal-getting, haulage, lighting and ventilation; for the maximum employment of coal-cutting and loading machinery and for a general reconstruction of surface plant. The modernization of existing collieries and the sinking of new ones were undertaken in the early years of nationalization as a preliminary to the preparation of a co-ordinated national plan for the industry.'[387]

Nationalization did in fact bring major improvements to colliery life: from 1952, pithead baths and provision of canteen facilities came to be regarded officially as part of colliery welfare. Improvements were also brought to colliery housing and safety standards, as well as workers' welfare and insurance.[388] But perhaps most importantly, nationalization provided a sense of employment security for pitmen throughout the country.

Initial jubilation over the change would prove to be short-lived, however, as it soon became apparent that, essentially, very little would be different under the NCB. By the end of the 1950s, the industry had already seen major decline, with County Durham being one of the hardest hit areas – between 1954 and 1956 alone, 4,000 Durham miners were forced to leave the county because of colliery closures.[389] Throughout the 1950s and 1960s, hundreds of mines across Britain were shut down, having been termed 'uneconomical' by the NCB, leaving hundreds of thousands of miners out of work – forced to move to another mining district, or find another livelihood.[390] Between 1957 and 1963, 264 collieries were closed nationwide, while the number of pitmen dropped by almost 30 per cent; the total workforce had fallen from over 750,000 in the late 1950s to 320,000 by 1968, and by 1979 only 250 of the approximately 950 collieries operating in 1947 were still running.[391] The nationalization of key industries had been the cornerstone of postwar Labour. From the beginning, however, many in the general public, and some miners, had been ambivalent regarding the virtues of nationalization, real or imagined.

Morgan has argued that contemporary observers of industrial workers in the 1950s, such as the sociologist Ferdynand Zweig, had already noted some apathy towards nationalization, even in the coal mines. He quoted Zweig's study, which observed:

> The miners have no doubt that nationalization was both necessary and beneficial, and has brought them a great many improvements, saying that one year of nationalization has brought them more advantages than their previous struggle for twenty years. Yet there can be no denial that at present the miners are disillusioned about the outcome of nationalization. They expected something else and something bigger.[392]

The expectation had been, as a NUM (Durham Area) annual report from 1956 stated: 'Our Industry is now publicly owned. No longer are we working for Colliery Owners. No longer are profits being paid to absentee Owners. No longer is it "They and Them" – it is "We and Us."[393] Throughout the 1950s and '60s, the traditionally strong links between counties like Durham and the Labour Party were threatened by the NCB's mine closure programme.[394] The relationship between miners, their national union and the Labour Party was undermined by Labour's blunders in the postwar period, often articulated in terms of betrayal – especially regarding the nationalization and eventual decline of coal; this disillusionment eventually led, in 1972, to the first national coal miners' strike since 1926.[395]

The ascendance of oil was one of the reasons for coal's precipitous decline from the mid-1950s onwards. Indeed, throughout the 1950s and '60s, successive British governments increasingly turned to oil for the nation's energy. The NCB had planned to combat the turn to oil by reorganizing and streamlining the industry, closing collieries with supposedly low productivity, high costs and declining resources. Jenkins argued that within two months of nationalization, there were 2,300,000 unemployed and £200,000,000 worth of exports 'down the drain,' due to a shortage of 'just 6,000,000 tons of coal'.[396] By the end of the 1950s, the industry had already seen major decline; by 1979, only 250 of the approximately 950 collieries operating in 1947 were still running.[397] Garside also noted that the NCB, in an attempt to attract workmen to areas deficient in manpower, introduced a scheme of payments to miners willing to undertake employment in other coalfields, which in Durham mainly meant the transfer of men to work in the West Midlands Division. A lodging allowance of 4s. per day was payable to employees with dependents; a 'settling-in' grant of 24s. 6d. was to be paid on a man's arrival at his new place of work, and provision was made for contributions towards the cost of travel and household removal expenses.[398] Garside asserted that 230 miners transferred from Durham to the West Midlands during 1952, of whom 119 were finally settled. Some returned due to dissatisfaction with lodging or colliery conditions; in the two years after 1954 nearly 4,000 miners left the area for work in other coalfields.[399]

According to Norman Emery, 'Miners increasingly saw themselves as "gypsies," moved around the county or to other coalfields as the government followed short-term policies, and new trends.'[400] In the West Midlands, by one 1960 estimate, 15 per cent of miners were leaving the industry each year, and in Yorkshire that number was 10 per cent.[401] Former miner Ron Rooney spoke of the way the mine closures affected him, describing the sense of displacement he and many others experienced as their pits closed and they moved cross-country: 'I was made redundant in 1952 from Wooley Colliery and was transferred to the Hole in the Wall Colliery in Crook. In 1964 I was made redundant again and I was transferred once more.'[402] Rooney described the feelings shared by many pitmen after nationalization, as hope gradually gave way to disillusionment:

> When nationalisation first started it was all right. It went the way the miners expected. But then it came to the position where it became a family affair. If you had a decent position on the Coal Board then your relatives also got a decent job, and it came about that there were more chiefs than there were Indians. This didn't go down well with the working class down the mine.[403]

Put simply: nationalization did not deliver the security it had promised. Far from it, and the growing anxiety for miners, their families, and communities increased exponentially throughout the 1950s and '60s. These fears were discussed in the *Newcastle Journal* in August, 1968:

> One burning question pushed all other topics of conversation aside in mining households all over County Durham last night. It was simply this – when will I lose my job? The Government's rejection of coal as the fuel for the Seaton Carew power station means that no miner in the county can sleep easy. In spite of assurances that it does not mean the end of the coal industry, miners will find it hard to understand how coal can survive when it has lost its most important battle for power.[404]

By October the same year, the *Journal* was rife with stories indicating that anxiety had given way to a deeply felt frustration with Harold Wilson's Labour government. Indeed, the miners' vexation had already spilled over at the Party's conference in Blackpool the previous month. The accompanying piece in the *Journal* on that occasion explained that 'Miss Jennie Lee, chairman of the conference, making her traditional chairman's speech, was stopped in her tracks when about 40 angry miners burst into the hall. Attendants were swept aside and an old lady was knocked to the ground as the miners stormed the barriers shouting and carrying banners demanding an end to "Butchery of the Mines."'[405] A second piece, written by *Journal* staff writer Michael Jamieson, took a more sympathetic approach to the miners' action:

> The despair and fear and desperate insecurity of Britain's miners spilled right over into the Labour Party Conference yesterday. Something snapped – and the men who for so long have shown such patient understanding that coal could no longer be kind, surged the Blackpool hall. It was an expression of their conviction that they are being betrayed; that the close-down of their pits is being hurried forward with insufficient concern for the resulting misery ... Yesterday, at Blackpool, however, emotion got the better of the men with the placards. 'Comrades,' shrilled a startled [Jennie] Lee, calling on them not to prevent discussion, 'we are all one movement, one history, one hope.'[406]

The exchange at Blackpool highlighted the growing tension between Labour politics, the postwar Left and the working class; this friction was communicated at Blackpool as it was in the cultural expressions of disappointment with nationalization. Indeed, after nationalization, the coal industry was defined in part by a profound sense of loss, as pit closures drove colliers from their homes and families in search of work. Their story was told in part through the folk revival in the 1950s and '60s, especially through performers from the Northeast. Indeed, the direct effect of pit closures on the close-knit villages of the Northeast was expressed powerfully through the folk music of the revival period. The folk revival played an important role in articulating a fundamentally very localized, yet powerful dissent, providing a compelling and empathetic voice for thousands of displaced coal miners.

A live recording of a pub concert at the Red Lion in Birtley, Durham, dated 19 August 1963, highlighted the vibrancy of the folk music scene in the Northeast. The recording was done in preparation for Lloyd's BBC Third Programme production, *Songs of the Durham Miners*.[407] Through both traditional and more contemporary industrial songs, the singers featured in *Songs of the Durham Miners* demonstrated the region's strong cultural and historical memory, and its exceptional musical tradition. These songs formed part of a living narrative of the region's unique twentieth-century challenges and distinct history, much of which centred on the fortunes of the coal industry. There were performances of humorous songs like 'My Lad's a Canny Lad' (sung by Johnny Handle) and 'In the Bar-Room' (Jack Elliott), but more telling were the songs detailing the joys and hardships of life in the mining community, which combined both traditional narratives of poverty, disaster and strikes – 'Trimdon Grange Explosion' (Louis Killen); 'Durham Gaol' (Mick Stephenson); 'I Wish Pay Friday Wad Come' (Killen); 'Oakey Strike Evictions' (Killen); 'Pound a Week Rise' (Unidentified male singer) – with current anxieties over mine closures in songs like 'Farewell to Cotia' (Elliott) and 'Farewell to the Monty' (Handle).[408]

Through this recording, and in the subsequent programme, Lloyd painted a picture of the community of folk singers in Tyneside. *Songs of the Durham Miners* was compiled from recordings from pubs throughout the area, and Lloyd stated in the first programme:

> The occasion was the regular Wednesday club night when colliers and their sons and wives and sweethearts get together to drink and sing. The lounge of the Three Tuns is large and grand – fitted carpet, coloured leather upholstery, a brilliant bar. And the colliers aren't obscure men in flat caps. They're smartly, even sharply dressed, and one might take them and their womenfolk for a superior roadhouse clientele. Until they open their mouths to sing.[409]

Although Lloyd offered an evocative description of the folk pub scene in places like Birtley, his account was still given from a distance, and was more than a little patronizing. He asserted that the music of twentieth-century miners took on a great variety of influences and styles:

> To traditionalists, folk song is mostly concerned with a loveable pastoral England lost beyond hope of recovery. But the folk songs of industry – if folk song is the word – deal with pleasures, anxieties and tragedies that are close – sometimes terribly close – to common life today. Their creators carried in their memory a mixed music baggage, of parlour ballads, music hall songs, some hymn tunes, a few scraps of opera, a smattering of traditional folk song.[410]

Lloyd argued for the unique importance of miners' songs in articulating the vitality of industrial folk song in the postwar period:

> Miners' songs have much to tell us about the social and cultural life of the industrial community. Many of them are invaluable as sources of history, for they give a far

more intimate view of attitudes and aspirations than ever the record of political speeches or the minutes of trade union meetings could offer ... Humbly, they record the conditions men worked under, the moments of disaster and triumph, the struggle towards some kind of security.[411]

The Red Lion recording is notable for its inclusion of most of the 'big' singers and groups to come out of Tyneside during the revival, and also one of the true local talents from the area, in Jack Elliott.

Elliott's story was one that underscored Lloyd's observations regarding the vitality of miners' songs after the war, as the industry crumbled. Elliott had attracted the attention of contemporary collectors like Lloyd, MacColl and Seeger, before he died in 1966; he was recorded, first with his extended family for the American Folkways LP *The Elliotts of Birtley: A Musical Portrait of a Durham Mining Family* (FW3565, 1962),[412] and then for a posthumous LP, compiled from many of his live performances, entitled *Jack Elliott of Birtley: The Songs and Stories of a Durham Miner* (Leader Sound, 1969). Reviewer John Makepeace, in a piece for *Sing* magazine entitled 'Treats from Tyneside', hailed *The Elliotts of Birtley* as 'a splendid way of presenting traditional material. The village, the mining community of which it is a part, the various members of the family, the singing style – all these are discussed in the notes with just enough scholarliness and without a trace of condescension.'[413] Makepeace's observations reflected the importance of the local tradition, as well as a *concern* with the relationship between the intellectual 'collector' – in this case, Ewan MacColl – and the folk singer. Of the disc itself, Makepeace argued that the 'unaffected, off-the-cuff singing and talking of the Elliotts is like a book you can't put down ... What a treasure chest is the Elliott's collective memory. All this oral tradition in one family lends weight to MacColl's claim that there is at least ten years of collecting to be done in the Durham coalfield.'[414] Indeed, Elliott encapsulated many of the ideals of the postwar folk movement, in his unassailable 'authenticity' as a working-class folk singer.

Michael Yates, in the EFDSS's *Folk Music Journal*, opened his review of Elliott's posthumous album by branding it 'authentic'; part of the recent trend, he claimed, which had been 'documenting certain localities which have for so long been isolated and unknown.'[415] Elliott, as his album title suggested, was inextricably tied to Birtley and Durham, and indeed the content of the album revealed his indebtedness to local influence; music in these small mining communities served to both entertain and celebrate local culture and working-class life more broadly; according to Makepeace, Elliott's work confirmed the folk revivalist, and broader postwar leftist hope, that 'the concerns, fears and interests of the working class could find expression in their own terms and language.'[416] Elliott's performances included a combination of mostly mining and drinking songs and stories, collected from local sources. He was a product of his environment, and his national popularity was often used paradoxically to pay tribute to the unique local culture of the pit village.

MacColl and Seeger's work, in collecting the songs of the Elliotts and others, followed a similar impulse to the collecting work of Sharp and others in the early part of the century. Indeed, both were concerned with preserving a culture that was perceived to be dying out; both presented an idealized notion of the folkways of working people in forwarding their political ideologies. Barron noted, 'The romantic image of the coal hewer … came to dominate the image of the miner in popular memory', that the typical Durham miner was 'suffused with a sense of dignity and nobility'.[417] Meanwhile, Arthur remarked on the underlying similarity between the early twentieth-century and postwar folk revivals, arguing that both were 'very selective in their cherry picking from popular culture, and both were intent on using it for their own ends. They were all on a political mission and felt that they knew what was best for the folk, and appear to have little sympathy for what real working-class people actually liked if it didn't fit their preconceptions'.[418] MacColl and others were interested, not just in the singing tradition of the Durham miners, but in presenting them as communicators of a political class consciousness.

MacColl and Seeger argued that Durham miners were 'a tough, hardworking body of men, and, like miners everywhere, they are extremely militant and politically articulate', that they were 'unanimous in declaring that they would fight any attempt on the part of any government to reverse the nationalization decision',[419] despite the trend of pit closures already begun at the time of the *Elliotts of Birtley*'s pressing in 1962. Johnny Handle echoed Lloyd and MacColl's assertions regarding the vitality and militancy of miners' songs in the Northeast, writing:

> The heritage of mining songs is nowhere so great as in the North East of England, and it was born of a militance against conditions which seem incredible when compared with our present times. Many kinds of songs were written, and still may be collected, about all aspects of the miner's life, but the hard core of songs narrate the grim history of the miner's struggle for a better way of life.[420]

In fact, the political consciousness expressed by Elliott and other miners through their music was much more ambivalent than MacColl and Handle's assertions suggested; the nationalization of the coal industry had markedly not delivered on the security it had promised, and thus, understandably, some miners were less than enthused about espousing its virtues. The notes for *The Elliotts of Birtley* ultimately hinted at the symbolic importance of song culture in the Northeast for people like MacColl, who were intent on creating and maintaining a connection between the folk revival – and more broadly the socialist Left – and the working class in the postwar period.[421]

There is little question that a great part of Elliott's appeal to audiences and critics alike was his status as an 'authentic' member of the folk. As a coal miner, his authority to sing mining songs was unassailable, even by the most cynical of critics. A contemporary article in the *Ashington Post* claimed that Elliott had 'soaked up the homely pleasures of generations of mining folk and brought them to life',[422] while the Geordie writer Sid Chaplin described him as 'part of the mining tradition. He was soaked in it … He learnt songs, stories and poetry from his father and from his workmates and passed them on, first to his family and then to a whole new generation of folk singers …. This man who worked only at one pit (Harraton) and lived all his life in one village (Birtley) has reached millions'.[423]

These superlatives reflected the high esteem in which Elliott was held as a singer and bearer of Northeast song tradition, but they also hinted at the keen desire amongst regional intellectuals to promote him as an ideal of working-class cultural expression.

Elliott's most well-known contribution to the postwar folk repertoire was the song he learned from Jock Purdon, a deputy at Harraton Colliery (known to locals as 'Cotia, after the coal-rich Canadian province of Nova Scotia),[424] where he had worked his whole life. It was written on hearing the news that the mine would be closed. The 'pit elegy' was a form unique to the English folk revival of the postwar period, which spoke both to the deep folk traditions of Tyneside and to the vitality and importance of coal. Purdon stated, in a short introductory description accompanying the song, that 'the' was good times and bad up at the 'Cotia pit. It somehow seemed to be a place we loved to hate, but the' was something about it and the men who worked there … [I] remember when we found out that 'Cotia was finished, [I] wrote "Farewell to 'Cotia" and stuck it up on the notice board at the pit. It's probably there yet, lying under the rubble.'[425] The song focuses on the uprooting of miners' lives as a result of pit closures, lamenting the subsequent loss of community, which actually underpinned much of the contemporary anxiety in the region:

> Ye brave bold men of Cotia,
> The time is drawing near
> Ye'll have tae change your language, lads,
> Ye'll have tae change your beer
> But leave your picks behind ye,
> Ye'll no need them again
> An' off ye go tae Nottingham
> Join Roben's Merry Men.
>
> Ye brave bold men of Cotia
> The time is drawing thus
> Ye'll have tae change your banner, lads,
> And join the exodus
> But leave your cares behind ye
> Yer future has been planned
> An' off ye go to Nottingham
> To Robens' promised land.
>
> Ye brave bold men of Cotia
> To you I say farewell
> An' somebody will someday the Cotia story tell
> But leave your cares behind ye
> The death knell has been tolled
> Cotia was the colliery
> Her men were brave and bold.[426]

The pride of working at 'Cotia' is evident in this song, although Elliott's voice betrays a sadness, which goes beyond the closure of the pit, and indicates an awareness of, and almost a resignation to, a way of life passing away. The song references the miners' imminent displacement – most often seeing them relocated to places like Nottingham, where huge, mechanized, 'super-pits' had been recently established – and also hints at the disdain many felt towards Lord Robens, chairman of the NCB from 1961, and nicknamed 'Old King Coal' for his high-handed approach.[427] Two more of Purdon's songs, 'The Cotia Banner' and 'The Echo of Pit Boots', also articulated the anger and disillusionment felt by many towards the government and the NCB as the closures continued: 'They're closing the pits that lie to the West/Times they are Changing they say for the best … Drape the 'Cotia Banner boys/And hang your head in shame/Ten million tons been left behind/And who the hell's to blame/That men or mine don't matter/In this economic game.'[428] Importantly, however, the pit elegy was not the singular domain of the pitman. Many other songs, eulogizing the decline of the pits, were produced by performers who had little or no direct experience of that life.

'Farewell to the Monty' (1959), written by Johnny Handle of the Newcastle folk group the High Level Ranters, told the story of the Montague pit in West Denton:

> For many long years the pit's done its best,
> And sets have rolled oot a' flats, north, east and west,
> And all of the rumours that closin' was due,
> They have all been put doon, for alas! it is true.
>
> A meeting was held to discuss the affair,
> And the manager said to us, right then and there:
> 'Let's have one last go before this pit is done,
> And show a good profit on each single ton!'
>
> Wey, profits were made, but with stock pilin' high,
> The Coal Board decided this pit has to die,
> And as output comes doon, we get drafted away
> To pits to the east for the rest of wor days.
>
> Wey, I've filled in yon Fan Pit, I've cut in the seam,
> In the Newbiggin Beaumont since I was fifteen,
> I've worked in the sections and in the main coal -
> Man, it's hot doon the Monty, she's a dusty old hole!
>
> So farewell to you, Monty, I knaa your roads well -
> Your wark had been good, and your wark has been hell.
> Ne mair to yor dorty old heap will aa come,
> For your coal is all finished, and your life it is done.[429]

Stephen Sedley hailed the song as a good example of Durham idiom, writing that, 'In Durham, the home of some of the greatest industrial songmakers of the last century, Johnny Handle commemorates the closing down of the Montague Colliery in the local idiom.'[430] The song paints a more overtly political picture than 'Cotia', focusing instead on the NCB's claims that 'Monty' had proven 'uneconomical'. Lloyd argued that songs like 'Monty' – written about working-class life by someone who was not strictly working class – highlighted the fact that '[t]he makers of the songs are but visitors to that area of traditional culture of which the folk singer is a more-or-less permanent inhabitant'[431]; in his review of the WMA's *Songs for the Sixties* – which featured 'Monty' – he argued that 'this is no place to raise the matter of whether pieces in "Songs for the Sixties" may be called folk songs or not ... But there can be no doubt that the songs are made, text and tune, under the influence of folk songs.'[432] He concluded, however, that 'THEY ARE SONGS WITH TEETH, THE KIND OF SONGS THAT HAVE THE POWER TO CHANGE A MAN'S WAY OF LOOKING AT THE WORLD ONCE THEY'VE TAKEN THEIR GRIP.'[433] Lloyd, then, had identified the crucial function of songs like 'Monty' and 'Cotia', in articulating a political and social ideology – and, crucially, an empathetic response to the closures – which would resonate beyond the immediate community of the singer.

Harker, conversely, saw Handle's commentary on the closure of 'Monty' as an overly sentimentalized attempt to cash in on a community's pain. The first problem with the song, he contended, was that Handle did not belong to the community about which he was singing, thus violating a cardinal rule for folk traditionalists, and highlighting again one of the central concerns of the revival more generally: 'Though the song is allegedly written from the stand point of the men – "we" and "us" – it's difficult to escape the feeling that the colliery workforce are being in some way patronized.'[434] In fact, Handle – born John Pandrich in Wallsend, Tyneside – had worked in the mines, but left in 1960 to become a teacher, and to sing with the Ranters. Still, Harker referred to him derisively as one of a group of 'former working class kids who got on (and out) into a secure, white-collar job, and who could look upon manual workers' troubles all the more dispassionately.'[435] He argued that 'Monty' was nothing more than an expression of 'romanticism, nostalgia, sentiment and tokenism.'[436] Harker's indictment echoed the conflict within the folk revival itself over authenticity and ownership of workers' songs amongst a largely middle-class artistic community. The music of the miners was arguably championed so strongly by the folk revival movement precisely because it expressed a 'class consciousness' consistent with the ideals of the socialist Left, which had been critical of the Labour Party's perceived abdication of empathy and responsibility in the face of the miners' struggles. Whether Handle's singing about the miners' dispossession fit, as Harker suggested, into a bourgeois appropriation of workers' culture, or whether it was simply a continuation of the folk process, it revealed the deeply fraught debate amongst participants and critics of the English revival as to what represented authentic folk song and who folk music in fact 'belonged' to: was it fundamentally the cultural property of the working class, the intellectual property of the middle-class Left, or could it comfortably straddle both?

Conclusion

Class has been the salient motif running through twentieth-century English society and culture; while 'affluence' was the general trend, it did not find everyone equally, and despite claims of an affluent society, based in part on the increased presence of modern consumer goods, many workers still perceived class boundaries and their place within them. This fact accounted for one of the essential differences between the

English folk revival and its American contemporary. In the United States, the postwar revival moved increasingly away from songs dealing with the struggles of labour and a persistent (indeed increasing) class divide, and became firmly entrenched in the causes of the New Left from the late 1950s onwards. As Peggy Seeger lamented, the postwar revival heralded the arrival of the middle class into folk music, in implicit opposition to the case in England. One of the central debates of twentieth-century folk revivalism has always centred on the relationship between the music and its 'working-class' origins; the tension within the English revival was largely focused on arguments over whether the movement itself had contributed to a romanticized leftist mythology surrounding working people, or whether it had helpfully publicized the plight of mining communities as England's industrial economy transformed itself, communicating an empathetic response to a wider audience.

The miners of County Durham were never the affluent workers of sociological study, and yet the 'pit elegy' chronicled a community and a society in transition; Jack Elliott and many thousands of others were being left behind as England's industrial infrastructure metamorphosed after the war – a fact which would eventually lead Jock Purdon to state sardonically that it was 'a funny feeling, being part of a lost era.'[437] The pit elegy and the folk revival also revealed an ambivalence towards nationalization rarely expressed by the British Left; songs like 'Farewell to Cotia' and 'Farewell to the Monty' have served to undermine the largely positive rhetoric surrounding the issue. Jack Elliott and Johnny Handle, from slightly different social backgrounds, representing in microcosm the social and political friction within the revival, together offered nuanced articulation of the hope – and disappointment – surrounding nationalization; ultimately, the folk revival and the pit elegy helped to elucidate the complex relationship between working-class culture and the Left in postwar Britain, personifying yet problematizing the Labourist dream.

4

'Accent Speaks Louder than Words':
Imagining Regional and National Community
through Folk Music

What makes a folksinger? Surely, above all his background.[438]

Introduction

'Where Have All the Voices Gone? They're in the North East Every One', read the cover of the January–February 1963 issue of *Sing*.[439] Benedict Anderson's notion of 'imagined community' has been central to the historiography of nationalism and identity in the modern era, as he famously argued that the nation was an imagined concept: an idea that arose as a response to, and consequence of, the great social, political and cultural changes taking place in the modern era. Applying Anderson's point to the English case, historian and Durham native Robert Colls argued that 'regions, no less than nations, are imagined communities.'[440] This chapter will examine the importance of the idea of 'community'. Through the folk revival's unique emphasis on 'industrial folk song', the North of England was promoted as the primary location of authentic folk culture after the Second World War – constituting a significant ideological departure from the bucolic Romanticism espoused by early twentieth-century collectors like Cecil Sharp. This chapter will analyse how and why the North – and more specifically the Northeast – of England came to be recognized as the location of authentic folk culture, as it seemed to encapsulate the ideals of both folk collectors and leftist intellectuals during the latter half of the twentieth century. It will also investigate how the folk revival's regional emphasis reflected a New Leftist 'anthropological turn', highlighting recurring tensions between province and capital in the postwar period. The celebration of regional identity was an integral part of the English folk revival, serving to distinguish between the various musical traditions of the country as well as to connect them in new ways.

Beginning in the nineteenth century, part of the imagination of national and regional community, in both Europe and America, was expressed through an evolving concept of folk culture; in the twentieth century, although the lives of traditional rural folk underwent significant and lasting changes, folklore and music were upheld as essential to understanding how a country's 'culture' creates and conveys a distinct identity. The local, regional – and, indeed, ultimately national – emphasis of the second revival in England revealed as much about the movement's political ideology as its musical heritage. Anderson has argued that 'vernacular' culture offers a particular expression of national sentiment, and he emphasizes the importance of language, broadly defined, in constructing and conveying communal relationships in the modern era: 'It is always a mistake to treat languages in the way that certain nationalist ideologues treat them – as emblems of nation-ness like flags, costumes, folk-dances, and the rest. Much the most important thing about language is its capacity for generating imagined communities, building in effect particular solidarities.'[441] Folk singers were often self-conscious bearers of the particular solidarities – of accent, dialect, ethnic background, occupation and class – that together form and bind community at every level: local, regional and national. The music that was promoted and performed throughout the postwar folk revival was to a great degree defined by the activities of folklore scholars in the early part of the twentieth century, who had collected what they perceived to be the quickly disappearing indigenous folk songs of their national communities; in many ways the postwar revival offered a self-conscious reaction to the regional and class biases of Sharp and the Folk Song Society (FSS).

Creating a national folk canon: The legacy of early collection

In the preface to his volume of *English Folk Songs*, collected largely in Somerset, Sharp argued for the rediscovery of the 'musical potentialities' of the nation, which, he asserted, had to come from looking at the 'musical utterances of those of the community who are least affected by extraneous educational influences; that is, we must search for them amongst the native and aboriginal inhabitants of its remote country districts.'[442] He was adamant that these folk songs be collected exclusively from the 'common people,' whom he defined – 'strictly in the scientific sense' – as 'those whose mental development has been due not to any formal system of training or education, but solely to environment, communal association, and direct contact with the ups and downs of life.'[443] Crucially, for Sharp, these common people were to be found in 'country districts' that had escaped the infectious reaches of modern life, industry and technology. He despaired that 'England, the land of Shakespeare,' would 'go down to posterity as the only nation in all of Europe incapable of original musical expression.'[444] Sharp's hope, and eventually part of his conflicted legacy, was to implement a folk music education programme in primary schools throughout England in order to instruct children about their national heritage, so to 'refine and strengthen the national character'; he lamented that 'our system of education is, at present, too cosmopolitan; it is calculated to produce citizens of the world rather than Englishmen. And it is Englishmen, English citizens, that we want.'[445] Following in the footsteps of Francis Child – who identified the origins of American musical tradition in the English and Scottish ballads – Sharp's search for the remnants of *English* musical tradition was initiated in the United States.

The Appalachian Mountains, running from as far north as Labrador (Newfoundland) to their southernmost point in Alabama, have long occupied that overlapping space in the Venn Diagram of Anglo-American cultural exchange. The mountain region is believed to have fostered, along with the Mississippi Delta, much of an authentically American music. However, the area was also characterized by nineteenth- and early twentieth-century collectors as a kind of pre-industrial Eden, where Anglo folk traditions had somehow been preserved, despite the wildness of their adopted continent.[446] In the twentieth century, the fascination with Appalachian folk continued unabated in the works of both American and English folklorists; a fascination partly predicated on the region's 'otherness'. Sharp spent a total of 46 weeks in the Appalachian region collecting music during the Great War – 9 weeks in 1916, 19 in 1917 and 18 in 1918 – writing down songs from a total 281 singers, and ultimately obtaining 1612 tunes representing approximately 500 songs.[447] Together with his English Folk Song Society colleague, Maud Karpeles, he visited five states – North Carolina, Kentucky, Virginia, Tennessee and West Virginia – with the majority of time spent, and tunes collected, in the first three. Karpeles noted that, 'on the whole, the most fertile ground was on either side of the big mountain range ... which separates the states of North Carolina and Tennessee, and this was, perhaps, to be expected, for it was in this region that the most primitive conditions prevailed.'[448] Sharp expressed an acute sense of urgency in visiting these 'mountain people', writing that '[t]he pressing need of the moment is to complete our collection while there is yet the opportunity – and who can say how long the present ideal conditions will remain unaltered? Already the forests are attracting the attention of the commercial world.'[449]

Sharp and Karpeles presented the Appalachians as a place where English pastoral traditions were still, albeit barely, alive – in a way that they feared was no longer true in England itself. Sharp's influence, and his choice of collecting locations, had significant implications for both the national and regional biases of the postwar revival. Not only had he set out to create a less cosmopolitan England, he had significantly focused his analysis of English folk songs in the rural south – of his own country, and in the United States. Postwar revivalists self-consciously offered a rebuttal to Sharp's theory that the last vestiges of English folk culture were to be found in Somerset, or indeed in the Appalachian range. They looked determinedly, instead, to the coalfields of Northeast England.

Regional identity and folk song in England

The idea of 'region' has been central to how historians, sociologists and folk collectors have documented postwar English history, especially relating to the Northeast and its coal mining communities. In the twentieth century, the idea of 'region' had necessarily been transformed as accelerating urbanization and new communications networks disintegrated old concepts of space and place. Sociologists Michael Pickering and Tony Green describe the state of social and cultural turmoil in England following the upheaval of the Second World War, as the spectre of an urban, and increasingly bureaucratized, mass culture, sparked a desire to rediscover the social and cultural roots of the nation, but also paradoxically to get back to a more localized concept of community. They argued that

> The disintegrative effects on the social basis of community life of the forces of mass production, centralized planning of housing patterns, geographical and social mobility, mass mediated forms of communication, the privatization of leisure and the rise of consumerism are incontestable. But these social developments have not reduced the 'need for roots', for indigenous popular association and a sense of belonging. They can indeed be said to have magnified that need even as its denials have in the twentieth century been the prerequisite for virulent nationalisms, centralized bureaucratic structures and the supremacist power of the nation-state, all of them rejections of the intimate and local.[450]

Regional identity has been part of the twentieth-century dialectic between province and capital, rural and urban; throughout the last century, many Americans and Europeans began, according to Andrew Cayton and Susan Gray, 'to take pride in their distance from perceived centers of political and intellectual power ... Romantic regionalism was all about transforming a perceived liability – that is, provincialism – into a perceived asset.'[451]

In England, especially, this was so – based on long-standing, almost endemic, regional distrust of London and the home counties – tied to a widespread resentment of that region's economic and cultural hegemony. The work of Doreen Massey et al. looks in part at the 'two nations' of England, dividing the 'old industrial "north" and a prosperous commercial "south,"' which has been at the centre of popular discourse in the country since (at least) the nineteenth century.[452] The writers assert that 'there is no single national identity – no one version of "Englishness" or "Britishness" – but competing national identities' within the country, further contending that 'Englishness' has been a historically contingent construction, 'a white culture, and a placed culture which only made sense in relation to the geography of parts of London, the home counties and the Empire.'[453] They argue, 'Place-identities are complicated things. Not only are they persistently multiple, but also they are formed inextricably out of the wider relations in which the places are set.'[454]

Robert Colls contends that Northern culture, in particular, came to be understood in opposition to 'Englishness' – meaning the culture of the home counties. He argues for the importance of regional over national identities; the region itself became 'a knowable imagined community ... British national identity resides in the south of England. The North East's human and material resources have been squandered because it is invited to share an identity which imagines that the real nation lives somewhere else.'[455] The collective power of regional and local identities has often been expressed through individual narratives: people tell stories about where they come from because it is fundamental to who they are, and in doing so they help to shape collective memory and identity surrounding a given region. Massey et al. have argued that spaces and places are constructed both materially and discursively, while Cayton and Gray have argued that 'regional identity is a form of storytelling', affirming the historian Katherine Morrissey's assertion that regions 'are "mental territories" in which "the boundaries that govern the residents are those they draw themselves."'[456]

Narrative has been fundamental to the way human beings organize experience, to how we express belonging to a certain place; often these expressions of regional identity present idealized notions of space, and place, within broader 'imagined communities'. Traditionally, folk performers had always been members of the community in and about which they sang. MacColl asserted that:

> In the past, the folksinger was a member of a small community and shared identical interests, accent, and vocabulary with every member of that community ... The modern urban folksinger, on the other hand, is rarely a member of a community in that sense. His audience is made up of strangers or of casual acquaintances about whom he knows little or nothing and whose experiences, accent, and social outlook may be very different from his own.[457]

Indeed, singers of folk songs had often been confined to local and regional variants of song. As Woods has argued, 'Folk music, by its very nature, is very much a local and regional phenomenon. A Somerset version of a folksong can differ considerably from a Shropshire version of the same song; and, by extension, Scottish and English variants can be even more radically different.'[458] When country folk moved to the factory or the city, and mass media enabled a very different kind of communication between performer and audience, the traditional relationship between folk performer and audience was transformed. And yet, in a more positive sense, folk music helped to bind disparate communities together, at the same time asserting regional uniqueness in an age of mass communication. The Second World War and its immediate aftermath forced an unraveling of previously held notions of an English 'imagined community', and yet ultimately provided an unprecedented opportunity for renewed cultural introspection. Historian Jed Esty has argued that the 'knowability' of English home culture was restored only after the country's world profile diminished.[459]

The desire for greater understanding of English 'home culture' – sometimes referred to as an 'anthropological turn' – was on full display at the 1951 Festival of Britain. The Festival signalled the renewed emphasis on introspective cultural and social study in England after the war – something seen in the plethora of sociological studies also emerging during the 1950s and '60s, some of which were discussed in Chapter 3; it celebrated the regional diversity of the country, according to Conekin, as part of 'a modern Festival of Britain, not a conservative volkisch rendering of "Deep England" ... resoundingly stressing the vast variety of this island nation,' and heralding Britain as a heterogeneous place of great regional diversity.[460] There was an apparently concerted effort to create a sense of Englishness that was 'not boastful, but sober and humble, not imperial but domestic,' to create a sense of belonging rather than Othering, looking inward, not outward.[461] This introspective impulse could be seen in the folk revival as well, developing at roughly this same moment of cultural rediscovery. Speaking to an audience of American university students at the 1960 Berkeley Folk Festival, MacColl asserted his belief that it had taken time for English people to embrace their own folk traditions, but that the moment had finally arrived.

He remarked that only after the war, belatedly, did England discover it was 'a fine country'; through the collective suffering of war, came an opportunity to discover the country anew.[462]

As the folk revival in England developed, there was a pronounced emphasis on the regional diversity and cultural richness within the country, with Sydney Carter asserting confidently, if rather naively, that there was an 'absence of class, national and racial barriers. A cockney, Geordie, Scots, West Indian or Irish accent is an asset rather than a liability.'[463] Woods, meanwhile, divided England into five musical regions for the purposes of understanding the revival: the Northeast, the Northwest, the Midlands, the South and East Anglia.[464] Revivalist performers were often classified in terms of their place of origin – whether through accent, instrumentation or choice of song – and many actively promoted the specific regional and local traditions in which they were raised. For many folk musicians and scholars during the revival, the local ties binding performer and audience were sacrosanct, with MacKinnon arguing, 'In the British folk tradition musical performance was tightly bound by locality.'[465] *Guardian* columnist Victor Keegan remarked in 1965, 'Folkists tend to sing traditional regional songs, best suited to their accents and gleaned from written collections, tape recordings, or discovered by going to public-houses and coaxing older people to sing songs recalled from their childhood. Industrial and mining areas, for instance Durham, yield particularly rich material.'[466] Keegan raised some of the salient issues of concern for the English revival in this remark: the emphasis on regional and local influence was of paramount importance, but equally revealing here is the singling out of Durham, and other 'industrial mining areas', as places where folk traditions were still seen to be thriving.

The Northeast had a very lively folk 'scene' during the revival; it was also a region where both coal mining and music were very important to the culture, and places like Tyneside held particular relevance for a folk revival that positioned itself firmly on the socialist left. The Geordie writer Sid Chaplin, in a *Guardian* article entitled 'The "Tyneside Sound,"' argued that '[w]e are having a revival of North-east word and song,' and noted that 'In Newcastle that singing pitman, Johnny Handle, dare not advertise his weekly gatherings of folk-songs and ballads. Two of our best folk-singers have turned full-time.'[467] Chaplin described the burgeoning interest in Northeast folk songs, although he lamented that 'none of them so far managed to sell that mere 100,000 which is what the Beatles' first record sold.'[468] He wrote of his 'self-indulgent' hope for a 'rebirth of the songs with the old words, songs with variations, and songs that hit you in the belly or cut to the heart.'[469] He cited the Birtley Elliotts as one of the few legitimate contemporary sources of honest song, but felt that even a 'regiment of Elliotts' were unlikely to break through the public consciousness.[470]

Topic Records, under A. L. Lloyd's direction, was interested in promoting the folk traditions from every part of the country, but especially the North and Northeast. In September 1962, *Sing* had already proclaimed that 'Topic is having quite a ball in the North East just now,' citing the recent release of EPs such as *The Collier's Rant* (TOP74) and *Northumbrian Garland* (TOP75).[471] In 1970, the label released the LP *'Owdham' Edge: Popular Song and Verse from Lancashire* (12T204), which featured, naturally, songs and performers from Lancashire. Amongst the song selection was the title song,

'Owdham Edge',[472] a song about a miners' strike ('The Miners' Lock-Out') and a song paying tribute to a particular local expression, in 'Nobbut a Cockstride Away'. The sleeve notes revealed the heavily regionalist emphasis of folk singing in postwar England: 'From the start of the postwar folk song revival, particular regions of England were at the forefront because of their abundance of material and the number of singers who were determined to revive and popularize their local songs and stories'.[473] The note writer(s) remarked on the particular richness of the Northeast, 'with its traditional and music-hall songs, mining ballads and, of course, distinctive pipe tunes', and the West Country, which 'had established itself very early in the folk revival in terms of quality, if not in quantity'.[474] They lamented that the 'industrial North-West' had been to date underrepresented, and argued that 'this omission seemed particularly strange in view of the fact that there is a strong tradition of dialect verse and song in Lancashire going back at least to the eighteenth century, and in more recent times, a multitude of fine music-hall entertainers'.[475]

In 1965, Topic had also released *New Voices*, which, in addition to boasting the recording debut of The Watersons and Maureen Craik of Newcastle, included six Lancashire songs sung by Harry Boardman of Manchester. The note writers for 'Owdham' claimed that 'the effect of [*New Voices*] in Lancashire was to encourage many younger singers to hunt for songs in libraries and perhaps more importantly, to seek out older dialect poets and singers; sometimes in dialect societies, sometimes in pubs. And here it must be stressed that in the "Lancashire Revival" there has been the closest contact between young and old'.[476] From this resurgent interest in regional songs, Topic gleaned the material for *Deep Lancashire: Songs and Ballads of the Industrial North-West* (12T188, 1968), which had been 'an immediate success'.[477] *Deep Lancashire* proudly exhibited the unique traditions of Lancashire, many of them centring on 'the industrialization of cotton', according to the sleeve notes – although the album also featured the song 'The Miners' Lockout'.[478] Apparently, the 'wide appeal of this very regional LP' led to its follow-up, 'Owdham'.[479]

The origin of a revival singer was a significant factor in how he or she was presented and received, a fact illustrated in a piece from a 1965 issue of *Sing* – 'You've Got to Have Roots' – in which author Stephen Sedley turned his piece into a pointed criticism of Scottish folk singer Alex Campbell, whom he felt had 'dumbed down' his material for the benefit of an audience not versed in folk tradition, while apparently downplaying his traditional roots:

> Alex Campbell is something of a mystery to me – not Alex himself, a relatively uncomplicated bloke who simply wants people to be as fond of him as he is of entertaining them, but Alex is a symbol. For years, in France and in Britain, he has been the darling of audiences who want their folk music spoonfed to them, laced with buffoonery and schmaltz … I still think, though, that roots make a folksinger. There is no reason why they should constrict him.[480]

Sedley instead praised the Liverpudlian Stan Kelly for his devotion to local tradition, despite his travels beyond Merseyside: 'Stan Kelly, son of the best plumber on Merseyside, Cambridge maths graduate and now a top computer man, has come as far as Alex Campbell has from his native territory, yet the songs he sings and writes have Scouse written all over them.'[481]

There was much to be gained by trading on one's roots. The performer who arguably benefited the most from his origins, however, was MacColl, who often promoted his roots in the industrial North of England and Scotland to great effect. His personal history was often accentuated, by himself and others, which lent him greater authority in the English folk community. For instance, Alan Lomax, as part of the narration for his BBC programme *A Ballad Hunter Looks at Britain* said of MacColl, 'Growing up in the heart of industrial England he has specialized in the songs produced by miners and factory workers. And not only has he found many new ballads, but he has composed some of his own, which have the old authentic ring.'[482] There is little doubt that authenticity was derived as much from what songs performers chose as where those songs came from. Although it was Northern England, in stark contrast to the first English revival, which was recognized by many postwar folk music collectors as the locus of a more authentic and vital folk culture, revival performers hailed from every county and region, and proudly represented their regional traditions, whether it was Shirley Collins of Sussex, Sydney Carter of London or Ian Campbell of Birmingham. Musicologist Ruth Finnegan observed that local folk musicians, even in a place like Milton Keynes, 'valued contact with "the regional roots" of their music ... and musicians liked to stress their own links with particular English or Celtic origins. They associated their music, and hence themselves, with "the folk" – ordinary people – in the past and present.'[483]

Derby actor and revival folk singer John Tams of the folk group Muckram Wakes, in a 1998 interview with Jan Rogers for the BBC's *Millennium Memory Bank* series, revealed much about the strength and uniqueness of regional association and identity in England, which often were more important than any national identification.[484] When asked whether he felt 'a kinship' with Derbyshire, Tams responded: 'Derbyshire is very important to me. I've never lived anywhere else. I've been abroad, obviously, working. I was in London for 10 years. But I only consider I was staying in London, I don't believe I was living there ... Although I had a flat down there, it was Derbyshire that was my home, and it's always been Derbyshire that I've come back to and always will, I think.'[485] Derbyshire, he asserted, was 'my identity.' Tams was then asked by Rogers if he considered himself an Englishman, to which he answered:

> Oh no, I have problems with that, I don't know what 'English,' what that means. I have to look at it culturally, and from my perspective ... I can understand people saying they're Irish, with some pride. And Scottish. And Welsh, even. And even Northumbrian ... I don't hear of many people who say ... they might say they're from Derbyshire, or they might say they're from Staffordshire. They might say, you know, they're Yorkshiremen (or women). But not necessarily English. I like the identity of knowing all the verses to 'The Derby Ram.' That suits me ... [Identity] wants to be personal, rather than nationalistic ... What is England, really? It's a football team.[486]

Tams's assertion of local identity, of region over nation, was by no means unique amongst folk singers during the revival period and since. His comments are especially noteworthy in terms of the implications for the relationship between 'the provinces' and London.

While London was often seen as a diluting bourgeois agent in folk music, it was also the place from which folk songs and performers, from various regions, were connected. Albums were recorded primarily in the capital, and many radio programmes were broadcast from there as well. All three strands of the BBC – Home Service, Third Programme and Light Programme – as well as regional stations, helped to broadcast folk songs and traditions from various parts of England and Britain after the war. Early programmes included *East Anglia Sings* (1947) and *Songs from the Four Provinces* (1948), as well as *As I Roved Out* (1953) and MacColl's *Radio Ballads* series, produced between 1958 and 1963, which focused on songs associated with particular themes, often highlighting music from a certain part of the country.

The BBC Radio programme *Folk Song Cellar* – produced in London from 1966 to 1967 and hosted by the Scottish folk singers Robin Hall and Jimmie McGregor – took great pains to represent the great variety of English and British folk music and song tradition. The programme presented three or four acts per forty-minute show, and almost every singer was introduced from a specific region, with most taking care to promote songs from that region. There was Shirley Collins from Sussex; Wag Puddefoot of Buckinghamshire; The Liverpool Spinners; The North West Three from Hampstead, London (NW3), as well as Sandy Denny of Wimbledon, and the Strawberry Hill Boys from Hounslow; Charlie Bate of Cornwall; The Leesiders of Birkenhead; Bob Cann and the Wayfarers from Devonshire; The Birmingham Foc's'les; the High Level Ranters and Louis Killen from Newcastle; The New Heritage Singers from Leeds; John Wright of Leicester; The Watersons of Hull; the Four Folk from Lancashire; Anne Briggs from Nottinghamshire; Tony Rose of Exeter; and Bob Roberts of East Anglia.

While programmes like *Folk Song Cellar* played a significant part in presenting the great variety of regional folk traditions in England and Britain, record companies were also important distributors of regional folk songs from all over England. Many of these BBC shows were broadcast separately on BBC Regional programming, which, Stuart Laing notes, was established to develop 'distinctive, if limited, areas of work' in the counties, while London – from whence the 'national service' – 'dealt with material of presumed universal and permanent significance'; Regions (or regional programming) remarked Laing, operated 'in a subordinate role', and the various programmes broadcasted under this umbrella revealed 'the everyday life and variety of the areas it served.'[487] He further commented that, in a bid to appeal to its base, the Northern Region programming included 'specific commitment to presentation of working-class experience and speech.'[488]

Utopian communities in the Northeast

Historian Hester Barron has argued that the use of 'community' as a tool of social analysis goes back a long time, citing Ferdinand Tönnies' concepts of *Gemeinschaft* and *Gesellschaft*; the former based upon interactive, culturally based and face-to-face relationships, linked by ties of kinship and descent and a similar occupational culture, and the latter which was characterized by relationships based upon the division of labour and contractual relations between isolated individuals, undertaken for their own self-interest.[489] The community spirit of the Northeast was celebrated again and again throughout the folk revival, as well as through the work of writers like Colls, Chaplin and the playwright Alan Plater. Singer Johnny Handle commented on the unique vitality of song traditions in the region, as he asserted that:

> The North East still has many of these industrial songs in tradition and it is from this that the singers of today in Northumberland and Durham are building and extending their repertoire. Although new songs are constantly being written, they reflect clearly the environment of song which has been a continuous thread from when the first coal came to bank, to the modern factory bench and Anderton shearer.[490]

The revivalist interest in the Northeast was based equally on its industrial identity as on its musical traditions; indeed, the two were inextricably linked in the minds of many.

Raymond Williams conceived of 'community' as a means of combating the anti-social effects of late capitalist society, creating 'structures of feeling' within a socialist framework. It was Williams who, according to Michael Kenny, 'returned to and transformed community as a political metaphor, fashioning a distinctive framework for his contemporary ideas, especially the belief that socialists had to broaden the scope of their social analysis and comprehend the interconnections between the lifestyles, consciousness and experience of social actors.'[491] The yearning for a return to this community, emphasizing cultural and political participation in social life, was particularly suited to the spirit of the folk revival. Indeed, this idea of community was central to much of the revivalist rhetoric, which was focused on creating authentic experience. Much of this leftist, and revivalist, yearning for community echoes Svetlana Boym's definition of nostalgia: 'a longing for home but often for a home that no longer exists or perhaps has never existed.'[492] This yearning could be perceived in the numerous eulogies for some long-lost ideal of community, penned by leftist intellectuals and folk revivalists alike throughout the postwar period.

For 'hippies,' argues Simon Frith, 'music was an experience of community as well as its expression.'[493] And not just hippies: folk musicians and leftist ideologues had long held the notion of community to be sacred to their overlapping causes. The *New York Times* pointed out, for instance, in its obituary for Pete Seeger (28 January 2014): 'For Mr. Seeger, folk music and a sense of community were inseparable, and where he saw a community, he saw the possibility of political action.'[494] Mr. Seeger's position on community reflected the position of the folk revival. Indeed, a lasting part of what the folk revival actually achieved was a revival of interest in community – not just as physical space, but as a social landscape. Anthony P. Cohen has argued '[t]he reality and efficacy of the community's boundary – and, therefore, of the community itself – depends upon its symbolic construction and embellishment … whether or not its structural boundaries remain intact, the reality of community lies in its members' perception of the vitality of its culture. People construct community symbolically, making it a resource and repository of meaning, and a referent of their identity.'[495] The idea of community had been a pre-occupation of the Left throughout the postwar period, tied to a fear of individual alienation. Like the drafters of the *Port Huron Statement* – a statement synonymous with the New Left in the United States – members of the Left in England expressed their concern over the increased isolation of the individual and the loss of community in the postwar world: 'Loneliness, estrangement, isolation describe the vast distance between man and man today. These dominant tendencies cannot be overcome by better personnel management, nor by improved gadgets, but only when a love of man overcomes the idolatrous worship of things by man.'[496]

It is clear that leftist and revivalist interest in the Northeast served an ideological purpose, recalling a time when Labour and labour enjoyed a more symbiotic relationship, bound in common political purpose. The idealization of Northeast communities tied into a broader leftist yearning for community, but was also part of a more particular idealization by folk revivalists, local writers and intellectuals. Throughout the 1950s and '60s, 'community' became a focal point for sociological and political discussion. Whether defined by class – as E. P. Thompson suggested – occupation, or ethnicity, 'community' has been contested as a term, but it was undeniably important, ideologically and symbolically, to the Left and to folk revivalists alike in the postwar period. It became politically expedient for the postwar Left to use the 'special' nature of mining communities – to promote them as homogeneously 'proletarian' – to understand the sociology of the working class in an age of affluence. Even as many Northeast natives lamented the romanticization of their region – Hoggart especially comes to mind – in their own writings, they often confirmed that romanticized vision of community, which many ascribed to the region. For instance, Colls recalled:

> As a child, what I was looking at from the window was indeed a 'community'. More, I saw that that community was, or had, or lived, or somehow encompassed, a culture. This flash of realization had everything to do with the book in front of me and nothing at all to do with what was happening down the street ... The book was *The Uses of Literacy* – a book with whole chapters devoted to people whom I took to be like those down there, saying that the lives they lived were cultured, and worthy of attention.[497]

Mining communities, arguably even more than the general population, were subject to this kind of romanticization.

However, Barron notes that, not surprisingly, mining communities were remarkably heterogeneous, citing significant regional and local variations, politically and culturally. Barron derided the tendency of earlier works 'to exaggerate the unity of a deeply class-conscious, proletarian workforce,' but likewise warned against 'the implication ... that the British miner struggled to identify with any sense of collective identity,' citing the importance of unions in particular.[498] County Durham, especially, Barron argues, needed to be approached with caution: 'Coal lay beneath every part of the county bar the far south and west, but the coalfield was home to a rich variety of terrains, both over and underground ... Such differences inevitably affected the social lives and relationships of colliery workers and their families.'[499] The great variety in landscape was often under-appreciated by sociologists and historians of the time, in favour of depictions of miners and their communities as a proletarian, communal whole. Indeed, folk music in the postwar period tied into increasingly politicized debates over the meaning of community, and the Northeast was often idealized as part of both a 'backward-looking romanticism' as well as the 'forward-looking socialism' which Joanna Bourke argued had become the only two options for discussing working-class communities in the twentieth century.[500]

Bourke has argued that the idea of 'working-class community' in the twentieth century has succeeded as part of these two separate, though not mutually exclusive, discourses. The folk revival in many ways reflected this tension, especially in its celebration of industrial – in many cases meaning 'Northern' – song traditions. In the extensive sleeve notes accompanying the Folkways album *The Elliotts of Birtley*, written by MacColl and Peggy Seeger, a significant amount of space was devoted to laying out the character of County Durham and its inhabitants. The landscape was described as 'a curious mixture of the pastoral and the industrial, of green fields and black pit-head gear, of small farms and large slag-heaps.'[501] The symbolic power of the landscape was made clear in these sleeve notes, as they incorporated a de-emphasized 'modernity' while asserting the industrial character of the horizon – tapping into both Sharp's romanticism and MacColl's Marxism. Significantly, the notes described the industrial Durham townships in many of the same terms as Sharp and Maud Karpeles had used to describe the rural villages of Somerset and the 'mountain people' of Kentucky at the turn of the twentieth century: 'The antiquity of the Durham coal-mining industry and the type of community created by it has done much to preserve popular traditions and customs which, in other types of communities, have tended to disappear.'[502] This statement marks an important aspect governing contemporary depictions of the pit villages and coal mining centres of the Northeast – they were thought to be disappearing, like the folk inhabiting them.

Contemporary writers often wrote about coal mining communities as a means of connecting to a home that in many ways could not be returned to. Colls, for instance, evocatively described the Durham pit village as 'a network of meeting places: Sunday mornings at the "Colliery Inn" corner; summer evenings squatted along the gable end; regular arms-folded chats in the sanctity of the back yard when the men were at work and toddlers were at your feet.'[503] Colls argued that much of the regional identity of the Northeast was bound up with being the nation's greatest coal producer. He argued, 'It was from the 1860s that the North East found its modern regional identity. Before then, the eighteenth century is different: sparsely populated and less able to communicate, while the early nineteenth century the outside image of the North East was dominated by metropolitan perceptions of a "Great Northern Coalfield" which kept London warm.'[504] Ron Rooney echoed the artistic and intellectual appraisals of the Northeast as a region of strong communities built around the pit which, as the pits closed, became increasingly threatened with extinction: 'In the pit community you could leave your back door open. You never locked your doors in the night. Folks came in, folks went out. On a weekend when they came away from the clubs and the pubs, you used to have a sing-song in the streets. Everybody joined in, everybody knew everybody.'[505] Finally, Colls argued that communities dried up and disappeared as pits closed, leaving a huge hole in the region:

> What I do know is that these days, when I go back to Eglesfield Road where I was first shown community, there are no old folk on the front steps; there are no kids on the back field, rebuilt now to look like a prison exercise yard; no gangs of men striding home for twelve o'clock dinner; no lines of washing; no knots of women holding the street as if they owned it. Whatever exists there now, and whatever aspects of this old civilization continue to exist in other places, it is not the street I knew. The world Hoggart described not so very long ago is a way of life as dead as that of the North American Plains Indian or the Mississippi sharecropper.[506]

Even as contemporary writers lamented, then, the romanticized depiction of the North and Northeast in many scholarly works, they still asserted the special and unique nature of the pit communities as they began to disappear.

Conclusion

In England, regional identities, and their expression in folk music, served to exhort a leftist notion of 'national' identity, congruent with Labour's hopes for the country – especially through the folk revival's emphasis on industrial folk songs and the Northeast. Distinct regional traditions were emphasized as part of the postwar 'anthropological turn,' and in large part through the re-emerging importance of industrial songs, the traditions of the North were promoted as the genesis of folk authenticity in England – in stark contrast with the initial efforts of Cecil Sharp. The celebration of the North and Northeast – and the industrial working class culture – was also tied implicitly to an underlying anti-capitalist (anti-American) feeling. In emphasizing the cultural and political traditions of the Northeast, folk revivalists arguably acted out their own 'invention of tradition,' recalling Hobsbawm's claim that traditions were invented as a means of establishing continuity with a 'usable' past: folk revivalists expressed a desire to return to an idealized notion of community, with its inherent associations of social, cultural and even political senses of belonging. The need to distinguish, according to Pickering and Green, between 'the retrogressive ideology of traditionalism' and the 'uncontrived involvement in the active indigenous usage of objects from the past for the sake of a progressively oriented social present' was perhaps nowhere else more at play in the postwar revivalists' need to preserve and broadcast the music of industrial workers as part of an authentic, almost quaint, proletarianism.

Regional and local identities have been increasingly imperiled as mass culture and communications rendered traditional human bonds and forms of connection mute. This chapter has explored the complex association between national, regional and local identities in postwar England, and folk music's role in negotiating those relationships. Local and regional associations were clearly highly symbolic in folk circles, not least amongst leading figures and collectors, from Ewan MacColl to the EFDSS to the BBC. In terms of favourable regional associations, none was more highly prized than the Northeast counties of Northumberland and Durham, known for their strong association with industrial labour – and coal mining, in particular. The Northeast was also singled out for its emblematic community spirit, a concept which became increasingly important to the Left during the postwar period. The twin ideals of community and labour solidarity were arguably what prompted Left-leaning folk revivalists to promote the music of the Northeast, of the miners, with such enthusiasm.

Folk Music and Cultural Exchange: The 'Shiny Barbarism' of Americanization

Introduction

The 1946 prediction of the journalist Walter Lippmann – that 'America is from now on to be at the center of Western civilization rather than on the periphery' – had seemingly come true by the early 1950s, as Alan Sinfield writes: 'The United States possessed institutional power – wealthy and prestigious universities, foundations and publishers ... and it seemed more vibrant, modern and important.'[507] However, this new American economic and cultural hegemony sparked a considerable degree of anxiety in Europe, and in England, many intellectuals became suspicious of an overweening American influence. The English Left – led by figures such as Richard Hoggart – took direct aim at the rising tide of popular consumer culture, advertising and the implicit Americanization of English culture,[508] while English folk revivalism played a significant role in defining 'English' and 'British' culture against the perceived onslaught of Americanization. This chapter will consider the complex cultural exchange of the revival period, as folk singers in both England and the United States chose repertoires and instruments – and even at times affected accents and tones of voice – that at times asserted, and sometimes subverted, both regional and national musical boundaries. As the American folk revival grabbed international attention, the English movement began to define itself *against* its American counterpart, almost as an ideological antithesis. Although the English folk revival owed a great deal, culturally and also politically, to the US revival, it also developed an identity as part of the antidote to Americanization in the postwar period. The Americanization of English culture was one issue of concern to postwar revivalists, reflecting, as in so many other facets, something much more significant for the country as a whole, and a subject of concern for left-leaning politicians and intellectuals alike, deeply rooted in the intersecting fears of commercialization and the political 'loss' of the working class.

According to Barnard, a preoccupation with 'how to protect the nation, and the nation's youth in particular, from the effects of supposed American economic and cultural imperialism' was a feature of both right- and left-wing opinion-formers in England throughout the late 1940s and 1950s.[509] The leftist suspicion of the capitalist trends of the 1950s led to a distinctive kind of cultural conservatism, which favoured folk music for its inherent authenticity as a 'native' cultural form. Hoggart wrote of the lamentable success of America's 'shiny barbarism' in postwar England, decrying the existence of the 'juke-box boys', who listened to records which 'seem[ed] to be changed about once a fortnight by the hiring firm; almost all [we]re American; almost all [we]re "vocals" and the styles of singing much advanced beyond what is normally heard on the Light Programme of the B.B.C.'[510] It was not only the military and political dominance of the United States that was troubling, but – much more nefariously – its cultural dominance, in the form of literature, film, television, fashion and, not least, music.

A symptom of the United States' economic might after 1945 was the proliferation of American 'cultural products' throughout the Western world. Ross McKibbin has argued that, 'English popular music was subject to relentless American influence. The English had always bought and listened to American ballads, novelty and nonsense songs – whether or not they were that year's craze.'[511] He further asserts, 'The effect of American soldiers on popular culture generally was profound: they were to "democratize" it everywhere by creating a music and dance which was not only thought democratic but associated in the popular mind with the immense material success of American democracy.'[512] Music – in the form of jazz, blues, rock 'n' roll and eventually folk – would prove to be particularly influential, especially as it found an audience in England's youth.

In England, according to Michael Brocken, 'alarm was expressed' amongst folk revivalists at the level of American domination of popular culture; many viewed American culture as manipulative, mass-produced pulp, which, during the Attlee era, 'created unrealistic expectations about material improvements during a period of austerity,'[513] and eventually spawned accusations of 'cultural imperialism'. Bernard Porter has argued that this cultural imperialism may have been more 'tyrannical in its impact' than traditional imperialism because it was in fact 'less responsible'; he contends that 'American imperialism, like American industry, was a whole stage ahead of its British predecessor; a fully developed, perfected, super-frog.'[514] One of the responses to this imperialism was an oft and increasing refrain – according to Howard Malchow, a 'defensive insistence on the "authenticity" of British (or English) form and content in just those genres where the transatlantic contexts are most obvious – commercial architecture and urban design, protest folk music and jazz.'[515] An authentically derived and self-consciously 'native' folk music became the riposte to Americanization in England.

Folk was, naturally, part of the socialist response to Americanization, with Sassoon arguing that they 'had to seek the protection of nationalism in a battle which operated largely through modern symbols.'[516] Established in both the writings of Williams and Hoggart and within the folk revival itself, this apotheosis of traditionalism and anti-American feeling came in the form of an official policy in many English folk clubs. Established first by MacColl at his London Singers' club, but copied in many others throughout the country, this policy reflected a deep concern within the revival movement for the preservation of 'authentic' English, or British, culture – stipulating that performers could only perform material from their own national background. In effect, the performance of foreign, and especially American, material was gradually snuffed out of many English folk clubs.

As American cultural products came to dominate the English market, many artists and intellectuals started to push back, although many others, it should be noted – especially skifflers and rock 'n' rollers – embraced the American influence. Sinfield has remarked that, although Americanization was perceived by many as a form of cultural imperialism, it also offered, for the 'teddy boys' and other working-class young people, 'a mode of resistance. They were deploying a fantasy image of US cultural power against a home situation that offered them little.'[517] It remained true, however, that a large part of the strength of feeling behind folk music, particularly, was that it presented a clear and vocal antidote to Americanization. Unlike jazz, blues and rock 'n' roll, folk was not necessarily an imported American style; there existed an equally distinct folk tradition in England as in the United States, one which revivalists and enthusiasts sought to uncover and celebrate in its own right.

As I established earlier on, English folk revival owed a great deal to American music; many young musicians came to know their traditional folk music through American forms like blues, jazz and especially skiffle. *The Penguin Book of English Folk Songs* (1959), for example, described the convoluted web of cultural influence between the English and American music: 'A search for the roots of jazz leads to American folk song, and a search for the origins of American folk song leads the astonished enthusiast back home to his own traditional music.'[518] The American folk tradition was replete with Anglo-Saxon and Celtic influence, and the English revival was inspired by its American counterpart both culturally and politically, through influential figures such as Woody Guthrie, Pete Seeger and Alan Lomax. Without the example of the American revival, and more particularly without the work of Lomax – who, during his time in exile in Britain in the 1950s, worked tirelessly at uncovering and recording its native folk song traditions – the 'second revival' in England would likely not have been so wide-ranging or successful.

The kind of 'nostalgic traditionalism' associated with the folk revivalists often involved ideological opposition to the United States. It was also closely associated with a desire to preserve an authentic culture in England; many 'cultural conservatives' on both the Right and Left, in this vein fought staunchly against American cultural influence. Williams, for instance, was unequivocal in his criticism of the nefarious power of American popular culture:

> In Britain, we have to notice that much of this bad work [of creating a synthetic culture] is American in origin. At certain levels, we are culturally an American colony. But of course it is not the best American culture that we are getting, and the import and imitation of the worst has been done, again and again, by some of our own people, significantly often driven by hatred or envy of the English minority which has associated the great tradition with itself. To go pseudo-American is a way out of the English complex of class and culture, but of course it solves nothing; it merely ritualizes the emptiness and despair. Most bad culture is the result of this kind of social collapse. The genuinely popular tradition is despised, the great tradition is kept exclusive, and into the gap pour the speculators who know how to exploit disinheritance because they themselves are rooted in nothing.[519]

It was in part the perceived decadence of American culture that alarmed both socialists and the folk establishment in England. In 1951 the Northern BBC broadcaster Wilfred Pickles created an interesting dichotomy between 'American modernity' – and also implicitly Southern English culture – and 'decent British working-class tradition' as he reported:

> Walking under the glare of the neon signs and the dazzle from the cinemas, pin table saloons and those chromium corridors where young men in broad jackets and loud ties sip coffees with their Americanized girl friends, I thought for a moment of the men down the pit at Brodsworth and Atherton. They would be on the night shift now in that black underworld that is so much cleaner than London.[520]

The influence of radio was a crucial factor in the important cultural exchange that underlay the revivals on both sides of the Atlantic. The BBC was generally on the front lines of defence. Barnard has contended that 'US-originated shows were quickly dropped from the schedules after the end of the war, and Alistair Cooke began sending his Letter From America in March 1946, a program which in part sought to redress the United States' culturally vulgar image (a task that could not apparently be trusted to American-born broadcasters).'[521] This 'insidious Americanization' had begun through the influence of the American Forces Network, which reached its height right before the Allied invasion of Europe as the numbers of US army and air force personnel stationed in England increased.[522] During the war, the BBC had broadcast material from the AFN, and also came to rely extensively on imported American records. The broadcaster also featured regular transmissions of US variety programmes, including performances by Bing Crosby, Bob Hope, the Andrews Sisters and Frank Sinatra.[523] However, after the war, the BBC consciously sought to distance itself from the American style of broadcasting; a style that their administration felt was commercially driven. As Barnard argued, behind this apprehension 'lay a sense of national economic inferiority, exacerbated by Britain's dependence on American finance for postwar reconstruction, and a feeling that Britain's cultural "superiority" over the United States (and the values reflected in its history and traditions) was under threat.'[524] Other radio stations and media – juke boxes, the cinema, television, as well as *Radio Normandie* and *Radio Luxembourg* – offered opportunities for English listeners to hear American music. *Radio Luxembourg*, in particular, was seen, writes Barnard, as 'either as an agent of American cultural imperialism or as a harbinger of cultural debasement, and often as both.'[525] Folk music in England very clearly presented an alternative to Americanization, for both its performers and audiences. According to Brocken, the folk revival became a 'national contingency plan … a counterforce to the onslaught of Americana.'[526]

Alan Lomax, while keen to promote American folk music abroad, was equally concerned that aspiring folk musicians in England re-discover their own music. He wrote of his conviction that, as musicians became more proficient, they would develop a desire to explore their musical roots: 'I have the greatest confidence in the world that their mastery of their instruments will increase, that they will get tired after a while of their monotonous two-beat imitation of Negro rhythm, and that, in looking around, they will discover the song-tradition of Great Britain.'[527] Lomax played a major role in the promotion of British folk music throughout the postwar period, establishing the *Columbia World Library of Folk and Primitive Music*, compiled with the help of folk singers Ewan MacColl and Seamus Ennis. Indeed, as Jeff Nuttall asserted, Lomax 'showed [Britain] what was left of [its] own folk music.'[528] Lomax has been credited with helping to ignite the English folk revival, especially through his collaborations with Lloyd and MacColl. Before he met Lomax, MacColl had been a struggling playwright and actor, but Colin Harper wrote that, 'inspired in 1950 by an encounter with [Lomax] ... MacColl had determined to devote his considerable energies to exploring and recording the indigenous folk music of the British Isles, with a notion to mustering its venerable authenticity to the furtherance of his socialist views.'[529] Lomax's work was significant in heightening public awareness of English folk music, and in promoting that music as an important part of a distinct national identity. Through programmes such as *A Ballad Hunter Looks at Britain* – discussed in Chapter 1 – and *Ballads and Blues*, Lomax worked hard to help English and British audiences understand the roots of their musical traditions.

Ballads and Blues was conceived as an educational programme for the North of England Home Service. It was billed as 'a series of programmes in which folk singers and jazz musicians find a common platform in modern and traditional folk music from both sides of the Atlantic.'[530] The list of episodes, all broadcast in 1955, included:

1. The Singing Sailormen (10 March).
2. Bad Lads and Hard Cases (17 March).
3. Song of the Iron Road (24 March).
4. The Hammer and the Loom (31 March).
5. Johnny Has Gone for a Soldier (7 April).
6. The Big City (14 April).[531]

A media release for the programme expressed its aim, which was to prove that folk music was very much still alive in England and Britain:

> Ever since Bishop Percy published his 'Reliques' in 1765 scholars have been lamenting the imminant [sic] extinction of British folk music. The ballad form in particular has been the subject of numerous obituaries and yet ballads continue to be written and the number of ballad singers up and down the country is increasing rather than diminishing. Furthermore, folk singers are no longer confined to the villages and out of the way places, they are just as liable to be found in a room off Sauchihall Street, in a locomotive repair shed in Manchester or at a trade-union-branch meeting in Hendon.[532]

Ballads and Blues also asserted the importance of American folk singers and collectors in bringing this revival about:

> It is to folk singers like Burl Ives, Woodie [sic] Guthrie, Josh White, and to folk-lorists of the calibre of John and Alan Lomax that the present revival owes most,

for they have largely succeeded in dissipating the aura of preciousness and sanctity with which 19th century folk-lorists shrouded popular music. The task of creating a new, wide audience for folk music was made comparatively easy in the United States by the fact that the American folk form is the blues and the blues not only formed the basis of jazz but has influenced all American popular music.[533]

For years, people like Lomax, Ewan MacColl and A. L. Lloyd had been promoting traditional folk song in England and Britain, but, Lloyd asserted, their efforts 'became properly fruitful only as the American example became clear.'[534]

Growing exposure to American popular culture in England had begun before the war; but although jazz had successfully crossed over to English audiences, American folk had been a relatively unknown entity. Pete Frame has asserted that '[in the pre-war] period ... only the skimpiest information about the folk scene drifted across the Atlantic. Here [in England] the folk tradition had been repressed and regulated almost to extinction.'[535] The war provided a unique opportunity for cultural exchange, as American soldiers stationed in England brought their musical traditions with them across the Atlantic. Frame described a 1946 meeting between a merchant marine friend and future folk singer John Hasted, in which the friend 'dropped by to play [Hasted] a 78 he'd picked up in New York: the Almanac Singers' recording of Woody Guthrie's Talking Union ... Hasted was galvanised; he had never heard anything like it before.'[536]

Lloyd credited the greater availability of American folk records after the war with helping to ignite the revival in England – he argued that the songs' simplicity helped to encourage young musicians to pick them up more quickly: 'When, after World War II, American recordings became more readily available in Britain, the influence of the transatlantic folk singers spread rapidly ... Some of the American material had an engaging impetuousness and a handy simplicity of harmonic structure, and youngsters found that with even the most rudimentary skill they could provide a passable performance.'[537] Indeed, as Britta Sweers has contended, the English revival was 'set in motion by a contradictory situation: it was, on one hand, a defensive reaction against domination of American culture, yet, on the other hand, it was also inspired by American models.'[538]

A revealing piece on attitudes to American folk music was included in the September 1959 issue of *Sing*, in which singer John Hasted – the same character in Frame's tale of wartime cultural exchange – expressed his views on the American 'dustbowl balladeer', Woody Guthrie: 'I'm going to write about Woodrow Wilson Guthrie, because SING has never carried anything to shout about on the greatest of the American folk song writers, because the information I can impart may inspire SINGers to find out more about Woody, and sing his songs, and because I saw and heard things myself last year while in the States which left a deep impression.'[539] While it is clear that Hasted greatly admired Guthrie, he is at pains to caution English folk singers against imitation of the Guthrie (Okie) style: 'Now don't try to imitate Woody or [American folk singer, and Guthrie emulator] Jack Elliott's accent, or flat vocal quality. Be content with your own accent. If you are not among the "rough people that are the best singers," find someone who is and let them sing ... In short, let Woody be your inspiration, not your model to imitate.'[540] Not only did Hasted caution against imitation of style, but he asserted that English folk singers and songwriters should use Guthrie's example in finding compelling material to sing about in their own backyards:

> When you string together your own songs, don't use Woody's style, use your own, and hammer it out of the life around you. In twenty years it may become as developed as Woody's, if you have managed to get as much life into those twenty years as he did. There's plenty of life right here around us; the coming of the thirty storey buildings, the exodus from Ireland, the greatest ports and ships in the world, the atomic power stations, the thousands of jobless, the march to Aldermaston ... All you have to do is live.[541]

This essay was telling for a number of reasons; while Hasted expressed a clear admiration for Guthrie, this was tempered with a clear warning against imitation. Often, this anti-imitation ethos was directed at American 'stylists' – but not always. Whereas in the United States people like Ramblin' Jack Elliott and Bob Dylan had made careers out of imitating Guthrie and others, in the English case this was definitely frowned upon – in fact, it may have been the ultimate folk *faux pas*. Much of this doctrine against imitation stemmed from the doctrine and formidable example of Ewan MacColl and Peggy Seeger.

MacColl's and Seeger's relationship, both professionally and personally, was immensely important to the success of the folk revival in England; apart from Lloyd, there were no other more influential participants. For the better part of the revival period, the two were hardly mentioned separately from one another. Both were keen promoters of Britain's folk traditions – and enthusiastic participants and producers at the BBC. They even collaborated on a Folkways LP, *Two Way Trip* (FW8755, 1961) – on which they swapped and compared national traditions through a series of duets. Their fruitful and influential relationship might not have been, however, were it not for the intervention of BBC producer Charles Parker, who wrote, in July 1958, an impassioned letter to his boss in the Features Department in order to secure Seeger a visa to live and work in the country. She had been deported on account of a recent 'political' trip to sing in China. Parker wrote: 'May I press, most strongly for your support in devising some means whereby Peggy Seeger ... can be established in Britain for at least a year, to inform what is, I believe, a newly emerging, truly popular, British music idiom. The problem will be to provide conditions of employment with the BBC.'[542]

Parker argued, remarkably, that the success of the burgeoning British folk movement depended on this young American woman: 'I consider that it is vital for the future health of British popular music and music-drama, that the problem is overcome ... The inescapable fact is, that we have, in this country at present, no comparable artists in this particular and vital field.'[543] He attempted to placate the policymakers at the BBC by arguing that Seeger wanted to stay in Britain to explore 'the well-spring of [her] own music (which is principally British in origin),' and to bring her 'instrumental technique and perception which is attuned at once to the especial genius of traditional British folk-song and to the vigorous rythms [*sic*] of the present day.'[544] Parker asserted that the BBC could have the opportunity to do something culturally very significant by sponsoring Seeger, intriguingly invoking the influence of Sharp in doing so: 'The

BBC has here, it seems to me, an opportunity of fathering the development of a fresh and vital musical form; and that recourse must first be had to America, is no more remarkable than that Cecil Sharp discovered some of the purest and most English folk-songs in the Appalachian mountains.'[545] True to Parker's hopes, the BBC helped to foster the English folk revival through numerous programmes involving Seeger and MacColl. In spite of wariness about the infiltration of Americanisms into British culture, the BBC – in consultation with English collectors like MacColl and Lloyd, as well as Alan Lomax – produced several shows which highlighted the similarities as well as the differences, and often the shared history, of English and American folk traditions.

Despite his work on programmes like *Ballads and Blues*, the popularity in England of the American revivalist material – especially the 'topical' or 'protest' songs written by the likes of Phil Ochs and Bob Dylan – was deeply upsetting to MacColl, who felt that the American music's popularity came at the expense of English and British traditions. In a 'preface' included in the liner notes to *Two-Way Trip*, MacColl and Seeger explained his thinking on this matter, writing that although he had a deep appreciation for the music of Texas Gladden and Woody Guthrie, he realized that he could not, and therefore should not, sing it with much conviction: 'I learned scores of American songs and ballads and made them work for my pleasure until they could work no more. The pseudo-American accent which I acquired … twisted the songs into mere parodies of themselves.'[546] It wasn't just MacColl who was behind banning Americanisms from the English folk revival. Many letters to the editor of music publications expressed similar sentiments. One man, Kenneth Blower of Leeds, wrote to *Melody Maker* in January 1963 to argue that 'the current vogue among British audiences is the "applause before you hear" system. What an aggravating and annoying Americanism this is! Aggravating to artists who are attempting to create a mood, and annoying to serious listeners who find the first bars of most medleys and request numbers drowned by emotional screams and handclapping. Let's resolve in 1963 to show our real appreciation at the correct moment.'[547]

An article in *Melody Maker*'s 22 June 1963 issue entitled 'If You Want to Get Ahead, Get an Accent' asked 'What's in an accent? For at least half the artists in the current Pop 50, the answer is short and very sweet – money. If you've ever heard a seaside singer cudgel a sometime American hit record in English accents, you realise what part the smoothly pleasant transatlantic tones played in the song's original success.'[548] Ross McKibbin argues that, above all, '[t]he Americanization of the language was almost as fraught a question as accent. The English had long been aware that their English was being permeated by American usage. Some regretted it, but most accepted it as a fact of life.'[549] As MacKinnon has here asserted, there was a feeling on the part of many revivalists that native English traditions were 'something that needed to be protected and nurtured. British traditional music was stylistically quite different, and in order to counter what they saw as a prevailing mid-Atlanticism many clubs adopted measures to promote a very English … idiom.'[550] He argued that the revival in England was partially based on 'the celebration of an ethnicity tied to a specific ideology. The content and forms of the cultural production of the genre serve to reassociate the adherents to a certain set of values.'[551] Eventually MacColl, and others who were influential in the

English revival, began to object to American material being performed in English folk clubs, fearing that something authentic in English music could be lost as a result of dependence on American songs and idioms.

The Policy

Reminiscing some years later on the revival and the life of Ewan MacColl, Peggy Seeger recalled:

> I do honestly believe that if our folk club [the Ballads and Blues Club, based in London] had not instigated what we called 'the policy' – that is, when you're onstage you sing folk songs from your own culture – I think it would have taken a much longer time for its folk revival singers to stop trying to sing like Leadbelly and Woody Guthrie. We have a wonderful revival in Britain ... and some absolutely superb singers and players. That would have taken a much longer time if Ewan and Bert Lloyd and myself had not taken that stance at our club.[552]

In the early 1960s, the folk revival split over song performance at folk clubs. On one side of the schism were those, like MacColl and Seeger, who exclusively performed material from their own 'national' backgrounds. MacColl, who ran the club at the Princess Louise pub in Holborn, was associated with several others as well, began a strict 'sing your own national music' policy at his club, and many who ran folk clubs across England and Britain followed suit. Woods wrote that 'MacColl's thinking at the Princess Louise became entirely national in that he decried the then British singers' habit of singing American (or Greek, or Israeli) songs, and insisted that an Englishman should sing English songs.'[553] He did not want, writes Lee Marshall, 'a bloke from Walthamstow pretending to be from China or from the Mississippi.'[554] Many disagreed with the policy, while others saw its potential benefits: folk singer and *Sing* contributor Lydia M. Fish, while not as doctrinaire as MacColl or Seeger, nonetheless lamented as late as 1963 that 'I have managed to sit through an entire evening in a London club without hearing one British song. Please don't misunderstand. I am all in favour of international song-swapping ... But when British singers start ignoring their own songs "because American songs are so much better," I, for one, feel that things are getting out of hand.'[555] Despite Marshall's assessment that MacColl spurred new levels of 'national creativity' by instituting this strict policy at his club, I would argue that the second folk revival reached its nadir with this policy.

In his autobiography, *Journeyman*, MacColl outlined the specifics of his and Seeger's aesthetic transition, which led to the policy rule at the Singer's Club. He wrote, 'As the months went by, we found that we tired of singing songs in a language we didn't speak fluently or, sometimes, didn't understand at all; or if the songs were from an alien culture or lifestyle, they began to lose their conviction. We felt no real sense of identity with them.'[556] 'Furthermore,' wrote MacColl, 'Peggy found it difficult to keep a straight face when she heard cockneys and Liverpudlians singing Leadbelly and Guthrie songs, pieces which she had drunk in with mother's milk. She felt that the songs didn't ring true and then it occurred to us that perhaps our own repertoire of foreign songs might not ring true to natives of the countries when those songs came. A polemic began.'[557] MacColl disputed the idea that they had been 'hostile' to 'foreign' songs, offering instead that 'we were eager to attract foreign performers to the club. Our problem was English, Scots, Welsh, Irish, and American performers singing songs whose idiom, whose language, they did not understand, hence mishandling the songs.'[558]

Further to this fear of material being 'mishandled' and disrespected, MacColl and Seeger were also very keen on proving that England 'had an indigenous folk-music that was muscular, as varied and as beautiful as any music anywhere in the world. We felt it was necessary to explore our own music first, to distance ourselves from skiffle with its legions of quasi-Americans'; the folk club, MacColl asserted, 'should be a place where our native music should have pride of place and where the folk music of other nations would be treated with dignity and respect.'[559] MacColl could get away with his no-compromise stance because he was perceived by many, including his brother-in-law Mike Seeger of the US group the New Lost City Ramblers, to be 'the best revival singer and contemporary writer in the English language.'[560] Karl Dallas meanwhile effused that, 'If the British revival can be said to have been started by one man, that man is Ewan MacColl. In fact, if we are to believe Pete Seeger, the American songwriting revival – about which Ewan is strongly critical – owes a great deal to his pioneering work as Britain's leading folk poet.'[561]

However, Colin Harper expressed a much more ambivalent view of MacColl and his formidable influence, stating that he 'imposed strict rules in his clubs but clearly bent them for his own performances; he championed the tradition with an iron grip but wrote some extraordinarily beautiful and enduring pop songs; and he had an opinion on everything and regularly gave the press controversy on a plate. He also knew exactly what he was doing.'[562] MacColl himself did not sing American songs; although he accepted the contemporary folk idiom, and sought to mix the old and the new in his own songwriting, he felt that national traditions were not to be hybridized. Most of MacColl's repertoire was of Scottish, or (Northern) English origin, in line with his upbringing, apart from departures such as *Two-Way Trip*. In the sleeve notes to that album, MacColl felt the need to explain the potentially suspect merger of styles while upholding his policy:

> During the time I have spent working in this field, I have rarely moved outside of my own musical tradition. At the hundreds of hootenannies where I have sung or acted as chairman I have made a point of insisting on the rule that singers do not sing anything but the songs of their own native tradition … And now I am not only singing American songs with Peggy but encouraging her to sing Scots and English songs with me! However, for the most part we confine ourselves to joining in the choruses of each other's songs.[563]

Revival singers Brian Byrne and Roy Harris described their personal introduction to folk music after the Second World War, and echoed MacColl's desire to eradicate pseudo-American style from English folk singing. Harris recalled that he had heard American greats such as Woody Guthrie, Burl Ives and the Weavers on American

Forces Radio during the war, and thus apparently had 'no conception' of English music at the time. He, like many others of his generation, came into English folk 'round the back way', thinking, he stated, that folk music was 'all American at the start'. Harris and Byrne started a club in Derby, where initially everyone was allowed to sing whatever they liked (he later admitted it was 'the blind leading the blind'); however, 'through time and persuasion', he came to the conclusion that all resident singers had to sing British music. Influenced by what MacColl had done at the Princess Louise Singers' Club, Harris and Byrne felt that 'this was the thing to do, rather than the pseudo-American thing'.[564]

MacColl allowed that his policy decision was unpopular at first. But the idea began to catch on at more traditionalist clubs throughout the country, as increasingly regional, and local, traditions became ascendant. One of the earliest converts to MacColl's policy rule was the club run by the High Level Ranters, Louis Killen and Johnny Handle, in Newcastle. As Anthea Joseph pointed out in her study of the club scene on Tyneside, the location of the club – in an area where folk tradition was very much alive, the club was given 'a pretty wide scope, for not only is the native Northumbrian tradition around them but there are large numbers of Irish and Scots, and even a sprinkling of Southerners, who have settled in the industrial belt along the "coaly tyne."'[565] The club soon developed an 'all-British' policy. Joseph claimed that this progression was 'natural', as 'why should they want to sing anything else when there is such a great store of their own traditions around them from which to draw?'[566] She further argued that the club's policy reflected the development and maturation of the club's organizers, and its audience. When Killen started the club in the autumn of 1958, the music presented was a mixture of American and British. Joseph wrote, 'All the regular singers and most of those from the floor had come to folk music via jazz and the blues, so it was natural that their repertoires should be overweighted with American material.'[567] However, by the early 1960s, this had changed, so that the club featured exclusively English and British music. In instituting such a stark change in policy and repertoire, the club risked losing its initial audience; however, argued Joseph, that was not what happened – numbers actually increased as 'audience, like singers, have developed, too.'[568]

On the other side of the debate were those who felt that folk song was part of a larger, global musical community, and that any kind of 'national' music was inherently a false construct. The increasing rigidity of the rules governing these clubs caused many performers to reject them, and in some cases to start rival clubs. MacKinnon has stated that 'those interested in American or other musics were either squeezed out or clear-cut divisions of clubs occurred. Folk clubs moved over to the native British tradition in a big way, and those clubs which formed at this time were created with the specific intention of traditional music revival.'[569] Unlike in the United States, where many immigrant folk cultures were synthesized into the folk revival[570] – something which was highlighted as a particular strength of the movement – Brocken has asserted that, for MacColl, 'Any form of cultural melting pot was total anathema to [his] secular religion of folk music.'[571] MacColl and Seeger, operating under this nativist ethos, laid down the framework for musical 'correctness' amongst revivalists, and insisted on 'traditional' performances showcasing an unaccompanied voice, or if necessary, fiddle and flute – never guitar or banjo.[572]

In an interview with fellow folk singer and songwriter Sydney Carter for *Sing*, entitled 'Going American?' MacColl and Seeger spoke about their commitment to the policy. In response to Carter's assertion that 'there's no doubt that a lot of English people like singing American folk songs ... I should be sorry to think that we must only sing our own things,' Seeger made reference to the negative influence of American cultural hegemony – 'Well, let's put it this way – how would you like it if everybody in the world spoke one language?' – while MacColl interjected, 'Or better still, suppose the dominant culture in the world was the Russian one, and we all sang Russian songs. How dull it would be.'[573] Carter tried again to suggest that cultural plurality was a virtue – 'Yes. On the other hand, we all speak different languages but we do borrow from each other' – to which Seeger countered that language and culture were distinctly national constructs:

> We all speak different languages because these have been built up over the years as separate. People have been proud of them and built them up as British, as French, as this and that. And it's not only language that has been built up, but a whole culture behind it, including music ... And to me, as an American, the fact that the Americans have built up a culture which is American, which is absolutely unique, is valuable to me. And that's why I sing American songs. Because they represented the particular struggle of a particular people at a particular point of time. But when I hear a British person singing a folk song from America I feel that there's an anachronism – a spiritual anachronism, if you want to put it that way – there's something which is not quite right.[574]

MacColl's last words on the subject were an emphatic rejection of a pluralistic or multicultural folk tradition in England: 'If we subject ourselves consciously or unconsciously to too much acculturation, as the anthropologists call it, we'll finish with no culture at all. We'll finish with a kind of cosmopolitan, half-baked music which doesn't satisfy the emotions of anybody.'[575] Putting aside its troubling racial subtext, the hardline approach taken by MacColl and Seeger did in fact pay some dividends with regards to knowledge of 'home-grown' folk traditions in England and Britain. Peggy's half-brother, Pete, in his regular 'Johnny Appleseed, Jr.' column for *Sing Out!*, commented on the changing focus of British folk music, which he observed during his national tour of Britain in 1961: 'Two years ago there was still a lot of imitation American singing. Nowadays you'll find a lot more appreciation of English, Scottish, and Irish songs.'[576] MacColl's policy in hindsight represents a folk revival unsure of its cultural roots, insecure about its tradition and authenticity. The coded language surrounding the defence of 'native' traditions is important in the post-imperial context of the folk revival. Was the revival asserting a 'indigenous' white, working-class Englishness for the post-imperial era?

Conclusion

After the Second World War, during a period when American economic and cultural hegemony was emergent, fears over Americanization particularly gripped the Left throughout Britain and Europe. In the works of leftist intellectuals, Americanization was implicitly – and sometimes explicitly – linked with fears of commercialization (a more well-established fear on the socialist left, going back to the nineteenth century). The work of people like Richard Hoggart and Raymond Williams sketched out the particular concerns of leftist intellectuals in Britain, as American cultural products threatened an already-fragile sense of national identity. The English folk revival was no exception; although the movement was in many ways closely linked, musically and ideologically, with the American revival, it nevertheless defined itself self-consciously against it – as an antidote to encroaching American influence. This eventually resulted in the controversial Ewan MacColl-led folk club 'policy', which limited the performance of songs in clubs to the national origin of the singer. Through this policy MacColl delineated much of the long-term legacy of the revival in England: although it was a policy designed to strengthen English folk singers' knowledge of their native traditions, it resulted instead, in a rather negatively defined, meanly exclusivist English revival.

6

'With Bob on Our Side': Folk Music, the Culture Industry and Commercial Success

Introduction

Almost since it first began to be collected, in the late nineteenth century, folk music has been understood explicitly in terms of its opposition to mass culture. The ideals of authenticity and truth were the pillars of folk revivalism in the twentieth century, and revivalists have self-consciously differentiated themselves from 'mass culture' and its entrapments. Music theorist Mike Marqusee has argued that 'unlike the mass counterculture of the late sixties that it helped to breed, [folk revivalism] was characterized by earnestness and restraint. It was self-consciously opposed to the glitzy superficiality and addled consumerism' often associated with American youth culture.[577] This 'jargon of authenticity' was applied to musical performance, artistic purpose, even personal style; Marqusee asserts that it 'coursed through the shared understanding of history, tradition, politics, the "folk" and the "people" and it levied existential demands.'[578] This chapter will address the uneasy relationship between folk music and mass culture after the Second World War, as the English folk revival sought to distance itself yet again from its louder, and more commercially successful, American counterpart. It will examine the problems created by the expansion and success of folk music within the matrix of a 'culture industry'[579] to which it would seem to be antithetically positioned, as an intrinsic set of folk values – focused on non-commercial and 'authentic' rendering of everyday life and struggle – came up against an emergent 'urban' folk culture, incubated within the context of an ascendant music industry commercialism and hungrier for success. Even before the Second World War, folk music had reached a global audience through the technologies of mass communication – by way of the radio and the record. However, this relationship between folk and mass culture was viewed with suspicion by many within the folk scene, who saw it as a threat to the folk community. For young folk fans, folk music offered an antidote to mass culture and capitalist society. According to Andrew Hunt, it was their 'search for authenticity in a world beset by war, overpopulation, environmental degradation, and corporate control of mainstream politics and media' which drove both the leftist movements of the 1950s and '60s, and, I would argue, the folk revival.[580] Folk music served to highlight the difficulties of cultivating authentic culture in a world dominated by mass media.

The paradoxical success of folk music in the late capitalist period echoed many of the concerns expressed by Marxist cultural theorists in the 1920s and '30s – and their less doctrinaire socialist descendants – as they sought to come to terms with the use and meaning of culture in commercialized society. Raymond Williams lamented, 'In the worst cultural products of our time, we find little that is genuinely popular, developed from the life of actual communities. We find instead a synthetic culture, or anti-culture.'[581] Richard Hoggart wrote about the effect of the culture industry on the working-class in particular: 'Mass culture gives the working classes cheap, sensationalist entertainment, enervating, dulling and eventually destroying their sense of taste; meanwhile, the working-class environment itself is being torn up and replaced by the cheap glitter of affluence.'[582] Finally, Theodor Adorno argued that under the influence of the culture industry, 'The masses are not primary, but secondary, they are an object of calculation: an appendage of the machinery. The customer is not king, as the culture industry would have us believe, not its subject but its object.'[583] Andreas Huyssen was, however, more hopeful for the critical and political potential of cultural products, and more specifically music, arguing that 'culture is a potentially explosive force and threat to advanced capitalism (and to bureaucratised socialism for that matter).'[584]

The idea of the culture industry as monolithic, however, fails to take sufficiently into account the agency of the audience and consumer. The extent to which the folk revival movements in England and the United States contributed to, or subverted, the domination of the masses has remained a matter for debate amongst critics and participants alike. The uneasy balance between the masses and mass culture was certainly highlighted during the folk revival in England, as (overwhelmingly white, middle-class) folk scholars and enthusiasts placed themselves in direct opposition to the evils of the culture industry. The road to understanding, and getting a sense of folk revivalists' and leftist intellectuals' anxieties regarding this paradox, inevitably leads through Theodor Adorno and the Frankfurt School. As I established in Chapter 2, the 'cultural Marxists' of postwar Britain were important advocates of folk music's usefulness as a tool for social and political awakening, in implicit opposition to the Frankfurt School – who saw almost all forms of popular culture in terms of their suppressive effects. Adorno's work is particularly interesting with regards to folk music precisely because he hardly mentioned it – he was much more concerned, theoretically, with American 'pop' and Jazz. Because of his influence on twentieth-century cultural theory, some discussion of Adorno's views is not only necessary, but perhaps also particularly useful for the subject of folk music. In essence, because folk music revivalists self-consciously perceived themselves, and their music, to be agents of subversive opposition to mass culture, Adorno's assertions regarding the sheer impossibility of that position remain significant.

For Adorno, popular music was the height of false consciousness. His and Max Horkheimer's *Dialectic of Enlightenment* (1947; trans. 1979) addressed the nascent political power of the mass media in the mid-twentieth century. Adorno and Horkheimer saw the culture industry as a force in which the critical tendencies of the listening audience were virtually eliminated. In the supposed 'enlightened' world of the twentieth century, Adorno and Horkheimer contended, '[i]magination atrophies';

it was a world, they argued, where 'the evolution of the machine has already turned into that of the machinery of domination.'[585] Indeed, for Adorno and Horkheimer, the modern world of technology and mass culture merely upheld the machinery of coercion and domination, and the 'culture industry' was on the same plane as the bomb and the automobile as a complicit partner in destroying social conscience and cultural creativity.[586] Fundamentally, the concern of *Dialectic of Enlightenment* was that 'The whole world is made to pass through the filter of the culture industry ... Real life is becoming indistinguishable from the movies. The sound film, far surpassing the theatre of illusion, leaves no room for imagination or reflection on the part of the audience.'[587] This was indeed a dangerous and frightening proposition – one that ultimately allowed, *Dialectic* implied, for the rise of fascism.

Adorno and Horkheimer (and a number of other Frankfurt Schoolers) were understandably wary of the power of mass communication for the furtherance of intolerance and the loss of social agency and subjectivity. Fleeing Germany in the late 1930s, Adorno eventually landed in the United States, where he was disappointed to find that '[the radio] collects no fees from the public, and so has acquired the illusory form of disinterested, unbiased authority which suits fascism admirably.'[588] In the United States, Adorno was more particularly concerned with the illusory autonomy of art under the schema of the culture industry. Music, for Adorno, represented the ultimate battleground between the culture industry and the consciousness of the masses, precisely because of its greater perceived autonomy, and thus was the subject of much of his theoretical work in the postwar period.

Adorno found popular music especially troublesome, and the worst betrayal (of many) perpetrated by the culture industry, precisely because of its revolutionary potential. As he argued, 'Music represents at once the immediate manifestation of impulse and the locus of its taming.'[589] Indeed, he famously stated, 'Music betrays all art.'[590] This betrayal largely resulted from music's susceptibility to the mass market. The entire purpose of the culture industry, argued Adorno, was to transfer 'the profit motive naked onto cultural forms, thus nullifying the autonomy of a work of art.'[591] One of Adorno's theoretical followers, Jacques Attali, argued that 'wherever there is music, there is money ... Music, an immaterial pleasure turned commodity, now heralds a society of the sign, of the immaterial up for sale, of the social relation unified in money.'[592] The rationalization and commercialization of a potentially truly popular cultural practice were the source of Adorno's anxiety regarding music. He claimed that 'music for entertainment seems to complement the reduction of people to silence, the dying out of speech as expression, the inability to communicate at all. It inhabits the pockets of silence that develop between people moulded by anxiety, work and undemanding docility.'[593]

Adorno blamed the phenomenon of the 'star principle' for the manipulative power of the popular culture industry over the masses, and his discussion of the corruptive force of celebrity also has implications for how folk music has been received and interpreted. Indeed, within the revivals themselves, the idea of celebrity became increasingly problematic. Fundamentally, folk revivalism was based upon the idea of the collective over the individual, which was why the notion of celebrity, for example, was anathema to folk revivalists. The commercial success of folk music made it possible for many people to make a living – sometimes quite a comfortable living – from being a 'folk singer'. However, as its popularity mushroomed, the idea of making money became a focal point of revivalist concern. Singer Sydney Carter, in an article entitled 'Pop Goes the Folksong' wrote, '"Folk" has now become a prestige word. Records which no teen-ager would have bought ten years ago now sell briskly with this magic label.'[594] In a subsequent interview with fellow singer Steve Benbow, Carter addressed folk music's new commercial appeal. Benbow unabashedly labelled himself a professional at a time when the term was associated with the worst aspects of folk's commercialization:

> Q: Steve, they say you're going commercial.
> A: I hope so! – If, by 'going commercial', they mean I am going to make money. I am a full time professional. But if they mean I'm spoiling songs just to make money, I am not. I'm singing the same sort of songs I always sang, and the same way as before.[595]

Making money ran completely counter to the ethos of some folk revivalists (although it was almost certainly a secret goal of most performers), which based itself upon the idea of un-mediated, authentic expression of everyday life.[596] For instance, singer Dominic Behan argued witheringly in 1965, 'There are some protest-song writers who're making more money out of peace than Krupps made out of war.'[597] As a result, 'professionalism' took on some seriously negative connotations, and instrumentation took on an almost political importance for many revivalists, especially in England.

In discussing the celebrity phenomenon at the centre of the culture industry, Adorno wrote:

> The star principle has become totalitarian. The reactions of the listeners appear to have no relation to the playing of the music. They have reference, rather, to the cumulative success which, for its part, cannot be thought of unalienated by the past spontaneities of listeners, but instead dates back to the command of publishers, sound and film magnates and rules of radio.[598]

In opposition to the American revival, the structure of the revival in England worked, according to Mackinnon, 'against stardom. There are stars, but their success has to be measured in terms other than financial success, or else they have to leave and work outside the folk scene. But this affects not only the pocket of folk "stars" but also their relationship to audiences. It prevents musicians aping the role models of other genres.'[599] Folk journalist Ed Badeaux addressed the mutual exclusivity of folk music and celebrity culture, as he saw it, writing that 'the star system is totally unrelated, totally foreign to folk music. A star is a super-person, an idea. A folksinger is common clay, the sort of stuff that everyday mortals are made of. The two have absolutely nothing in common.'[600] Badeaux's assessment then took a turn for the Adornian, as he argued that actually the commercial turn of folk music was representative of society as a whole: 'For we live in a faceless, corporate, materialistic society, spoon-fed electronic pap to crush whatever might remain of our individuality, and make us indeed the wheel of the system.'[601] The existence of folk 'celebrities' encapsulated the anxieties of the movement generally.

The question of folk music's place in an age of mass communication has troubled not only the critical theorists of the Frankfurt School, but folklorists and scholars throughout the twentieth century. The anonymous composer of folk songs past could no longer exist in the technological world, and thus any true conception of folk music must take into account the means of its production: 'In the process of traversing the technological present, many of the folk's past ideological precepts have metamorphosed ... the anonymous author of folk's past has given way to a revival of authorship and ownership in which a politics of experience plays fundamental roles in constructions of authenticity.'[602] Indeed, in a world where sounds and images are easily transferrable and where 'authorship' and ownership have been increasingly contested, the implications for folk music have been multitudinous.

Since the nineteenth century, folk music and technology have been on an ideological collision course. In the mid-twentieth century, that tension reached its zenith. Jacques Attali has argued that throughout the twentieth century, 'the phonograph record would ... disrupt the network of music. The genealogy of these phenomena is of cardinal importance: the grinding deformation of the social position of the musician, the rerouting of usage toward the spectacle in the interests of exchange.'[603] Folk music in the twentieth century has had to contend with the rise of consumer culture, and come to terms with its paradoxical aversion to – and need for – the technologies of mass communication. American folklorist John Lomax once asserted that the radio had been 'chiefly responsible for the active interest in folk music.'[604] Indeed, a key ingredient in the development and success of the folk revival movements was the invention of machines for sound recording, which made a new kind of cultural documentation possible. The ability to record 'in the field' revolutionized folk scholarship and collection, and ultimately allowed for a greater variety of voices to be heard.[605] As Maud Karpeles feared during her return visit to the Appalachians in the early 1950s, radio and a growing mass media had indeed transformed folk music. Anxiety over the meaning of 'oral tradition' in an age of 'technological reproducibility' became an increasing issue of debate amongst folk revivalists (many of whom, it should not be forgotten, had learned their songs from records or radio programmes).

The sanctity of oral tradition for many folk revivalists was paramount, and was at the centre of these fears about technological mediation. Philip Bohlman argues that oral tradition 'fosters both the creativity and the stability of folk music. So strong is the correlation of oral tradition with folk music that most definitions treat oral tradition as fundamental to folk music, if not its most salient feature.'[606] Bohlman remarks further that 'modernization' – in the form of radio and the record – 'often affects most directly the musical and structural aspects of folk music, by altering the way in which oral transmission occurs, for example, or by providing a technology that refashions the role of the performer', and that '[t]echnological advances have always presaged folk music revivals.'[607] The introduction of recording technology also inarguably altered the relationship between singer and audience, and thus the nature of folk music performance and oral tradition. Frith has argued that, once recording technology was introduced into the performance equation, it was nearly impossible to experience the same intimacy between singer and audience. He writes, 'If in other musical experiences the musicians and their audiences are joined by the speed of sounds, for recorded music the link is an elaborate industry. Between the original music and its final listener are the technological processes of transferring sound to tape and disc and the economic processes of packaging and marketing the resulting product.'[608]

Peggy Seeger lamented this development, and its role in the folk revival. She stated that, because of the presence of the phonograph and radio, there would be no true folk music in the future, because the audience would then inevitably say 'that isn't how it goes'.[609] There were indeed incidents where this type of thing occurred, as fans began associating songs and arrangements with certain performers or recordings.[610] Seeger also lamented the lack of contact between field and revival singers, stating that too many revivalists had learned songs from records, rather than actually living amongst the singers they were trying to emulate.[611] She argued that this was a particular problem in the United States, where there was no opportunity to hear good 'traditional' singers singing 'traditional' songs – there was 'no BBC, with Herring fishermen and As I Roved Out'.[612] Edith Fowke likewise argued, 'Multimedia has largely killed traditional folk singing. It's harder and harder to find people who have learned the old traditional songs and who still sing them,'[613] while Alan Lomax bemoaned the mass mediated turn of postwar revivalism, which he associated with a decline in the social and political consciousness of the music and its audience. He wrote, 'The modern American folksong revival began back in the thirties as a cultural movement with overtones of social reform. In the last ten years our gigantic amusement industry, even though it is as yet only mildly interested in folk music, has turned this cultural movement into a small boom.'[614]

Benjamin Filene highlights the tension between technology and folk music in the postwar period, but hints at the naivety inherent in the revivalist ideal of uncommercial and unmediated music:

> The notion held by early folklorists ... of an unself-conscious, unmediated and wholly uncommercial mode of musical expression strikes me as fundamentally flawed: almost all musicians, after all, are influenced by others and make use of their talent in social settings. Since the turn of the century, even seemingly isolated musicians have spent their afternoons listening to phonographs and dreaming of recording contracts.[615]

Michael Scully meanwhile asserts that, since the beginning of the modern process of folk music collection – in which the collector took on a more active role in discovering, and often recording, field singers – most close observers had 'come to understand that there never existed any pure, unmediated, unselfconscious folk music, springing organically from the collective consciousness of isolated communities.'[616] I would argue that this is true: measuring the 'degree of transmission' seems a false enterprise. All music is a mediated, subjective product of human experience. While some were content to merely point out the naivety of the revivalist rejection of technology, however, others suggested that there was a more insidious hypocrisy in that position.

Brocken notes this underlying hypocrisy governing folk revivalists' attachment to the 'purity' of unmediated folk songs, arguing that this ideal was ultimately unhelpful in understanding the popularity of folk music in the twentieth century: 'Oppositions to mediation only further the concept of musical apartheid. All song is mediated as soon as somebody sings it, never mind collects it.'[617] American folk singer John Cohen, too, undermined the purist positions of some within the revival movement by highlighting the central role Alan Lomax himself had played in presenting folk music to a mass audience, using mass technology: 'Lomax suggests that the use of books and records has been inadequate and unfortunate in that these sources have not communicated the singing style and emotional content of the folk songs. Yet these very books and records have been the products of the work of folklorists such as Alan Lomax for the last twenty years.'[618] In fact, the very success of folk music in the twentieth century, and especially after the Second World War, depended on its being recorded and distributed on a large scale. In significant ways, technology altered the relationship between singer and audience, but also challenged traditional modes of collection, authorship and ownership of songs in ways that sat uncomfortably with many revivalists.

Marshall McLuhan's *Understanding Media* (1964) argued that technological advancements, and the proliferation of art and culture through the mass media, allowed for the democratization of the public sphere, and for greater popular participation in cultural and political events. McLuhan's theorization of the world as a 'global village' and his famous assertion that 'the medium is the message' have been helpful in dealing with folk music as a mass-produced form. McLuhan wrote that Western civilization in the early 1960s had reached 'the final phase of the extensions of man – the technological simulation of consciousness, when the creative process of knowing will be collectively and corporately extended to the whole of human society, much as we have already extended our senses and our nerves by the various media.'[619] A crucial aspect of technology's advancement, for McLuhan, was its new inclusiveness:

> As electrically contracted, the globe is no more than a village. Electric speed in bringing all social and political functions together in a sudden implosion has heightened human awareness of responsibility to an intense degree. It is this implosive factor that alters the position of the Negro, the teen-ager, and some other groups. They can no longer be contained, in the political sense of limited association. They are now involved in our lives, as we in theirs, thanks to the electric media.[620]

Media, then, became a vehicle through which these social and political issues could be understood, and people on the margins of society could be heard. The implications of this new involvement and awareness of political events through media, for the activist movements of the New Left, were considerable.

Folklorist Richard Dorson echoed McLuhan's optimistic assessment of the mass media's influence on culture (and social and political consciousness), writing that the 'new oral-aural ambience of the media' returned folk culture to its status, as part of an 'early tribal community'.[621] However, Pickering and Green more pessimistically contended, 'The penetration of capital into many areas of human need and relationship, the growth of a multinational culture industry, the massification of the means of communication, all these render highly problematic an interest in small-scale, localised forms of cultural performance.'[622] Indeed, in much the same way that Sharp and Karpeles lamented the encroaching influence of industrialization and technology – which by the time Karpeles made a return visit after the Second World War, had indeed transformed the area and many of its inhabitants[623] – postwar revivalists concerned themselves with the transformative evil of mass technology, even as they exploited that technology.

Addressing a major problem facing folk revivals in the twentieth century, Pickering and Green wrote that interest in amateur song performance was 'retreatist and regressive when it is simply a blind reaction to capitalist development, when it involves a wilful refusal to acknowledge the use and aesthetic values of much commercially produced popular music, or when it is a sentimentalization of the songs of an idealized past.'[624] There was, certainly, some truth to this argument – many folk enthusiasts ignored, or expressed deep disdain for commercially produced music on principle. However, it was by no means universal, and this tension would underpin many of the movement's greatest debates over direction and scope, which were often tinged with inflammatory accusations of inauthenticity, and coloured by the same anti-American feeling that had often been a prominent feature of English folk revivalism in the postwar period. Much of the tension was centred on the paradoxical dependence of folk music on the machinery of the 'culture industry' during periods of revival; the very nature of 'revival' problematically implied greater distribution and reception within the schema of mass culture.

Folk music and the culture industry

During the English folk revival, the antagonistic relationship between folk and mass culture was highlighted and contested at length amongst its participants. For many of its adherents, folk music offered a much-needed refuge from mass culture. Frith has argued, 'Folk was a particularly attractive alternative for musicians unwilling to commit themselves to a life of apparent manipulation and exploitation by the pop moguls.'[625] He contends further that 'folk ideology not only confirmed (the do-it-yourself) culture but politicised it: folkies were anti-commercial pop, rejected the star system and were proud of their integration of performer and audience.'[626] The folk revival therefore offered an intriguing paradox: the movement expressed a focus on mass participation and a desire to 'get people singing', while simultaneously trying to keep the influences of mass culture out. MacKinnon pointed out the inherent contradiction of this position, as a 'scene' whose 'central organising ethos' was that ordinary people could make music independent of commercialization, which then produced 'a generation of professionals.'[627] Indeed, as we will see, the anti-commercial ideal of folk revivalism had long been rendered unlikely if not altogether untenable; since the earliest days of folk music collection, going back to the nineteenth century, the mass media, the interlocution of technological reproduction, had been a problem that folk collectors and performers needed to solve.

The issue of copyright was one of the battlegrounds of folk's image crisis in the mid-twentieth century, as arguments abounded over the ethics of collection, ownership and authorship of material. Pete Seeger acknowledged the role of the collector, and technology, in making the folk revival possible: 'We were handed on a silver platter some of the world's best songs, by folklorists who dug the gold out of the hills and presented it to us ... LP records made it possible to hear this music performed by people who knew it well.'[628] Tunes for new songs were often taken from older ones, as part of the 'folk process'. For some, this process was the means through which the music maintained its vitality – through adaptation and renewal – but for others it was merely stealing. Arguably, the re-appropriation of tunes by different singers served both to de- or re-politicize and reinvigorate previous material and update it for current situations and contemporary audiences. However, Arlo Guthrie – son of Woody, himself a prolific borrower – asserted that the term 'folk process' 'is a good word for plagiarism or something like it, people stealing tunes and ideas from each other.'[629]

Sing contributor Ken Lindsay was incredulous over what he perceived to be the creative theft rampant within the revival and, in an article entitled 'Finding's Stealing,' asked: 'Why do you hate each other? You folk-type people. Why don't you know that before you can carve and share a chicken it needs to hatch out an egg. Why do you condone the robbery of folk – this finding of songs and tunes from old-timers and the copyrighting of same to your own best advantage and for the benefit of the trust funds.'[630] Indeed, the pages of folk magazines and periodicals were replete with arguments over copyright. *Ethnic* warned in its inaugural 1959 issue, 'At the moment the folksong world is rife with rumours of copyright being enforced in the US by British collectors, and, nearer home, of attempts to claim household Scots songs such as "The Four Marys" as the copyright property of one single Scots singer.'[631] For his part, A. L. Lloyd argued that one of the most important problems to be raised out of the commercialization of folk music was copyright. In an article reprinted in *Sing Out!*, entitled 'Who Owns What in Folk Song', he asserted that 'at present, here as in America, every other folknik and city-billy who makes a record is claiming copyright on the items he sings, even if he "collected" them from a library book or off someone else's record. Or if he doesn't, his agent will.'[632] Lloyd argued that, given the interest of 'big business' in 'the hitherto remote planet of folk song,' it would seem imperative 'that a proper and just law be devised concerning the ownership and use of material.'[633]

Sydney Carter's composition, 'A Reel of Recording Tape,' emphasized the often fraught and ethically dubious relationship between folk singer and collector, as new media made the act of collection easier and the songs more easily reproducible:

> As I went out one morning
> I was singing a country song,
> I met a man with a microphone
> And oh, he did me wrong
> He sat me on a grassy bank
> And whipping out a tape,
> He took my country ditty down
> Before I could escape.
>
> To Tin Pan Alley he took my song
> And there he chanced to meet
> A publisher who cleaned it up

And gave the tune a beat,
And now they rock and now they roll
And now they pay a fee
To that false young man with a microphone
And nobody thinks of me.

I'll sell my rock and I'll sell my reel
And buy a steel guitar,
I'll take a ticket to London Town
And sing in a coffee bar,
I'll sing until I'm famous
And when I'm on TV
I'll tell the world of that false young man
And what he did to me.

Never trust a collector, girls
Whoever he may be
When his hand's upon his microphone
And not above your knee,
He's thinking of your melody
And not about your shape
And he'll rob you of our copyright
With a reel of recording tape.[634]

Carter's song detailed the exploitative relationship between singer and collector, and negatively portrayed London as the epicentre of that exploitation. He also hinted at the importance of instrumentation in making folk's authenticity, in contrast with the steel guitars of Tin Pan Alley, with electrified music. However, Carter's song has an unsettling sexism about it as well – in the last verse he suggests that a female singer should feel insulted that the collector was not thinking about her 'shape' – with a hand placed above knee – but only about taking her song. Nevertheless, the song illustrated widespread revivalist concerns about copyright.

Bill Eitman, in a *Sing Out!* article from 1960, called for a policy on copyright for the folk scene: 'On folk-song copyrights, let's grant that copyrights of altered versions of songs in the public domain are legally valid.'[635] Eitman lamented that it had become 'common practice among publishers and now, (sadly enough) among folksingers and arrangers deliberately to alter a melodic phrase or add a new verse, not for any aesthetic or intellectual reasons, but merely as a device to protect their authorship claims.'[636] He called copyright claims a matter of personal honesty and integrity, and suggested that

if ethics are to be our guiding light from here on in, a good beginning would be to ask that John Lomax be removed from 'Goodnight Irene.' Too many negroes suffered too much to create Irene, and they would sleep more peacefully if Leadbelly, who brought Irene to womanhood, could have his name standing along on the page, unaccompanied by the name of his generous benefactor.[637] In fact, the problematic relationship between Leadbelly and John Lomax went beyond copyright. It was also rife with a patronizing racism.

While some revivalists welcomed the mass distribution of folk song as a means of forwarding the revivalist community ethos, others, emphatically, did not. Not surprisingly, Ewan MacColl took exception to the idea that folk's commercialization was a positive partner in creating a wider folk community. He wrote,

> There are those, active in the folk revival, who, without reserve, welcome this growing 'interest' on the part of the A & R men. 'Folk music,' they argue, 'is not really folk music at all unless all, or a large majority, of the folk are familiar with it.' This point of view implies that there was once a time when everybody knew all the songs and every other person could sing them. THERE IS NOT ONE SHRED OF EVIDENCE TO SUPPORT THIS ASSUMPTION.[638]

MacColl was correct, of course; folk music had historically been a relatively 'local' phenomenon, and many traditional songs were only parochially understood in many parts of England and Britain. MacColl thus challenged the idea that folk music had to be popularized to be 'folk'. But his statement also hinted at his belief in maintaining a more exclusive folk culture in England.

A letter to the editors of *Melody Maker*, included in the 12 January 1963 issue, sparked a debate about 'folk or fake?' with regards to the English folk scene. The original author, John Kirkham, of Keighley, Yorkshire, echoed MacColl's worst fears, as he wrote:

> I cannot understand how anyone can listen to an overgrown teenager dressed in corduroys and a tartan shirt whining about the misfortunes of a Northumbrian miner or a Scottish navvy, and take this music seriously. Folk music is supposed to be sincere and non-commercial. Yet the performers sing songs which are British adaptations of songs sung in the Southern States of the USA and also adopt phoney stage names which are taken from American blues singers ... To all the folk singers who wish they had been born black and sing pseudo-American ballads about the boll weevil, the chain gang and other things they have never seen, I say: 'Come off it, or join the Black and White minstrel show.'[639]

Respondents to this initial letter were equally passionate: in the next week's issue, several people, among them a couple of folk singers, took issue with Kirkham's remarks. Steve Benbow (Old Couldsdon, Surrey) argued,

> In his banal and unoriginal remarks, John Kirkham accuses them of singing British adaptations of songs sung in the Southern States of the USA. He forgets to mention, or perhaps doesn't know, that the majority of these songs originated in Britain anyway. In reply to the accusation that some folk singers take their stage names from American blues artists, all the singers I know sing under their own names – for example Robin Hall and Jimmie Macgregor, John Baldry, Stan Kelly, Dominic Behan, Alex and Rory McEwen.[640]

Meanwhile, Paul Marsden (Hillingdon, Middlesex), asked, 'What great folklorist told Kirkham that folk music is "supposed to be sincere and non-commercial"? It isn't supposed to be anything. It is simply the idiom of the people singing and creating songs because they enjoy doing it.'[641] Finally, another folk singer and songwriter, Sydney Carter (London, WC1), asked:

> Folk or fake? – a good question, if you're in the antique business. But are we? Melody Maker is concerned with entertainment. What we have to think about is (a) art, and (b) making money. Some folk addicts collect old songs like bits of Roman pottery. This can be fascinating – you can even make money out of it, as you can from stamp collecting. But it hasn't much to do with art. Robin Hall and Jimmie Macgregor make use of folk material – but as artists, not archaeologists. They know enough about folk music to be aware that what they're doing on 'Tonight' is not always pure 'folk'. They can do that, too; but if they did it all the time they wouldn't be so welcome on 'Tonight'. If it's nothing but 'genuine' folk song with all the cracks and wormholes that you want, don't go to Jimmie or Robin. They are not in the antique business. They are entertainers, and you can't fake entertainment. It's either good or bad, but never 'fake'.[642]

The debate over instrumentation and how a song was interpreted musically was another issue of concern for many. Carter observed that Benbow sang his songs 'with a guitar and a strong rhythmic backing,' and asked him, 'Is that a proper way to treat English folk song?'[643]

Speaking about 'Folksong Accompaniment: Types and Tastes' at the 1960 Berkeley Folk Festival, MacColl and Seeger differentiated between 'Traditional Sound' and the 'Professional, Night-club type sound' of artists.[644] Seeger spoke of the controversy, as she saw it, regarding the commercialization of accompaniment, and argued that it was difficult to sing in a traditional (i.e. 'correct') way without traditional accompaniment.[645] She further stated that she felt there was a fear amongst 'commercial' folk groups, of chordal simplicity, dissonance and singing without a rhythm. She stated that she felt 'divorced' from the American folk scene for this reason, and its tendency to have accompaniment override the song.[646] American revival singers in particular, according to Seeger, sang all the verses the same (because of an implicit fear of improvization), and she argued that 'If you take a chord outside the tradition it's no longer folk music.'[647] MacColl and Seeger spent a lot of time educating young folk singers – at events like the Berkeley Festival, and later as part of their Critics' Group – about the 'correct' way to perform a song, which for them reflected a singer's 'respect for the material.'[648]

For instance, a Critics Group class recorded in September, 1972, set out to establish the reasons people sing folk songs. MacColl asked the participants why they sang folk music. At first, the responses were timid and spare. The first singer on the tape answers that she 'just enjoy[ed] singing,' and that she didn't like pop music, or opera. A second singer, Lorna, claimed to sing folk songs because she 'always [had] done'; she enjoyed the fact that one didn't need as much training to sing folk songs.[649] The lone male singer in the group, Tony, claimed not to have heard any folk music until the age of 15 or 16, when – 'unsatisfied by rock and roll' – he went to a 'traditional' folk club.

He argued that folk music spoke to his worldview; he wanted to stop being 'just a listener' – to be more involved in the causes that were important to him.[650] Pushed on why they enjoyed hearing and performing folk songs, the class participants offered interesting and varied responses. One woman, Victoria, admitted to wanting to be the 'centre of attention', and that she felt great when people asked for songs they'd heard her sing before. She particularly enjoyed folk music, she said, because 'all you need is your voice – you can do it anywhere.'[651] Leslie enjoyed the theatricality of folk music, and enjoyed having 'other people in the palm of your hand,' who would stop and listen. She stated that, 'for a short time, you have control – it's gratifying. To be able to capture an audience. Like acting.'[652]

The English revival, as this book has established, often defined itself in terms of difference from the American revival. MacColl stated that the English revival was 'so much healthier' than the American one, because of its emphasis on amateurism. As opposed to many of their American counterparts, English and British folk singers were guardedly amateur. MacColl, for his part, insisted that 'in particular areas in England ballads are still sung – not by professionals, but by people at the pub, people at football matches, gypsies.'[653] To illustrate this point, Fred Woods took stock of the expense figures of Glaswegian singer Alex Campbell for 1975: 'Fares £1,817.71, Accommodation £375, Food £884, Commission £797.15, Publicity £219.50, Accountants' fees £113.99, Postage £161.99, Instruments £96.92, Telephone £351.57, National Insurance £128.82 (Total £4,946.65).'[654] Woods elaborated:

> Those expenses were accumulated in the course of travelling 42,205 miles in nine countries. In that year, Campbell made two records, appeared at two festivals, did six radio broadcasts in three countries and a television documentary. He made 215 live appearances, 2 at festivals, 29 concerts and 184 club bookings. He spent 257 days and nights away from home, spent 1,438 hours 55 minutes travelling, 305 hours 50 minutes on stage and an estimated 620 non-singing hours in clubs.[655]

Frankie Armstrong and Brian Pearson, writing for the *History Workshop Journal* in 1979, offering a post-mortem for the revival – a retrospective examining its goals, successes and failures as a movement – argued that the folk revivalist repertoire had 'been created by the "common people" themselves. Organized by enthusiasts in their spare time, it has few impresarios and receives no subsidies from the authorities. It appears to be the model that we have all been waiting for and yet in many ways it is seriously flawed.'[656] This description of the movement highlights, implicitly, the differences between the English and American folk scenes: the American revival representing the brash apotheosis of mass commercial appeal, the English revival supposedly remaining an amateur endeavour, centred on socialist values.

MacColl claimed that the revival in England was a 'spontaneous revival,' which attempted to keep field singers in the public eye. Mike Seeger affirmed the grassroots strength of the revival in England and Britain as opposed to the one in the United States, when he wrote that 'we need more informal (less show-biz like) outlets such as the very popular community folk clubs in Britain, more small local folk festivals, and we need to become a greater part of community and college cultural programs in the South as well as the North. Only then can the diverse potentialities of current folk song activity be fully realized.'[657] MacColl and Seeger were not the only concerned parties. Mike Aston wrote, 'The American folk music scene has expanded so rapidly in the last two years that some of us in Britain are becoming just a little horrified. What is an "instant hootenanny kit"? Why do thousands of fans flock to see Bob Dylan? Joan Baez? Peter, Paul and Mary? Where does the jug band fit in?'[658] Aston asked, 'What's happened to the people who started it all – the Lomaxes and the Weavers for instance? ... The big question is whether we are going to find ourselves following the same pattern in Britain. The commercial boys are already looking for a successor to the beat music ... Tipped for the top is folk music, define it how you will. And that's the trouble. They will do the defining, not the singers.'[659]

The differentiation between the English and American revivals at times centred on individual personalities. It was no secret, for instance, that the central figure of the English revival – Ewan MacColl – had nothing but disdain for Bob Dylan, whom he saw as the embodiment of folk music's commercialization. While some English music publications were hailing Dylan as being 'among the great American progressives, the Guthries and Seegers – even the Steinbecks',[660] MacColl reserved a special vitriol for Dylan, once stating dismissively that 'I have watched with fascination the meteoric rise of the American idol [Dylan] and I am still unable to see in him anything other than a youth of mediocre talent. Only a completely non-critical audience, nourished on the watery pap of pop music, could have fallen for such tenth-rate drivel.'[661] MacColl referred derisively to the 'cultivated illiteracy' of Dylan's topical songs and his 'embarrassing fourth-grade schoolboy attempts at free verse.'[662] However, Robert Colls rightly points out the hypocrisy in MacColl's distaste for Dylan, writing that 'Ewan MacColl (born Jimmie Miller, Coburg Street, Salford) had called Bob Dylan (born Robert Zimmerman, Third Avenue East, Duluth, Minnesota) a "youth of mediocre talent," but the shame was that MacColl failed to recognize that Zimmerman had travelled in search of his authentic self no less than Miller had travelled in search of his.'[663]

In an interview with folk journalist and singer Karl Dallas, MacColl asserted that the folk revival was 'artificially created and it won't be over until big money has been made by the people who created it. We're going to get lots and lots of copies of Dylan – people who have one foot in folk and one foot in pop.'[664] When asked by Dallas, 'Isn't it a good thing he writes songs about war and peace, even if he doesn't say too much about what should be done about it?,' MacColl answered dismissively: 'He doesn't say anything President Johnson could disagree with. He deals in generalisations – that's always safe.'[665] But MacColl was not alone in his contempt for Dylan and his betrayal. Many English folk fans expressed a sense of betrayal at Dylan's changing style – and many came to his defence.

Michael Dewdney-York, treasurer of the West Country Folk Club, commented that 'Dylan will never be remembered for his protest songs 40 years from now. The flavour of his songs is communistic but he lives like a capitalist, having been pushed into a mould by the people behind him.'[666] In response to a reader who claimed that Dylan was 'trying to tell us something and ... failed miserably', Dan Atherden, of London (N8) wrote to *Melody Maker* with the following in February of 1966:

Once upon a time there lived a little boy called Bob Dylan who used to entertain his little friends with tales of freedom of the individual and all his friends (called folk fans) were impressed and gathered in circles and talked about the freedom of the individual and how narrow minded and critical were the outsiders. One day Bob decided to test his theories and began to sing with a rock and roll backing and all the folkniks forgot about the freedom of the individual and screamed Traitor! – and ran back to their holes (folk clubs). They began raving over a new roving rambling ex-accountant who sang about the freedom of the individual and they were happy again.[667]

The strongest reactions against Dylan seemed to be sparked by his May 1966 tour of Britain. A (former) fan wrote in to *Melody Maker* that month, lamenting that 'I have just attended a funeral at Bristol's Colston Hall. They buried Bob Dylan, the folksinger, in a grave of electric guitars, enormous loudspeakers and deafening drums. It was a sad end to one of the most phenomenal influences in music. My only consolation is that Woody Guthrie wasn't there to witness it.'[668]

Largely because of Bob Dylan's popularity, 'folk music' had a global profile by the mid-1960s. Dylan became the symbolic figure of this increasingly problematic relationship between folk music and mass culture, in both the United States and England. According to Josh Dunson, 'Dylan had forced his songs and his contemporaries into the mass media.'[669] Indeed, the success of 'Blowin' in the Wind' – popularized, not by Dylan himself, but by the likes of Peter, Paul, and Mary, the Staples Singers and Sam Cooke – had proved that 'a great deal of money was to be made from songs of the protest movements.'[670] It was especially Dylan's abdication of his prescribed role of 'spokesman as a generation' – evident to folk circles in his abandonment of topical material – which upset the folk establishment in the United States and elsewhere. *Sing Out!* editor Irwin Silber, in a now-infamous 'open letter' to the singer, published in the magazine, lamented that Dylan's new songs 'seem to be all inner-directed now, innerprobing, self-conscious – maybe even a little maudlin or a little cruel on occasion.'[671] He blamed the 'American Success Machinery,' which he felt 'chew[ed] up geniuses at a rate of one a day and still hungers for more.'[672] This letter identified the central rupture within the folk scenes in both England and the United States, but also revealed the crucial importance of Dylan, both in helping to create the postwar folk boom on both sides of the Atlantic, and in almost single-handedly dismantling it. In essence, Dylan self-consciously created a version of the modern 'authentic self' – even as he was imitating Woody Guthrie – and then almost viciously denied the very possibility of that authentic self. Dylan's mid-sixties work, in particular, deconstructed the notion of authenticity or truth in the world.

I believe that the reason so many in the folk world were disappointed with Dylan was because his use of technology was necessarily opposed to the sense of community folk music was supposed to create. Frith has argued that, amongst folk performers, the feeling was that 'amplification alienates performers from their audiences. The democratic structure of the folk community was thus unable to survive a situation in which the singers came to monopolize the new means of communication – electrical power. By "going electric" Bob Dylan embraced all those qualities of mass culture that the folk movement had rejected – stardom, commerce and manipulation.'[673] The direct line between performer and fans was fatally disrupted by the amplification of the instruments.

The sense of betrayal people associated with Dylan was extended from either side of the Atlantic. Indeed, one need not look any further than his 1966 tour of Britain – captured so well in Martin Scorsese's *No Direction Home* documentary – to see that. It was infamously in Manchester that an audience member yelled out 'JUDAS!' into a silent Free Trade Hall before Dylan's performance.[674] In fact, the entire tour was a battleground between folk ideals. The tour footage, which informs a large portion of Scorsese's narrative, encapsulated the extreme responses which Dylan's performances engendered – he would perform the first half of a show by himself, on acoustic guitar; the second half was backed by his touring band, The Hawks (later The Band) – and ultimately sheds light on the importance of Dylan as a figure in both folk revivals.

The reactions to Dylan's new sound have become part of twentieth-century music lore – there were booing, insults, people walking out. During the concerts, audience members shouted invectives towards the stage: cries of 'Go home!' 'What happened to Woody Guthrie, Bob?' 'Get off, Bobby!' filled the silence between numbers. In one instance, Dylan responded, bored, 'These are all protest songs, now, come on. This is not British music; this is American music, come on.'[675] The negativity towards Dylan's new direction – and, it was feared, the direction of folk music – was exemplified in a few post-concert interviews, where people offered honest appraisals of Dylan's career trajectory. In Newcastle, one wounded young fan lamented, 'He's just changed altogether. He's changed from what he was. He's not the same as what he was at first'[676]; another explained, 'He went really commercial with this backing group, and I didn't like that very much. I don't know what he's trying to do. I think he's conceding to some sort of popular taste. I think it's a bad thing – I think he's prostituting himself!'[677] Yet another fan stated, 'It makes you sick, listening to this rubbish now.'[678] Dylan also received death threats – 'I don't mind being shot, but I don't dig being told about it', he responded.[679]

Melody Maker's coverage of the 1966 tour illustrated the deeply divided reactions it garnered amongst Britain's folk fans. Before he had even arrived, the magazine proclaimed that Dylan would not be alone; that he was bringing his 'American backing group with him. The group – just called The Group – will play all Dylan's British dates with him.'[680] Once Dylan *had* arrived, the controversy only grew. Journalist Max Jones wrote, 'Having read that he was booed at a US concert last year when he emerged with an electric guitar for the second half, and greeted by mass shouts of "We want the real Dylan," I wanted to know if he'd be using an amplified guitar over here. "I'm not sure if I will or not," was the best I could get.'[681] In the same issue, Vincent Doyle wrote:

After an hour of the opening Dublin concert on Thursday, Bob Dylan, the folk-poet genius who is credited with re-routing the entire cause of contemporary folk music, suffered the humiliation of a slow hand-clap. It was a climax of growing mutual contempt … It was sad to see the tiny figure with the desolate barbed-wire hair trying to make it a night to remember for the two thousand who came to hear him. But for most, it was the night of the big let-down.[682]

Sing got in on the act as well, printing this song – 'With Bob on Our Side' – in its February 1966 issue:

> Come all you young rebels who sing in the street
> And tap out the rhythm with dirty bare feet
> If some crooked agent takes you for a ride
> You're never alone, boy, with Bob on your side.
>
> There's money in protest – the word's got about
> They don't give a damn what you protest about
> Promoters and agents take this in their stride,
> They'll still make a million with Bob on their side.
>
> If I were a blackbird, I'd whistle and sing
> Of bloody red rivers and a big golden ring,
> If I caught the wind then I'd sail with the tide –
> It has to mean something, so Bob's on my side.
>
> I don't give a damn if I'm not in the charts,
> My song is of freedom, not flowers and hearts,
> But money brings freedom, it can't be denied,
> So I'll keep on trying, with Bob on my side.
>
> Now Bob is big business – I think they've caught on –
> On his latest hit record the words have all gone,
> The sound is distorted, the meaning to hide …
> Oh, close the lid tightly, for Bob is inside.[683]

The song expressed many of the criticisms against Dylan from within the folk community, and the disappointment many felt with the direction he had taken the revival. At the same time, there is some recognition of the way Dylan himself was taken advantage of. The 'crooked agent' of the first verse is undoubtedly a reference to Albert Grossman, Dylan's manager, a Colonel Tom Parker-type figure who also managed Peter, Paul and Mary. The second verse references the commercial appeal of protest in the mid-1960s, not just for songwriters and performers, but for the promoters and agents who sold the product. In the final verse, the indictment of Dylan's deliberate obfuscation of meaning in his mid-1960s work – 'the sound is distorted, the meaning to hide … ' – spoke again to just how far Dylan had travelled from his early days as a Guthrie imitator to existentialist poet in the span of just four or five years.

Badeaux decried the evils of Dylan-worship (as symptomatic of a greater weakness in the American folk scene), and pondered the decline of the folk revivalist movement in the United States (but not, pointedly, in England), in a piece entitled 'The Spectacle Moves On':

Dylan, as was to be expected, exploded the bomb ... [but] where are the audiences of yesteryear? Why does England seem to have such a stable scene, while we here have to depend on the caprices of the general audience? What had become of all the guitar and banjo pickers who flooded the concert halls, the festivals, who bought all the albums?[684]

He asserted that, in the United States, 'the national craze for folk music (or what was thought of as folk music by the public at large) was about as serious and meaningful as the national craze for hula hoops. Period.'[685] Finally, Badeaux mocked 'those dedicated idealists who saw this national revival as but the first step towards a gigantic American awakening to true musical values,' who were 'just victims of their own enthusiasms, blinding themselves to the truths of the American commercial music scene.'[686]

Dylan's rise to fame became emblematic of mass culture's treachery; his break with folk music, so starkly laid out at Newport and in Manchester, led to several retrospectives on the problem of folk's success within the matrix of the culture industry. 'The spectacle has moved on,' Badeaux wrote, but its effect, its significance for the meaning of folk music and oral tradition in the twentieth century, still remained to be debated; could folk music exist alongside, and thrive within, the matrices of mass communications and the culture industry, or would it be necessarily compromised? In many ways, this was the central issue facing the English (or any) folk revival, and goes back to the question which started this thesis: what happened to the folk?

Conclusion

Folk culture's separation from the mass media was central to revivalist identity. Indeed, English folk revivalism, especially, was wary of the influence of a 'culture industry' on what it considered to be a grassroots, amateur, movement. Often, this anxiety regarding mass culture involved an implicitly anti-American feeling, centred, particularly, on the person of Bob Dylan – the physical embodiment of the nefarious influence of the mass media on folk musicians. Dylan's betrayal of the folk world was felt almost equally in Britain as in America – his 1966 tour highlighted the vehemence of the response to his 'going electric': silence, booing, heckling, and even semi-racial epithets (JUDAS!) could be heard in concert halls throughout the country. While Dylan provided a lightning rod for these debates in folk circles on both sides of the Atlantic, he also inspired a new genre and direction for folk revivalists looking to break free of traditionalist constraints of the earlier movement. As mass media became not only helpful, but essential, to the distribution of folk music in the twentieth century, the subversion of oral culture, the role of the collector and accusations of theft became prominent issues for revivalists in both England and the United States.

Conclusions

After the Second World War in England, folk songs and culture – for so long associated with rural peasantry, and largely excluding the industrial working classes – reached new heights of popularity, helped in part by a surging consumer economy, and flourishing as part of the postwar leftist political culture. The folk revival helps to tell the political and social story of postwar England, and also contributes to narratives of regional, national and transnational identity, mass culture in the modern world and the phenomenon of 'Americanization' in postwar Europe. It offers new perspectives on the history of leftist political culture and the postwar Labour Party in England, as well as the persistent influence of class in English society and culture.

Folk music has been, according to Thomas Gruning, a 'potent vehicle in struggles for social change', while at the same time reinforcing the power relations that undermined that change; the evocative imagery of the folk music form, 'of love and loss, rural pasts', coupled with its continued insistence on an (increasingly nebulous) ideal of authenticity have meant that the form was also used as part of the 'continual reprocessing of nostalgic fictions' throughout the twentieth century.[687] Although Gruning was referring here to the American folk revival, his observations reflect the central paradoxes of twentieth-century folk revivalism generally, which have made it a particularly rich cultural form for study.

The folk revival in England was constantly fighting against the impulse to create 'nostalgic fictions' from both within and without the movement, but not always succeeding. The 'politics of image' described by Gruning did indeed play a powerful role in the English folk revival, as it sought to assert itself both on the domestic cultural stage, and, perpetually, in relation to its American counterpart. This book set out to answer the following questions: How can we measure the influence of folk music in postwar England, not only culturally, but politically and socially as well? Why did the English folk revival happen when it did? Was it a movement born out of celebration, or crisis? What, in effect, was being 'revived'? And what, finally, can the revival tell us about postwar English history?

Folk music provided a trusted medium for the articulation of a multitude of social and political anxieties, often implicitly related to a perceived deterioration of traditional human bonds and relationships. The postwar revival in England signalled a renewed popular interest in, and greater commercial success for, folk music in a world increasingly dominated by mass technology, and many revivalists self-consciously viewed it as part of a preservation of socialist communality within a world of growing anomie; somewhat more cynically, folk songs have also been part of a twentieth-century 'invention of tradition' – used by collectors, scholars, performers and politicians alike to forge links with a 'usable' past, to conserve certain notions of identity and to restore political positions where ideological connections had become frayed.

Histories of postwar Britain and England have largely ignored the folk revival; it has been an under-appreciated and under-studied part of the postwar English historical landscape. Not only was the revival a unique and powerful cultural event in its own right but it also contributed significantly to many of the most important social and political events of the postwar period: the fight for nuclear disarmament, the social fallout from mine closures, Labour's 'cultural turn' – our understanding of these events, and their cultural and social impact, would be demonstrably poorer without the English folk revival. This work has firmly established the importance of the folk movement in the political, social and cultural history of postwar England, and analysed the ways in which it was both influenced by and contributed to its historical moment. Through the music of the English folk revival, as well as through the expressed (and undergirding) ideologies of its leading figures, the salient social and political issues of the postwar period were not only illuminated, but also, crucially, complicated: the triumphs and conflicted legacy of the welfare state, the subsequent crisis of leftist politics, the essential and continuing importance of class divisions – the folk revival highlighted all of these issues and provided a significant cultural voice for their articulation in the public sphere.

In providing another arena for the cultural expression of complex social and political processes – and for itself embodying many of the same – the folk revival has offered something compelling and unique to the historiography of postwar England. Overall, this book has stressed the many ways in which the English folk revival can contribute to our understanding of the country's postwar trajectory. In doing so, it has contributed to several overlapping yet disparate historiographical discourses, none of which have attempted to fully contextualize and explain the English revival in historical terms: the existing revival historiography provides important information on the postwar movement's cultural inheritance and significance, but fails to tie it to the broader social and political history. This book has been an attempt to understand the folk revival on its own terms, but also as part of the historical fabric of the postwar period, not simply in a 'cultural studies' vacuum.

Through each stage of this work, I've tried to highlight the most important factors – as I have seen them – contributing not only to the revival of folk music in postwar England, but also, just as importantly, to explain why the folk revival matters to our understanding of this history. From the scaffolding of the movement – the folk clubs and societies, record labels, radio and folk festivals – which helped to create and maintain its essential small-scale, grassroots feel, to an examination of its political and social dimensions, the first three chapters aimed to get to the heart of who and what the folk revival was. Who, and what, did it serve? The affluent society left many behind – among them the coal miners whose livelihood was no more secure after nationalization than before; through the case study of the 'pit elegy', this portion of the book looked at the disappointment many miners felt with the Labour Party and its nationalization programme.

From there, the book looked to discussions of place – of roots and regional identity – in building folk revivalism in postwar England. As part of the nation's 'anthropological turn', which saw the renewed interest in regional culture in the midst of postwar recovery, the folk revival celebrated every region of England in its quest to uncover the musical roots of the nation; with the help of the BBC, and Topic Records, folk music from every part of the country was collected and distributed to a growing audience. This regionalist emphasis belied the traditional distrust between province and capital, rural and urban society, but also revealed the symbolic significance of different regions as they were perceived and presented by the Left. In this respect, no region more than the Northeast was emphasized. Linking the folk revival with the political establishment, the Northeast was central both to the Labour Party's nationalization programme and to the folk revival's focus on industrial folk songs. The region became the focal point for leftist and revivalist hopes and disappointments in the postwar period, the authentic counterpoint to America's 'shiny barbarism'. Chapter 5 focused on one of the central, underlying, tensions of the revival – the fear of Americanization. This chapter discussed the feeling both amongst revivalists and the broader leftist establishment that English (and British) culture was being snuffed out by American cultural hegemony in the postwar period.

All music, but *especially* folk music, I would argue, is fundamentally a narrative about human experience. In the twentieth century, technology allowed that experience to be transmuted from the individual to the collective – via radio, record or indeed live performance. In some ways, it is miraculous that the complex and nuanced range of human emotions could be given a melody and delivered in a three-minute song; conversely, some might describe this phenomenon as perverse. Chapter 6 examined the longstanding hostility between folk music and mass culture in the twentieth century, which was exacerbated as the technologies of mass media in fact made the folk revival possible. The dichotomous relationship between folk and mass culture was part of a twentieth-century discussion about the nefarious effects of the 'culture industry' on popular art forms. Although the central figures of the English folk revival maintained its separation from commercial culture, the fact is that folk revivalism in England had long depended on the forces of mass communication for success. Once again, this anti-commercialism was inextricably entwined with a certain anti-Americanism, as shown through the vehement response to Bob Dylan and his supposed betrayal of folk music. Indeed, on both sides of the Atlantic, Dylan's electric turn was viewed as the ultimate victory of the culture industry, and in the American case, signalled in effect the end of their revival.

Primarily, what the folk movement in England 'revived' was a popular interest in tradition. To some extent this tradition had been 'invented' by twentieth-century collectors like Cecil Sharp, and later A. L. Lloyd and Ewan MacColl. The music that was presented to audiences throughout the revival was hugely influenced by their ideological decisions. The particular revival, in the English case, of 'industrial song' was what largely distinguished the postwar movement from both its early twentieth-century and American counterparts. Indeed, Lloyd and MacColl's resurrection of workers' songs arguably reflected a leftist 'invention of tradition' after the war, as the early promise of a welfare state gave way to a crisis of confidence in an increasingly 'affluent' society. The same conservative impulse which guided Cecil Sharp in rediscovering the 'musical potentialities' of the nation amongst the rural peasantry of Somerset also guided Lloyd and MacColl's collection of industrial workers' songs in regions like Durham, Northumberland and Lancashire in the 1950s and 1960s. The bucolic romanticism of Sharp's revival gave way, after the war, to a new kind of socialist romanticism, this time prizing the music of the industrial working class – especially in the miners' songs of the Northeast.

A significant part of this project involved looking at the English folk revival as a movement with important transnational dimensions. English and American folk music shared a long, intertwining history: going back to Francis James Child and Cecil Sharp, folk scholars had accepted and, even to a certain extent, promoted the cross-cultural influences. Much of the American folk canon had descended from the Anglo-Saxon tradition, and the influence of American music – jazz, skiffle, rock 'n' roll and folk – on the second English revival was in turn considerable. And yet, although the two postwar movements maintained close ties through magazines and recordings, English revivalists – encouraged by some of their most prominent personalities – gradually moved away from the performance of American material. The desire to promote a native English tradition, as well as a concern over the nefarious influences of commercial culture (symbolized by the fate of the American revival) limited the possibilities of transnational cultural exchange, undoubtedly affecting the nature and trajectory of the English revival.

Although the zenith of the postwar folk boom occurred auspiciously during a relatively weak period in the history of popular music – between Elvis Presley's departure for the Army and the start of Beatlemania – record sales figures remained relatively weak compared with those of Tin Pan Alley; the implicit question being, therefore, to what extent we can speak of a popular revival of folk music. Although many millions more rock 'n' roll records were sold than folk, there was indeed a marked increase in the availability and purchase of folk records after the Second World War – to say nothing of increase in programmes focused on folk music on both radio and television, as well as the exponential growth of folk magazines, societies and clubs. But the importance of the movement should not be confined to a study of sales figures, or magazine subscriptions. As Steve Strauss has argued, 'Somewhat like the nineteenth century return to the abandoned, mythic cultural values, the folk music revival grew out of a recognition that human sensitivity was trampled and perverted by the icy competitiveness and complexity of the cold-war world.'[688] Indeed, folk music had a cachet and a power which resonated beyond economics, especially amongst members of a younger generation, many of whom would go on to align themselves with the causes of an emergent New Left, whose yearning for 'authentic experience' in a consumer-driven late capitalist society drove them to seek out a form of cultural expression that adequately espoused their evolving social and political ethos.

The emergence of topical songwriting, as it related to the development of the so-called New Left, in many ways clashed with the central hope of the English folk revival; namely, that it would be a truly grassroots, social movement. Recalling the central question posed at the beginning of this book, as to where 'the folk' were as their music was being 'revived', I think this book has shown that the folk were part of the folk revival, even if they have not lasted in the public memory in the same way as those who collected and performed their songs. The relationship between the grassroots movement and the commercial revival of folk music associated with topical songs of the New Left has been one of the issues this book has been most concerned with. The political culture of the New Left took the folk revival in a direction, and on a journey or trajectory which necessitated the distinction – not least in the minds of many folk scholars – between folk songs, and songs in the 'folk idiom', as expressed by folklorist Edith Fowke in the introduction.

There is an inherent tension between the revival's emphasis on the grassroots nature of the movement, and the fact that folk music experienced a boom in popularity at a specific time, as a (largely generationally-important) yearning for authenticity pushed it up the charts. It was a tension between, on the one hand, the local and amateur, and on the other, the global and topical – two visions of folk music and its purpose which – while not necessarily mutually exclusive – caused much anxiety amongst the revival's leaders and thinkers. I am not sure that this tension can, or should, ever be resolved. The form's flexibility, its elasticity and inclusiveness are what have allowed it to endure, quite apart from its commercial appeal. I don't think that the English – or American – folk revivals occurred coincidentally during periods of increased social and political upheaval, nor that folk music 'mattered' more during the postwar period; rather, the political adaptability of folk music had been apparent for some time before the Second World War, but its commercial and communicative viability only became apparent once mass recording and distribution technology became part of the picture. The commercial and the political capabilities converged in the 1950s and 1960s.

The question is, how and to what extent did these two, rather disparate halves of the folk revival movement, become reconciled? Where were the folk? Did these new compositions belong in an ever-evolving folk canon, or were they an anomalous development, which obscured the true meaning of folk music? This was the crux of Chapter 2, although I think ultimately the answer to these question lies beyond the scope of this book. It is possible that the concurrent, commercial, growth of folk music and the New Left provided an unprecedented, and ultimately irresistible, opportunity to make money at singing folk songs. This could certainly be seen in some of the Critics' Group responses to the question, 'why sing folk music?' – they knew folk music would sell, and they wanted to be heard, to express their budding political ideals. Even Bob Dylan admitted that he wrote 'protest songs' – specifically 'The Times They Are a-Changin' – because he knew that they would sell. However genuine this statement might have been, it hinted at the conflict between the grassroots and the political folk revival.

What does this study tell us about the relationship between music and 'politics', then, more generally? Before rock 'n' roll became a self-consciously political medium (not discounting the sheer subversiveness of 'race music' in the early 1950s), folk music had proven its political usefulness. Indeed, from individual expressions of defiance to songs of mass-protest, folk music has been an important voice for the politically disaffected, and the socially and economically vulnerable. Political meaning is not just derived from lyrics – the location of the performance, choices of instrumentation, intonation and melody, the background of the singer, sometimes just the act of singing becomes 'political'. Think back to MacColl's policy – where even the presence of a banjo became political.

I think there is an interesting parallel story to be found in the importation of American rock 'n' roll styles to Manchester and Liverpool during the postwar period. As the folk revival fought against American influence – even as it acknowledged its indebtedness – English youth across Britain embraced it. The story of the North, and Northeast, brought out through folk revivalism – the uniqueness of the region's culture, the tension it created between London and the provinces – shared some similarities with the story of the Mersey Beat sound. Michael Watts argued that the Beatles's 'emphasis on their Liverpudlian origins … showed rare candour in an idiom which until then despised provincialism. But in addition to this, it served to relax the constricting monopoly which London held on the British entertainment industry.'[689] There is a worthwhile project here, involving the story of American music in Northern England (and perhaps Scotland) in the postwar period, and why rock 'n' roll enjoyed so much success amongst Northern England's (working-class) youth, contrasting the very guarded, uneven and complex importation of folk styles during the same period (and by and large by more affluent youth).

The gradual fading of the folk revival from popular culture returned the folk, as Gruning put it, 'to its status as a marginalized musical community', a position many within the revival apparently, and somewhat counter-intuitively, preferred. The folk revival in England did not end, in the same way as its transatlantic cousin, by way of some epic conclusory event (that is, the 1965 Newport Folk Festival). Like many socio-cultural movements, it gradually faded from public consciousness, and went back underground. The folk revival in England lasted longer than its American counterpart, at least into the early 1970s. In accounting for this, several interesting stories come together. First, the relative longevity of the English movement would seem to validate its participants' claims regarding the fundamentally grassroots nature of their revival, in contrast to the American case; because the English revival really did not have the celebrity clout from across the ocean, it was able to maintain a humbler, more locally and regionally vibrant movement, incubated in the public houses central to many communities. Remarkably, that infrastructure largely still remains intact: it is still possible, on any given night, to find a folk club in the back or upstairs room of a pub in most cities and towns throughout England.

Notes

Introduction

1   Quoted in Peter Eckersley, 'Folk-Song without Folk', *Guardian* (13 November 1961), 7.

2   The creation and performance of folk music in England existed well before the revival period, and continued after commercial interest began to wane, by the late 1960s. I chose the period between roughly 1945 and 1965 because that covers the germination and development of large-scale interest in folk music in England. By 1965, the introduction of the 'singer-songwriter' and the revelation of rock 'n' roll's social conscience had both helped to push folk music out of the cultural spotlight; although folk-rock groups such as Fairport Convention, Steeleye Span and the Albion Band enjoyed success into the 1970s, the folk *movement* was sapped of much of its energy and relevance by the mid-sixties. This periodization also covers most of the important socio-political developments concerning the revival, including the transition from 'austerity' to 'affluence' as well as the decline of the coal industry, the impacts of increased immigration and the Labour Party's 'cultural turn'.

3   Eckersley, 'Folk-Song without Folk', 7.

4   Ibid.

5   Sam Hinton, quoted in Kristen Baggelaar and Donald Milton, *Folk Music: More than a Song* (New York: Thomas Y. Crowell Company, 1979), 133.

6   Karl Dallas, 'The Roots of Tradition', in eds. Dave Laing, Robin Denselow, Karl Dallas and Robert Shelton, *The Electric Muse: The Story of Folk into Rock* (London: Methuen, 1975), 125.

7   Ibid.

8   See Chris Waters, *British Socialists and the Politics of Popular Culture, 1884–1914* (Manchester: Manchester University Press, 1990) and Donald Sassoon, *One Hundred Years of Socialism: The West European Left in the Twentieth Century* (New York: The New Press, 1996), for more on the early history of British socialism.

9   For more on the first English folk revival, see: Georgina Boyes, *The Imagined Village: Culture, Ideology, and the English Folk Revival* (Manchester: Manchester University Press, 1993).

10 The American folk revival – associated with figures such as Pete Seeger, Bob Dylan, Joan Baez and Phil Ochs – has been closely intertwined with the history of the New Left, student and civil rights movements, and was covered extensively in the mass media and popular press – everywhere from *Time* to the *New York Times* – causing its leading figures to become global celebrities. There are many good histories of the American revival, in retrospectives such as Robert Cantwell's *When We Were Good: The Folk Revival* (Cambridge, MA: Harvard University Press, 1996) and Ronald D. Cohen's *'Wasn't That a Time!' Firsthand Accounts of the Folk Music Revival* (Metuchen, NJ: Scarecrow Press, 1995), as well as newer histories such as Gillian Mitchell's *The North American Folk Music Revival* (Burlington, VT: Ashgate, 2007). Other important

studies of this movement include: Benjamin Filene's *Romancing the Folk: Public Memory and American Roots Music* (Chapel Hill: University of North Carolina Press, 2000); Kristin Baggelaar and Donald Milton's *Folk Music: More than A Song* (New York: Thomas Y. Crowell Company, 1979); Regina Bendix's, *In Search of Authenticity: The Formation of Folklore Studies* (Madison: University of Wisconsin Press, 1997).

11 Lawrence Black, *Redefining British Politics* (London: Palgrave Macmillan, 2010), 1.

12 Lawrence Black, *The Political Culture of the Left in Affluent Britain, 1951–64: Old Labour, New Britain?* (Hampshire: Palgrave Macmillan, 2003), 1.

13 Ibid., 4.

14 Ibid., 6.

15 Ibid., 4.

16 'Labourism' and 'Labourist' are terms which I understand to mean an ideology of social reform, which sought to bring about a successful socialist state in postwar England. They can be used to describe the practical idealism of the Labour Party during the postwar period. For more on Labourism, see Black, *The Political Culture of the Left*, 3.

17 Regina Bendix, *In Search of Authenticity: The Formation of Folklore Studies* (Madison: The University of Wisconsin Press, 1997), 7.

18 Ibid., 21.

19 Dave Harker, *Fakesong: The Manufacture of British 'Folksong' 1700 to the Present Day* (Milton Keynes: Open University Press, 1985), ix.

20 Niall MacKinnon, *The British Folk Scene: Musical Performance and Social Identity* (Buckingham: Open University Press, 1995), 1.

21 Michael Brocken, *The British Folk Revival, 1944–2002* (Burlington, VT: Ashgate, 2003), 31.

22 Ibid., 15.

23 Thomas R. Gruning, *Millennium Folk: American Folk Music since the Sixties* (Athens: The University of Georgia Press, 2006), 41.

24 Ewan MacColl, quoted in Karl Dallas, 'Focus on MacColl: The MM Folk Correspondent, Karl Dallas, Talks to Ewan MacColl', *Melody Maker* (18 September 1965), 23.

25 Ibid.

26 J. P. Bean's *Singing from the Floor: A History of British Folk Clubs* (2014) offers a more comprehensive study of the social base of the revival via oral history.

27 Benjamin Filene, *Romancing the Folk Public Memory & American Roots Music* (Chapel Hill: University of North Carolina Press, 2000), 11.

28 Ibid., 13.

29 Boyes, *The Imagined Village*, 63.

30 Simon J. Bronner, *American Folklore Studies: An Intellectual History* (Kansas: University Press of Kansas, 1986), 11; 15.

31 Krishan Kumar, *The Making of English National Identity* (Cambridge: Cambridge University Press, 2003), 208.

32 Waters, *British Socialists*, 106. This kind of 'subtle' paternalism could be seen again after the war, for instance in the BBC's three-tiered approach to broadcasting (discussed in Chapters 1 and 2).

33 Ibid., 103. While socialists migrated to folk music, other contemporary musical forms were more maligned. Music Halls had become perhaps the most visible manifestation of the new leisure industry in nineteenth century, and as such were suspect. The first music hall was established in London in 1840, and, as Derek Lamb has argued,

'remained unrivalled as the British working people's entertainment for almost one hundred years.' (Derek Lamb, 'The British Music Hall', *Sing Out!* 15, No. 4 (September 1965), 34). Music halls had grown up exponentially in the latter half of the nineteenth century, between 1850 and 1900, and these cultural institutions incubated many of the musical traditions that would eventually help drive the postwar revival. For more on the influence of music hall on the English folk revival, see A. L. Lloyd, 'Songs and Stories of the Durham Miners', programme 1 of 2 (BBC Third Programme, 27 January 1964. Prod. Douglas Cleverdon, avail. BBC Written Archive); Johnny Handle, 'Industrial Folk Music and Regional Music Hall in the North East', *English Dance and Song* (October, 1965), 139.

34 Sassoon, *One Hundred Years of Socialism*, 16.

35 Dave Harker, *One for the Money: Politics and Popular Song* (London: Hutchison, 1980), 147.

36 Ibid., 148. Sharp's legacy has been highly contested in the twentieth and twenty-first centuries, although it has generally been acknowledged that his censorship of songs, as well as his reported racism, served to damage it.

37 Britta Sweers, *Electric Folk: The Changing Face of English Traditional Music* (New York: Oxford University Press, 2003), 7.

38 A. L. Lloyd, *The Singing Englishman: An Introduction to Folk Song* (London: Lawrence and Wishart, 1944), 3–4; 22.

39 Pete Seeger, quoted in Smithsonian Folkways Recordings, Folkways Collection Podcast, 'Subterranean Homesick Blues Part I' (Originally broadcast 25 July 2006).

40 Cited in A. L. Lloyd, *Folk Song in England* (London: Lawrence and Wishart in Association with the Workers' Music Association, 1967), 15.

41 Many revivalists expressed an anxiety regarding the relationship between 'oral' and 'aural' traditions, and how these affected the folk tradition. These anxieties will be discussed in much more detail in Chapter 6.

42 Richard A. Peterson, *Creating Country Music: Fabricating Authenticity* (Chicago: The University of Chicago Press, 1997), 198.

43 G. D. Towner, 'Letter to the Editor', *The Observer* (22 September 1963), 38.

44 Neil Alan Marks, 'Reliving the "Golden Years" of Folk Music', *New York Times* (2 November 1980), D23.

45 Ewan MacColl, 'Recollections on Creation of Radio Ballads BBC Recording, "Singing the English" with Charles Parker', British Library Sound Archive, Ewan MacColl and Peggy Seeger Collection, 1CDR0001754-1755 S1 BD2-BD7 NSA (Recorded 1961–1962).

46 Ibid.

47 Eric Hobsbawm, *The Invention of Tradition* (Cambridge: Cambridge University Press, 1992), 1.

48 Ibid.

49 Ibid., 2.

50 Fred Davis, *Yearning for Yesterday: A Sociology of Nostalgia* (New York: Free Press, 1979), 31.

51 Ibid., 32–3; 49.

52 Ron Eyerman and Andrew Jamieson, *Music and Social Movements: Mobilizing Traditions in the Twentieth Century* (Cambridge: Cambridge University Press, 1998), 30.

53 Ibid.

54 Hugh Latimer, 'Skiffle Intelligentsia', *The Observer* (16 June 1957), 21.

55   Ibid.

56   Ibid.

57   See Billy Bragg's *Roots, Radicals and Rockers: How Skiffle Changed the World* (London: Faber and Faber, 2017) for more on the importance of skiffle.

58   Stephen Barnard, *On the Radio: Music Radio in Britain* (Milton Keynes: Open University Press, 1989), 37.

59   Not only did prominent British folk revivalists such as Martin Carthy and Stan Kelly start their careers in skiffle bands, but so too did the Beatles, the Hollies and many other British rock groups.

60   Iain Chambers, 'A Strategy for Living: Black Music and White Subcultures', in eds. Stuart Hall and Tony Jefferson, *Resistance through Rituals: Youth Subcultures in Postwar Britain* (London: Unwin Hyman, 1976), 162.

61   Eric Hobsbawm, *The Jazz Scene* (London: Weidenfeld and Nicolson, 1989), 247.

62   George McKay, *Circular Breathing: The Cultural Politics of Jazz in Postwar Britain* (Chapel Hill: Duke University Press, 2006), 16.

63   Ibid., 25.

64   Ibid., 26.

65   Ibid., 19.

66   Ibid.

Chapter 1

67   Simon Frith, *The Sociology of Rock* (London: Constable, 1978), 185.

68   Robert Shelton, 'Britain's Folk Scene: "Skiffle Craze" to Clubs in Pubs', *New York Times* (6 March 1966), X23.

69   In *The Structural Transformation of the Public Sphere* (1962), Jürgen Habermas explored the effects of capitalist production on social relationships and cultural expression in modern society. Habermas traced the gradual democratization of the public sphere in the Western world. Habermas's work has significant implications for studying the community of folk singers, collectors and enthusiasts involved in the postwar revivals, and for the threatening commodification of that community and its socialist ethos.

70   Frankie Armstrong and Brian Pearson, 'Some Reflections on the English Folk Revival', *History Workshop: A Journal of Socialist Historians* 7 (Spring 1979), 95. Peggy Seeger also volunteered, in conversation, that the pub-based folk club was the single-most important distinguishing element of the English folk revival.

71   Bean, *Singing from the Floor*, 146.

72   The Village became the epicentre of a national movement, contained in the ubiquitous shops and cafés along MacDougal St. Places like the Café Wha?, Gerde's Folk City and the Gaslight fostered the burgeoning folk community in the Village, and attracted folk performers from all over the country as well. These folk club/coffee shops were often called 'Basket Houses'; performers were not paid a flat rate, but would pass a breadbasket around following each set.

73   Steve Benbow, 'Focus on Folk: If the Beatles Turned to Folk …', *Melody Maker* (11 January 1964), 11.

74   Shelton, 'Britain's Folk Scene', X23.

75   Eric Winter, 'Focus on Folk', *Melody Maker* (16 March 1963).

76   Louis Killen, quoted in Fred Woods, *Folk Revival: The Rediscovery of a National Music* (Poole: Blandford, 1979), 58.
77   A. L. Lloyd, 'The English Folk Song Revival', *Sing Out!* 12, No. 2 (April–May 1962), 34.
78   Anthea Joseph, 'A Singers' Notebook: Dovetailing into the Treats on Tyneside', *Sing* 6, No. 5 (January 1962), 48.
79   Ibid.
80   Ibid.
81   Eric Winter, Advertisement for Birtley Folk Club, *Sing* 7, No. 1 (September 1962), 6.
82   John Mann, 'A Singer's Notebook: Forest Folk at Southampton', *Sing* 6, No. 8 (April 1962), 85.
83   Ibid.
84   Ibid.
85   Harker, *One for the Money*, 152.
86   Woods, *Folk Revival*, 88. Woods likely converted the admission costs from old to new pence. For the most part, this work makes use of the monetary system in use in Britain before 1971, as this is what most of the revival's participants would have used. Britain abandoned the old penny on Decimal Day, 15 February 1971, when one pound sterling became divided into 100 'new pence'. The British shilling was replaced by the 5 new pence coin, worth one-twentieth of a pound.
87   Ibid. See also Bean, *Singing from the Floor*, 123–5.
88   Ibid., 104.
89   Michael Pickering and Tony Green, 'Towards a Cartography of the Vernacular Milieu', in eds. Michael Pickering and Tony Green, *Everyday Culture: Popular Song and the Vernacular Milieu* (Milton Keynes: Open University Press, 1987), 32.
90   Laing, Denselow, Dallas and Shelton, *Electric Muse*, 143. This policy will be discussed in detail in Chapter 5.
91   Ibid.
92   Eric Winter, 'A Singer's Notebook: Unaccompanied Singers', *Sing* 6, No. 4 (December 1961), 34.
93   Ibid.
94   Shelton, 'Britain's Folk Scene', X23.
95   Ewan MacColl, 'Why I Am Opening a New Club', *Sing* 5, No. 4 (August 1961), 65.
96   *Sing* 6, No. 9 (May 1962), 89.
97   Ibid., front cover.
98   Ibid., insert.
99   I am using the term 'provinces' here as the editors of *Sing* used the term – i.e. places located outside of major urban centres, not just London. For the full list from this insert, see Appendix I.
100 Brocken, *British Folk Revival*, 114.
101 The EFDSS had offices in Cambridge, Haywards Heath, Birmingham, Kettering, Liverpool, Darlington and Exeter.
102 Armstrong and Pearson, 'Some Reflections', 96.
103 EFDSS leaflet, Richard Reuss Folk Music Ephemera Collection, Library of Congress, American Folklife Center (AFC 1983: 005), box 3 of 15.
104 EFDSS advertisement and information related to booking service (dated 1965), in Ibid.
105 Woods, *Folk Revival*, 92.
106 Sweers, *Electric Folk*, 39.

107   Eric Winter, 'Focus on Folk: TV Trip for New York Folknik', *Melody Maker* (19
       January 1963), 12.
108   Chris Roberts, 'Suddenly – It's Folk!: Special Report from New York', *Melody Maker*
       (24 August 1963), 13.
109   Ibid.
110   Eric Winter, 'Focus on Folk', *Melody Maker* (31 August 1963), 16.
111   Author Unknown, 'Folk? No Boom Here, Says Dusty Springfield', *Melody Maker* (14
       September 1963), 18.
112   *Melody Maker* (12 September 1964), 4.
113   This did not mean that broadside culture had entirely disappeared either. Journalist
       Stephen Sedley told the story of John Foreman, the 'broadside king', who began
       selling broadsides of new folk songs in 1958 in Petticoat Lane on weekends.
       (Stephen Sedley, 'The Folk Laureates', *Observer* (5 July 1964), 29).
114   EFDSS *Folk Music Journal* 1, No. 1 (December 1965), ii.
115   Winter, '*Sing* Mission Statement', *Sing* 1, No. 1 (May–June 1954), 2.
116   Ibid.
117   Alan Bush, in Ibid., 10.
118   *Sing* 8, No. 3 (April 1965), 12; 14. One of the most popular American subjects for
       Sing articles was Pete Seeger, especially in the extensive coverage of his dealings
       with the House Un-American Activities Committee (HUAC). See the August,
       1961, issue of *Sing* for more. Seeger's 1961 tour of Britain was also covered
       comprehensively by the magazine. (Karl Dallas, 'Seeger Is Here', *Sing* 6, No. 3
       (November 1961)).
119   Winter, *Sing* 1, 2.
120   *Ethnic* 1, No. 1 (January 1959), 2. The etymology of the word 'Ethnic' and how it
       was used has been slightly problematic. In the context of folk music, even, there was
       no consensual definition of the term. In the United States, Folkways Records used
       it to describe world music, but in the case of *Ethnic*, it meant a much more national
       focus, as the magazine's statement alluded to. Magazines such as *Melody Maker*
       and *Sing* used the term 'ethnic' to stand in for 'authentic'. Bruce Woodley wrote
       for *Melody Maker*, about the New York folk scene, 'On the subject of ethnics, over
       there they don't knock folk-rock, or the pop-folk, or whatever you want to label it.
       The Village ethnics would never think of doing this kind of music – but they don't
       knock it. None of that write-a-letter-to-the-MM bit complaining that Bert Jansch
       uses an electric plectrum on his new album and is he getting too commercial?'
       (Bruce Woodley, 'Seeker Bruce on the New York Scene', *Melody Maker* (29 January
       1966), 9).
121   Ibid.
122   Ibid.
123   Reg Hall, *Ethnic* 1, No. 3 (Summer 1959), 3.
124   Ibid.
125   David A. Callister, 'note to BBC producer D.G. Bridson', BBC Written Archive,
       R19/2, 140/1 'Folk Music' (12.12.63).
126   John Kaneen and David Callister, 'Editorial', *Folk Review* 1, No. 1 (December
       1963), 1.
127   Ibid.
128   Ibid.
129   Ibid.
130   Ibid.

131   *Sing* 8, No. 1 (1964).

132   Ed. Beryl Davis, *Folk Songs from Spin*, No. 3 (Cheshire: Spin Publications, 1974), inside cover.

133   Ed. Beryl Davis, *Folk Songs from Spin*, No. 2 (Cheshire: Spin Publications, 1969), inside cover.

134   Ed. Davis, *Spin,* No. 3, inside cover.

135   Ibid.

136   Richard Reuss, from a compiled list of English folklore and folk music serial publications, Richard Reuss Folk Music Ephemera Collection, Library of Congress, American Folklife Center (AFC 1983:005), box 4 of 15. Other, smaller, magazines, listed in a *Sing* 8, No. 1 (1964), included *Folk Music* (a monthly, edited by Karl Dallas, which sold for 2 shillings), and *Heritage Broadsheet* (occasional publication of the Oxford University Heritage Society).

137   *Sing Out!* was the clearest example of this; the magazine's readership rose from about 500 in 1951, to 1,000 in 1960, to, at the height of circulation in 1964, 25,000, before dwindling to about 15,000 by the early 1970s (Cantwell, *When We Were Good*, 280).

138   Winter, appeal for funding, *Sing* 1, No. 6 (March–April 1955), 117.

139   Ken Phine, 'For the Record', *Sing* 6, No. 1 (September 1961), 8.

140   Ibid.

141   Ibid.

142   Brocken, *British Folk Revival*, 55; 60.

143   Harker, *Fakesong*, 238.

144   Ibid., 237.

145   Dave Arthur, *Bert: The Life and Times of A. L. Lloyd* (London: Pluto Press, in association with the EFDSS, 2012), 327.

146   1969 advertisement for Leader Sound, Richard Reuss Folk Music Ephemera Collection, Library of Congress, American Folklife Center, AFC 1983: 005, box 3 of 15.

147   Harker, *One for the Money*, 157.

148   *Sing* 9, No. 1 (February 1966), 4.

149   Ibid.

150   Eric Winter, 'Discussion: Scotland the Brave', *Sing* 5, No. 2 (December 1959), 39.

151   Ibid.

152   Ken Phine, 'For the Record: Thin Time for Folk-Disc Fans', *Sing* 6, No. 6 (February 1962), 64.

153   Eric Winter, 'Focus on Folk', *Melody Maker* (16 March 1963), 20.

154   Ibid.

155   This was especially true of the relationship between Topic and Folkways, as each label worked to promote artists from across the ocean.

156   Phine, 'For the Record', 8.

157   Robert Shelton, 'Folkways on Record', *Sing* 5, No. 4 (August 1961), 69.

158   Ibid.

159   In the United States, in the early days of FM Radio and before the advent of National Public Radio, folk music – especially the more traditional material – found limited space on national airwaves, although local radio stations all over the country were important in building the folk revival. *Sing Out!* editor Irwin Silber recalled, 'Every city has its own radio station [,] has some kind of radio program that deals with folk music. It not only plays the latest hits according to the Billboard

charts but also plays what we would call either traditional songs or songs sung in traditional styles. In the largest cities, a day cannot pass by in which you cannot hear some kind of folk music radio program.' (Silber, 'The Size of the Revival', in 'The Folk Music Revival: A Symposium', *New York Folklore Quarterly* 19, No. 3 (June 1963), 109). Silber also co-hosted the *Sing Out!* radio programme in New York with folksinger Barbara Dane.

160   The broadcaster famously refused to play 'Lucy in the Sky with Diamonds' because it was thought to glorify the use of hallucinogenic drugs. Appearing at the Newport Folk Festival in 1966, singer Donovan Leitch told the crowd that the BBC had also refused to play his song 'Ballad of a Crystal Man', because of its lyrics criticizing the Vietnam War.

161   Woods, *Folk Revival*, 18.

162   Barnard, *On the Radio*, 17.

163   Ibid., 4.

164   Ibid., 5.

165   D. G. Bridson, *Prospero and Ariel: The Rise and Fall of Radio, a Personal Recollection* (London: Victor Gollancz Ltd., 1971), 222.

166   Ibid., 222–3.

167   Ibid., 223.

168   Reg Hall, 'The Fifties: 1947–1963', *Root and Branch* 2 (1999), 4.

169   Woods, *Folk Revival*, 19.

170   BBC Written Archive, R46/598/1 'As I Roved Out', File 2 (1956).

171   BBC Written Archive, R46/26/1 'As I Roved Out', File 1A (1953–54).

172   'As I Roved Out', File 2.

173   Sweers, *Electric Folk*, 88.

174   'Reactions in Brief: As I Roved Out', Memo from Head of Audience Research Robert Silvey to Mr. Harold Rogers, dated 17.06.55. BBC Written Archive, R46/26/2 'As I Roved Out', File 1B (1955).

175   Memo from Controller, Light Programme (16.02.54). BBC Written Archive, R46/26/1 'As I Roved Out', File 1A.

176   Hall, 'The Fifties', 4. Robin Hall and Jimmie MacGregor were the popular co-hosts of the BBC programme *Folk Song Cellar* (1966–67), which featured both traditional and contemporary performers from all parts of Britain.

177   BBC Written Archive, A. L. Lloyd Program Catalogue.

178   Ibid.

179   BBC Written Archive, *A Ballad Hunter Looks at Britain*. Transcript for Program 1, 'Come Listen to My Song' (1.11.57).

180   Ibid.

181   Ibid.

182   Ewan MacColl interview for the Oral History of Recorded Sound, British Library Sound Archive, C90/76/03 C1 (Recorded June, 1985).

183   Ibid.

184   Ibid.

185   'Recollections on the creation of Radio Ballads BBC Recording, "Singing the English" with Charles Parker', British Library Sound Archive, Ewan MacColl and Peggy Seeger Collection, 1CDR0001754-1755 S1 BD2-BD7 NSA (Recorded 1961–62).

186   Alan Sinfield, *Literature, Politics, and Culture in Postwar Britain* (Berkeley: University of California Press, 1989), 264.

187 MacColl, Oral History of Recorded Sound interview, British Library Sound Archive, C90/76/03 C1.

188 Stuart Laing, *Representations of Working-Class Life 1957–1964* (London: Macmillan, 1986), 165.

189 P. J. Waller, 'Democracy and Dialect', in ed. P. J. Waller, *Politics and Social Change in Modern Britain: Essays Presented to A. F. Thompson* (New York: St. Martin's Press, 1987), 8–9.

190 MacColl, *Oral History of Recorded Sound*, British Library Sound Archive, C90/76/03 C1.

191 Bill Holdsworth, 'Songs of the People', *New Left Review* 1, No. 1 (January 1960), 48.

192 Eric Winter, 'Ballads and Bravery', *Manchester Guardian* (16 October 1958), 7.

193 BBC Radio Ballads, 'The Big Hewer'. Lyrics and Music by Ewan MacColl; Arrangements and Musical Direction by Peggy Seeger; Production by Charles Parker. BBC Written Archive, Ewan MacColl programme catalogue.

194 The programmes, in order, included 'The Ballad of John Axon' (2.7.58), 'Songs of the Road' (5.11.59), 'Singing the Fishing' (16.8.60), 'The Big Hewer' (18.8.61), 'The Body-Blow' (27.3.62), 'On the Edge' (13.2.63) and 'The Fight Game' (3.7.63).

195 Keenan and Callister, 'Radio Ballads Axed', *Folk Review* 1, No. 1 (1963), 27. The Elliotts will be discussed in further detail in later chapters.

196 *The Song Carriers* 1–3, British Library Sound Archive, 1CDR0002705 C200/231 (recorded 1965, BBC Midland Home Service). MacColl also explained that the difference between a 'good' and 'bad' revival singer was whether they transformed or extended the tradition.

197 *The Song Carriers* 11–12, British Library Sound Archive, 1CDR0002710 C200/233 (Recorded 1965).

198 Notes to contributors for IFMC-EBU joint project, 'Polyphony in Folk Music', BBC Written Archive, R34/1322, 'Policy – International Broadcasting Arrangements – Folk Music 1966–1972' (23.12.66).

199 The Newport Folk Festival, premiering in 1959, was by far the most popular folk festival of the era. Organized by George Wein, the festival became a forum for the great diversity of American musical styles that, together, were part of the American folk revival. Newport organizers prided themselves on the diversity of styles presented at the festival. Newport was not just about a confluence of city and country – styles of the North and the South, East and West were all presented, alongside workshops on style and songwriting.

200 Eric Winter, 'Focus on Folk', *Melody Maker* (6 July 1963), 16.

201 Ibid.

202 Ibid.

203 A. L. Lloyd, quoted in Robert Shelton, 'Britons Enliven Fete at Newport', *New York Times* (25 July 1965), 68.

204 Sweers, *Electric Folk*, 209.

205 *Ethnic* 1, No. 3 (Summer 1959), 2.

206 Woods, *Folk Revival*, 91.

207 Arthur, *Bert*, 333.

208 *Sing* 8, No. 5 (November 1965), 10.

209 Ibid., 13.

210 Victor Keegan, 'Money No Object at Festival of Pure Folk', *Guardian* (17 July 1965), 14.

211 Ibid.

212 Dave Laing and Richard Newman, *Thirty Years of the Cambridge Folk Festival* (Ely: Music Maker, 1994), 1; 5.

213 Ibid., 8.

214 Ibid., 14.

215 Ibid., 25.

216 Ibid., 16. By 1974, attendance had reached 10,000 over the course of the weekend.

217 Ibid., 23.

218 Woods, *Folk Revival*, 91–2.

Chapter 2

219 Holdsworth, 'Songs of the People', 49.

220 Alastair J. Reid, 'The Dialectics of Liberation: The Old Left, the New Left and the Counter-Culture', in eds. David Feldman and Jon Lawrence, *Structures and Transformations in Modern British History* (Cambridge: Cambridge University Press, 2011), 261.

221 Lin Chun, *The British New Left* (Edinburgh: Edinburgh University Press, 1993), xiii.

222 Gordon Friesen, 'Songs of Our Time from the Pages of Broadside Magazine', in eds. David A. De Turk and A. Poulin, *The American Folk Scene: Dimensions of the Folksong Revival* (New York: Dell Publishing Co., 1967), 131.

223 Richard A. Reuss and JoAnne C. Reuss, *American Folk Music and Left-Wing Politics, 1927–1957* (Lanham, NJ: Scarecrow Press, 2000), 185.

224 Brocken, *British Folk Revival*, 50–1. The London Youth Choir had significant links with the CPGB, as did Lloyd, Eric Winter and other members of the WMA.

225 Ibid., 19–20.

226 Workers' Music Association, *Pocket Song Book* (London: Lawrence and Wishart, 1948), Back Cover.

227 Harker, *Fakesong*, 234.

228 Ibid., 231.

229 Gareth Stedman Jones, *Languages of Class: Studies in English Working Class History, 1832–1982* (Cambridge: Cambridge University Press, 1983), 240.

230 Sassoon, *One Hundred Years of Socialism*, 58.

231 Ibid., 126; 140. See also Ross McKibbin, *Parties and People: England 1914–1951* (Oxford: Oxford University Press, 2010), 144.

232 J. M. Keynes, quoted in Eric Shaw, *The Labour Party since 1945: Old Labour, New Labour* (Oxford: Blackwell, 1996), 20.

233 Hugh Armstrong Clegg, *A History of British Trade Unions since 1889, Vol. 3 1934–1951* (Oxford: Clarendon, 1994), 324; 327.

234 Steven Fielding, '"To Make Men and Women Better than They Are": Labour and the Building of Socialism', in ed. Jim Fyrth, *Labour's Promised Land? Culture and Society in Labour* Britain *1945–51* (London: Lawrence and Wishart, 1995), 18.

235 McKibbin, *Parties and People*, 141.

236 Sinfield, *Literature, Politics, and Culture*, 238.

237 Ed. Steven Fielding, *The Labour Party: 'Socialism' and Society since 1951* (Manchester: Manchester University Press, 1997), 2.

238 Martin Pugh, *Speak for Britain! A New History of the Labour Party* (London: The Bodley Head, 2010), 302. For more on the limits of the affluence thesis – especially

relating to the Labour Party's evolving relationship with the unions – see also Keith Laybourn, *The Rise of Labour: The British Labour Party 1890–1979* (London: Edward Arnold, 1988); Andrew Thorpe, *A History of the British Labour Party* (New York: Palgrave, 2001); Shaw, *The Labour Party since 1945 Old Labour*; and Leo Panitch and Colin Leys, *The End of Parliamentary Socialism: From New Left to New Labour* (London: Verso, 2001).

239 Michael Kenny, *The First New Left: British Intellectuals after Stalin* (London: Lawrence and Wishart, 1995), 1. See also Panitch and Leys, *The End of Parliamentary Socialism*, 2–3; Dennis Dworkin, *Cultural Marxism in Postwar Britain: History, the New Left, and the Origins of Cultural Studies* (Durham, NC: Duke University Press, 1997), 51.

240 Stuart Hall, 'Editorial', *New Left Review* 1, No. 1 (January–February 1960), 1.

241 C. Wright Mills, 'Letter to the New Left', *New Left Review* 1, No. 5 (September–October 1960), 18; 23.

242 Ralph Miliband, 'The Sickness of Labourism', in Ibid., 5.

243 Ibid.

244 Thorpe, *A History of the British Labour Party*, 163.

245 Black, *The Political Culture of the Left*, 68.

246 Leon Rosselson, 'Battle Hymn of the New Socialist Party', in eds. Nathan Joseph and Eric Winter, *New English Broadsides: Songs of Our Time from the English Folk Scene* (New York: Oak Publications, 1967), 70.

247 Emily Robinson, 'Radical Nostalgia, Progressive Patriotism, and Labour's English Problem', *Political Studies Review* 14, No. 3 (2016), 378.

248 Ibid., 379.

249 Ibid., 380.

250 Morris first linked the causes of art and socialism in an 1884 speech to the Leicester Secular Society. This idea – that art could be used to further the socialist cause – was crucial to the ethos of the English Left after the war, cited by key figures such as Williams and Hall, and discussed at length in the pages of the *New Left Review*: See Raymond Williams, *Culture and Society* (1957), and Stuart Hall's editorial in the first issue of the *NLR* (1/1, January–February 1960), for example.

251 Hall, *New Left Review* 1, No. 1.

252 Dworkin, *Cultural Marxism*, 4.

253 Simon Frith, *Performing Rites: On the Value of Popular Music* (Cambridge, MA: Harvard University Press, 1996), 20.

254 Black, *The Political Culture of the Left*, 83.

255 Michael Frayn, 'Festival', in eds. Michael Sissons and Philip French, *Age of Austerity, 1945–1951* (London: Hodder and Stoughton, 1963), 319–20; Black, *Redefining*, 43.

256 Black, *Redefining*, 43.

257 Becky Conekin, *The Autobiography of a Nation: The 1951 Festival of Britain* (Manchester: Manchester University Press, 2003), 2.

258 Martin Daunton, *Wealth and Welfare: An Economic and Social History of Britain 1851–1951* (Oxford: Oxford University Press, 2007), 608–09; 610.

259 Frayn, 'Festival', 337–8.

260 The project emerged out of a 1960 TUC motion (No. 42, hence the moniker), drafted by Wesker and writer Bill Holdsworth, which urged greater attention to culture on the part of the unions. (Black, *Redefining*, 139). The motion was passed, part of what Black has argued was the 'rising trade union concern with cultural matters in this period'. (Black, *Redefining*, 149).

261   Black, *Redefining,* 145–6.
262   Jeff Nuttall, *Bomb Culture* (London: MacGibbon & Kee, 1968), 59; 62.
263   Black, *Redefining,* 145–6.
264   Ibid., 152.
265   Sinfield, *Literature, Politics, and Culture,* 263.
266   Ibid.
267   Sedley, 'The Folk Laureates', 29.
268   *Melody Maker,* 11 September 1965, cover.
269   Pete Seeger, 'Johnny Appleseed, Jr', *Sing Out!* 12, No. 1 (February–March 1962), 58.
270   Richard Taylor, *Against the Bomb: The British Peace Movement 1958–1965* (Oxford: Clarendon Press, 1988), 1.
271   Ibid., 50.
272   Ibid., 275.
273   Leon Rosselson, 'Dear John Profumo', Leon Rosselson and Stan Kelly, Topic Records Collection, BBC Sound Archive, 1CDR0004225.
274   Ibid.
275   Nuttall, *Bomb Culture,* 53.
276   Colin Irwin, 'Aldermaston – Birth of the British Protest Song', *Observer* (10 August 2008).
277   Pete Seeger, 'From Aldermaston to London – They Walked and Sang for Peace', *Sing Out!* 10, No. 4 (December–January 1960–61), 14.
278   Ibid., 15.
279   Ian Campbell, 'The Sun Is Burning in the Sky', in eds. Joseph and Winter, *New English Broadsides,* 17.
280   John Brunner, 'The H-Bomb's Thunder', in Ibid., 18.
281   This was especially apparent in the work of the Glasgow Songwriters Guild, a group that contributed many songs to the cause of nuclear disarmament, particularly relating to the presence of nuclear submarines off the Scottish coast.
282   National Youth Campaign for Nuclear Disarmament, *1961 Aldermaston March Leaflet* (London: Columbia Printers, 1961), back side.
283   Michael Brake, *Comparative Youth Culture: The Sociology of American Youth Cultures and Subcultures in America, Britain and Canada* (London: Routledge, 1985), 105–6. Although the CND was the largest and most often-cited of the New Left initiatives in Britain, there were several other organizations which sprang up in response to the social and political conditions of the country, including the British Council for Peace in Vietnam (BCPV), founded in May 1965 by Fenner Brockway; and the Vietnam Solidarity Campaign (VSC), founded in 1966 by American activist Ralph Schoeneman, personal secretary to Bertrand Russell.
284   Nuttall, *Bomb Culture,* 63.
285   Mike Marqusee, *Wicked Messenger: Bob Dylan and the 1960s* (New York: Seven Stories Press, 2005), 55.
286   Bob Dylan, quoted in dir. Martin Scorsese, *No Direction Home: Bob Dylan* (2004).
287   Ewan MacColl, 'Ballad of Ho Chi Minh', *Sing* 1, No. 3 (1954), 57.
288   *Sing* 8, No. 4 (July 1965), 10–11.
289   Ibid., 10.
290   Ibid., 11.
291   This was the same tour depicted in D. A. Pennebaker's documentary *Dont Look Back* (1967).
292   Bill Schwarz, '"The Only White Man in There": The Re-Racialisation of England, 1956–1968', *Race and Class* 38, No. 1 (1996), 73–4.

293   Tom Nairn, *The Break-Up of Britain: Crisis and Neo-Nationalism* (London: New Left Books, 1981), 277.

294   Shirley Joshi, quoted in ed. Hanna H. Meissner, *Poverty in the Affluent Society* (New York: Harper & Row, 1966), 8.

295   Ibid.

296   Wendy Webster, *Englishness and Empire 1939–1965* (Oxford: Oxford University Press, 2005), 150.

297   Arthur, *Bert*, 212.

298   Cliff Hall, interview for *Millennium Memory Bank*. British Library Sound Archive, C900/07564 C1 (Recorded 27 January, 1999 for BBC Radio Kent at Hall's home).

299   Ibid.

300   Ibid.

301   Kathleen Paul, *Whitewashing Britain: Race and Citizenship in the Postwar Era* (Ithaca, NY: Cornell University Press, 1997), 139.

302   Webster, *Englishness and Empire*, 165.

303   Stuart Hall, 'ULR Club at Notting Hill', *New Left Review* 1, No. 1 (January–February 1960), 71.

304   Ibid.

305   Paul, *Whitewashing*, 155.

306   Bridson, *Prospero and Ariel*, 254.

307   Ibid., 255.

308   *Sing* 5, No. 1 (September 1959), 15. Cochrane was born in Antigua and moved in 1954 to London, where he settled in Notting Hill and worked as a carpenter. While walking home, shortly after midnight on 17 May 1959, the 32-year-old Cochrane was set upon by a group of white youths, who stabbed him with a stiletto knife. Three other men arrived on the scene, and the youths ran off. The three men took Cochrane to hospital, where he died an hour later. His funeral was attended by more than 1,200 people.

309   Ibid.

310   Ibid., 19.

311   *Sing* 8, No. 4 (July 1965), 14.

312   Peggy Seeger and Ewan MacColl, 'Jimmy Wilson', *Sing* 5, No. 1 (September 1959), 18.

313   Ibid.

314   Vanessa Redgrave, 'Hanging on a Tree', *Sing* 8, No. 1 (1964), 6. The following description accompanied the song: 'Vanessa Redgrave composed this song and sang it at an anti-apartheid meeting last December. Now Topic has issued it as a single (STOP111). Vanessa's poem expresses the agony of thinking about South African citizens in a direct manner … If you believe that apartheid is evil, the song will move you – if you are undecided, it will convince you.' (6).

315   'Sunny South Africa', *Sing* 8, No. 4 (July 1965), 7.

316   'Birmingham Anti-Racism Concert', British Library Sound Archive, Topic Records Collection, 1CDR0004901 (Recorded 16 April, 1962).

317   Ibid. A recording of the concert was to be sent to Martin Luther King Jr.

318   Stuart Hall, 'Black Diaspora Artists in Britain: Three "Moments" in Postwar History', *History Workshop Journal* 61 (Spring 2006), 16–17. The ripple effect of Notting Hill was not entirely negative; the riots served to galvanize London's immigrant communities – especially those of West Indian origin – to assert their place and identity as part of English society. Notting Hill also led to the

organization, in 1959, of a West Indian carnival at St. Pancras Town Hall, which evolved by the mid-1960s into the Notting Hill Carnival. The events in Notting Dale, Shepherd's Bush and Paddington can be interpreted as a powerful moment of change in the politics of English identity, and particularly English urban identity. The growth of rights groups, such as the Committee of Afro-Asian-Caribbean Organizations (CAACO), the Coordinating Committee Against Racial Discrimination (CCARD) and the Campaign Against Racial Discrimination (CARD), in the wake of the riots, was an equally important development, no doubt inspired by the gains of groups like the NAACP, SNCC, SCLC and CORE in the United States.

319   Black, *Redefining*, 7–8.
320   Ibid., 142.

Chapter 3

321   E. P. Thompson, *The Making of the English Working Class* (London: Gollancz, 1965), 832.
322   Edward A. McCreary, *The Americanization of Europe: The Impact of Americans and American Business on the Uncommon Market* (Garden City, NY: Doubleday, 1964), 24.
323   Daunton, *Wealth and Welfare*, 410.
324   Prime Minister Harold Macmillan, at a speech in Bedford in 1957, stated: 'Let us be frank about it: most of our people have never had it so good.'
325   Anthony Sutcliffe, *An Economic and Social History of Europe since 1945* (London: Longman, 1996), 146. This was a trend that was largely repeated throughout Western Europe. For more on the economic state of Europe after the Second World War, see Tony Judt, *Postwar: A History of Europe since 1945* (New York: Penguin, 2005).
326   Kenneth O. Morgan, *Labour in Power 1945–51* (Oxford: Oxford University Press, 1984), 25.
327   John Clarke, Stuart Hall, Tony Jefferson and Brian Roberts, 'Subcultures, Cultures and Class: A Theoretical Overview', in eds. Stuart Hall and Tony Jefferson, *Resistance through Rituals: Youth Subcultures in Postwar Britain* (London: Unwin Hyman, 1976), 21.
328   Laing, *Representations of Working-Class Life*, 29.
329   Malcolm Bradbury, *All Dressed Up and Nowhere to Go: The Poor Man's Guide to the Affluent Society* (London: Max Parrish, 1962), 15. Bradbury was offering a satirical study of the leftist response to affluence.
330   'The Future Labour Offers You', quoted in Lawrence Black, '"Sheep May Safely Gaze": Socialists, Television and the People in Britain, 1949–1964', in eds. Lawrence Black et al., *Consensus or Coercion?: The State, the People and Social Cohesion in Postwar Britain* (Cheltenham: New Clarion Press, 2001), 29.
331   Stuart Hall, 'A Sense of Classlessness', *Universities and Left Review* 1, No. 5 (Autumn 1958), 26.
332   Joanna Bourke, *Working-Class Cultures in Britain, 1890–1960: Gender, Class and Ethnicity* (London: Routledge, 1994), 5.
333   Stedman Jones, *Languages of Class*, 241.

334   Clarke et al., 'Subcultures', 22.

335   Sinfield, *Literature, Politics, and Culture*, 21.

336   Mark Abrams, *The Teenage Consumer* (London: London Press Exchange, 1959), 5; 10.

337   Ibid., 7.

338   Ibid., 10.

339   Ibid., 13. Simon Frith, in a complementary argument, asserted that teenaged consumers of rock music were largely working class. For more, see Frith, 'Youth and Music', in *Taking Popular Music Seriously: A Collection of Essays* (Hampshire: Ashgate, 2007), 18.

340   Dominic Sandbrook, *Never Had It So Good: A History of Britain from Suez to the Beatles* (London: Abacus, 2006), 181.

341   Mike Savage, 'Sociology, Class and Male Manual Work Cultures', in eds. Alan Campbell, Nina Fishman and John McIlroy, *The Postwar Compromise: British Trade Unions and Industrial Politics 1945–64* (Monmouth, Wales: The Merlin Press, 2007), 25.

342   Ibid.

343   Ibid., 26.

344   Ferdynand Zweig, *The Worker in an Affluent Society: Family Life and Industry* (London: Heinemann, 1961), 8–9.

345   Ibid., 133.

346   Ibid.

347   Ibid., 133–4.

348   Arthur Marwick, 'Images of the Working Class since 1930', in ed. Jay Winter, *The Working Class in Modern British History: Essays in Honour of Henry Pelling* (Cambridge: Cambridge University Press, 1983), 215.

349   Janet Howarth, 'Class and Culture in England after 1951: The Case of Working-Class Women', in eds. Clare V. J. Griffiths, James J. Nott and William Whyte, *Classes, Cultures, and Politics: Essays on British History for Ross McKibbin* (Oxford: Oxford University Press, 2011), 86.

350   Richard Hoggart, *The Uses of Literacy: Aspects of Working-Class Life, with Special Reference to Publications and Entertainments* (London: Chatto and Windus, 1957), 5.

351   Ibid., 6.

352   Ibid., 170.

353   Sinfield, *Literature, Politics, and Culture*, 253.

354   Sandbrook, *Never Had It So Good*, 186.

355   Keegan, 'Money No Object', 14.

356   Peggy Seeger, quoted in Irwin Silber, 'Peggy Seeger – The Voice of America in Folksong', *Sing Out!* 12, No. 3 (Summer 1962), 7.

357   Ironically, however, her own family, including her older half-brother, Pete Seeger – easily the American revival's most respected elder statesman – were of a decidedly upper-class ilk.

358   Johnny Handle, 'Industrial Folk Music', *English Dance and Song* (August 1965), 106.

359   Ewan MacColl, *Sing Out!* 17, No. 6 (December–January 1967–68), 29.

360   MacColl, quoted in Irwin Silber, 'Ewan MacColl – Folksinger of the Industrial Age', *Sing Out!* 9, No. 3 (Winter 1959–60), 9.

361   Ewan MacColl, 'The Singer and the Audience', *Sing Out!* 14, No. 4 (September 1964), 17–8.

362   MacKinnon, *British Folk Scene*, 127.

363   Ibid., 43–4.

364   Ibid., 130.

365   Arthur, *Bert*, 212.

366   Harker, *One for the Money*, 153.

367   Ibid., 155.

368   Ibid., 156.

369   Peter Jenkins, 'Bevan's Fight with the B.M.A', in eds. Sissons and French, *Age of Austerity*, 247.

370   Robert Colls, 'Born-Again Geordies', in eds. Robert Colls and Bill Lancaster, *Geordies: Roots of Regionalism* (Newcastle-Upon-Tyne: Northumbria University Press, 2005), 11. The importance of Robert Colls's work to understanding ideas of region, community and identity – especially with regards to the Northeast – is considerable. Colls's historical and personal observations on the resonance of community and regional identities straddle contemporary observation with historical distance, and are deeply influenced by personal experience as a South Shields native.

371   Ibid., 19.

372   Lloyd, *Folk Song in England*, 316.

373   Harker, *One for the Money*, 149.

374   Lloyd, sleeve notes for *The Iron Muse* (Topic 12T86, 1963).

375   Lloyd, *Folk Song in England*, 316.

376   Harker, *One for the Money*, 150.

377   A. L. Lloyd, *Come All Ye Bold Miners: Ballads and Songs of the Coalfields* (London: Lawrence and Wishart, 1978), 11.

378   Ibid.

379   Ibid., 20.

380   Fielding, *The Labour Party*, 5.

381   Ibid., 258.

382   W. R. Garside, *The Durham Miners 1919–1960* (London: George Allen & Unwin Ltd., 1971), 388.

383   Jenkins, 'Bevan's Fight', 247.

384   Garside, *The Durham Miners*, 389.

385   Clegg, *A History of British Trade Unions*, 345.

386   W. Hamish Fraser, *A History of British Trade Unionism 1700–1998* (London: Macmillan, 1999), 227.

387   Garside, *The Durham Miners*, 414.

388   Ibid., 469.

389   Ibid., 488.

390   David Howell, '"Shut Your Gob!": Trade Unions and the Labour Party, 1945–64', in eds. McIlroy et al., *The Postwar Compromise*, 137; Garside, *The Durham Miners*, 486–9.

391   Charles Kernot, *British Coal: Prospecting for Privatization* (Cambridge: Woodhead Publishing Ltd., 1993), 66–7; Fraser, *A History of British Trade Unionism*, 227.

392   Ferdynand Zweig, *Men in the Pits* (London: Victor Gollancz, 1948), quoted in Morgan, *Labour in Power*, 158–61.

393   Quoted in Garside, *The Durham Miners*, 389.

394   Martin Bulmer, 'Politics in County Durham: Introduction', in ed. Martin Bulmer, *Mining and Social Change: Durham County in the Twentieth Century* (London:

Croom Helm, 1978), 91. Durham was the first English county to elect a Labour majority, in 1919. The Northeast had always been a traditionally 'safe haven' for Labour, with the help of the National Union of Mineworkers. Not surprisingly, the Attlee Labour government had a particularly strong relationship with the unions, with the peak of workers' support for the party coming in 1950–51 (Howell, 'Shut Your Gob!', 121–3; 132).

395 Howell, "Shut Your Gob!", 137–8.
396 Jenkins, 'Bevan's Fight', 247.
397 Kernot, *British Coal*, 66.
398 Garside, *The Durham Miners*, 486–7.
399 Ibid., 487–8.
400 Norman Emery, *The Coalminers of Durham* (Stroud: Sutton Publishing, 1992), 115.
401 John Hughes, 'The Nation's Coal', *New Left Review* 1, No. 2 (March–April 1960), 50.
402 Ron Rooney, 'Changing Times', in eds. Terry Austrin et al., *But the World Goes on the Same: Changing Times in Durham Pit Villages* (Whitley Bay: Erdesdun, 1979), 38.
403 Ibid., 37.
404 'For Miners – One Burning Question', *Newcastle Journal* (22 August 1968), 2.
405 'Miners Storm to Success', *Newcastle Journal* (1 October 1968), 5.
406 Michael Jamieson, 'Despair That Drove the Miners to Blackpool', *Newcastle Journal* (1 October 1968), 6. Notably, Lee had previously been associated with Centre 42.
407 The programme consisted of two episodes, broadcast in January and May, 1964. It was later re-broadcast on BBC Radio Durham. Transcripts available at the BBC Written Archive.
408 'Songs of the Durham Miners', British Library Sound Archive, A. L. Lloyd Collection, 1CDR0002717 (Recorded 19 August 1963, Red Lion Pub, Birtley, Durham).
409 BBC Written Archive, transcript for *Songs of the Durham Miners*.
410 Ibid.
411 Ibid.
412 The recording was done in the Elliotts' kitchen by Peggy Seeger and Ewan MacColl over three sessions during the summer of 1961. MacColl and Seeger also recorded several other tapes of the Elliotts, in which they discuss life in Birtley, life in the pit and their musical heritage. These are contained on the British Library's Elliotts of Birtley Tapes 1–10, most of which were recorded in 1961 and 1962. British Library Sound Archive, Ewan MacColl and Peggy Seeger Collection, 1CDR0001296 (C102/29-31); 1CDR0001298 C102/33; 1CDR0001298 C102/34; 1CDR0001298 C102/35; 1CDR0001300 C102/38; 1CDR0001299 C102/36.
413 John Makepeace, 'Treats from Tyneside', *Sing* 7 (1962), 11.
414 Ibid.
415 Michael Yates, 'Review: Jack Elliott', *Folk Music Journal* 2 (1970), 68.
416 Ibid.
417 Hester Barron, *The 1926 Miners' Lockout: Meanings of Community in the Durham Coalfield* (Oxford: Oxford University Press, 2010), 15.
418 Arthur, *Bert*, 170.
419 MacColl and Seeger, sleeve notes for *The Elliotts of Birtley: A Musical Portrait of a Durham Mining Family* (FW3565, 1962).
420 Handle, 'Industrial Folk Music', *English Dance and Song* (New Year 1966), 6.

421   It is worth noting that Seeger and MacColl often received praise from other
      revivalists for their note-writing abilities, especially in their roles as collectors. *Sing*
      editor Eric Winter, reviewing an LP of songs by the fisherman Sam Larner, *Now
      Is the Time for Fishing* (Folkways FG3507), wrote that 'Ewan MacColl and Peggy
      Seeger have done a better job of presentation than I have ever seen. The notes
      are masterly. The man, the singer, the village (Winterton), the music, the singing
      style – all are detailed with analytical quotations from the tunes of the songs. There
      can be no doubt that this is the way to record a traditional singer. The notes are
      scholarly but never dry, authoritative but not dogmatic.' ('**DISC**USSION: Larner
      and Teacher', *Sing* 6 (January 1962), 50).

422   *Ashington Post*, 'The Elliot Family Present a Tribute to Jack' (17 July 1969).

423   'A Note on Jack Elliott', University of Newcastle Archive, Sid Chaplin Papers, SC
      1/5/7 (dated 26 June 1969).

424   In *Songs of the Durham Miners*, Lloyd spoke of the importance of Nova Scotia
      as a bridge between mining and musical traditions of Canada, the United States
      and Britain: 'One of the main swapping-posts for miners' songs is the Glace Bay
      coalfield in Nova Scotia, where many English and Scottish colliers migrated and
      met miners from the anthracite industry of Pennsylvania and the bituminous pits
      of the Appalachians. We've been able to trace the route of British pit songs to Glace
      Bay, and of American songs via Nova Scotia to Durham and East Fife, through the
      reminiscences of miners' families.' (Transcript, BBC Written Archive).

425   Jock Purdon, *Songs of the Durham Coalfield* (Chester-le-Street: Pit Lamp Press,
      1977), 13.

426   Ibid.

427   Lord Robens was presented with a copy of *Jack Elliott of Birtley* in July, 1969, during
      a visit to the Northumberland NCB headquarters at Ashington (Newcastle *Journal*,
      'Record of Miner's Life', 17 July 1969). The article noted that more than 1,000 copies
      of the LP had been sold to date, requiring a re-pressing. Another story, in the
      Ashington Post, noted that Robens, on accepting the gift, said: 'This whole industry
      has a very long and very honoured history but as we move to the end of this
      century, the old pit village feelings are about to disappear and mining communities
      are not isolated any more.' The article went on to state, 'The NCB chairman said
      Jack Elliott captured the family associations in mining life, when even the pit was
      called "She". Something which cannot be captured today.' (*Ashington Post*, 'The
      Elliott Family Present a Tribute to Jack' 17 July 1969).

428   Purdon, *Songs*, 5–6.

429   This song was printed in the January 1962 issue of *Sing* (volume 6, page 49).
      Other pit elegies included 'Cheer Up, Lads' and 'Lament for Albert'. Durham
      native and former pitman Dave Douglass included an unattributed song about
      the disappointments many felt regarding the realities of nationalization, written
      in 'the closing weeks' of Wardley Colliery's life. Lines in the song included: 'We
      have survived the great sweeping hand of Robens and his gang,/To each and every
      gaffer's trick we stood firm to the man /And now the wage is just worthwhile, bad
      fate does us befall/For the only face that has our hopes has hit a great white wall.'
      (Dave Douglass, 'The Durham Pitman', in ed. Raphael Samuel, *Miners, Quarrymen
      and Saltworkers* (London: Routledge & Kegan Paul, 1977), 209).

430   Sedley, 'The Folk Laureates', 29.

431   A. L. Lloyd, 'Review: *Songs for the Sixties*', *Sing* 6 (1962), 82–3.

432   Ibid.

433   Ibid.
434   Harker, *One for the Money*, 177–8.
435   Ibid.
436   Ibid., 180.
437   Purdon, *Songs*, 5.

Chapter 4

438   Winter, 'Dublin – By Dominic', *Sing* 6, No. 4 (December 1961), 32.
439   Winter, 'Tees-Tyne Tops and Trads', *Sing* 7, No. 4 (January–February 1963), 39.
440   Eds. Colls and Lancaster, *Geordies*, 1.
441   Benedict Anderson, *Imagined Communities: Reflections on the Origins and Spread of Nationalism* (London: Verso, 1983), 133.
442   Cecil Sharp, *English Folk Songs: Some Conclusions*, 4th ed. (East Ardsley, Yorkshire: EP Publishing, 1965), 1.
443   Ibid., 4.
444   Ibid., 164.
445   Ibid., 173.
446   Jane S. Becker, *Selling Tradition: Appalachia and the Construction of an American Folk, 1930–1940* (Chapel Hill: University of North Carolina Press, 1998), 5.
447   Ed. Maud Karpeles, *English Folk Songs from the Southern Appalachians, Collected by Cecil J. Sharp, Comprising two hundred and seventy-three Songs and Ballads with nine hundred and sixty-eight Tunes, Including thirty-nine Tunes Contributed by Olive Dame Campbell*, Vol. 1 (London: Oxford University Press, 1932), xii. These figures are the total of both volumes of this work. The original volume (1916) comprised 122 songs.
448   Ibid., xv.
449   Sharp, 'Introduction', in ibid., xxxvii.
450   Pickering and Green, 'Towards a Cartography', 5.
451   Andrew R. L. Cayton and Susan E. Gray, 'The Story of the Midwest: An Introduction', in eds. Andrew R. L. Cayton and Susan E. Gray, *The Identity of the American Midwest: Essays on Regional History* (Bloomington: Indiana University Press, 2001), 5.
452   John Allen, Doreen Massey and Allen Cochrane, *Rethinking the Region* (New York: Routledge, 1998), 9; 11.
453   Ibid., 29.
454   Ibid., 82.
455   Eds. Colls and Lancaster, *Geordies*, xv.
456   Cayton and Gray, 'The Story of the Midwest', 4.
457   MacColl, 'The Singer and the Audience', 18.
458   Woods, *Folk Revival*, 77.
459   Jed Esty, *Shrinking Island: Modernism and National Culture in England* (Princeton, NJ: Princeton University Press, 2004), 7.
460   Conekin, *Autobiography*, 33; 130.
461   Ibid., 31.
462   MacColl, speaking at the Berkeley Folk Festival (Workshop II, recorded 1 July 1960, 9:30 am). American Folklife Center, Library of Congress (AFS 19, 451 LWO 12, 960).

463   Sydney Carter, 'Faith, Doubt and Folksong', *Sing* 8, No. 3 (April 1965), 8.

464   Woods, *Folk Revival*, 78.

465   MacKinnon, *British Folk Scene*, 67.

466   Keegan, 'Money No Object', 14.

467   Sid Chaplin, 'The "Tyneside Sound,"' *The Guardian* (16 November 1963), 14. This small mention of Handle's professionalization is not insignificant, although Chaplin seems more proud than unnerved by Handle's success – many others, notably historians such as Harker, have held the opposite view.

468   Ibid. Chaplin's description of the Beatles revealed both a deep distrust of rock 'n' roll and a grudging respect for the band's magnetic appeal: 'There was a bit of blessed Liverpool nasal in their patter; but the "Merseyside Sound" turned out to be only the slave trade getting a belated revenge on the port and the people … With their narrow, conventional range, the Beatles are splendid performers. Like the bull dancers of Crete they live in the teeth of time … Listen to the words. Get that beat. Then watch those faces.'

469   Ibid.

470   Ibid.

471   Makepeace, 'Treats from Tyneside', 11.

472   'Owdham' Edge is a colloquial pronunciation of Oldham Edge – a well-known vantage point from which can be seen, according to the sleeve notes, 'on the one hand, a great vista of industry and endless rows of terraced houses, and on the other, the wild moors of the Pennines.' (Anon., liner notes for *'Owdham' Edge: Popular Song and Verse from Lancashire*, 12T204, 1970).

473   Ibid.

474   Ibid.

475   Ibid.

476   Ibid.

477   Ibid.

478   Lesley Boardman, sleeve notes for *Deep Lancashire: Songs and Ballads of the Industrial North-West* (12T188, 1968).

479   Sleeve notes for *'Owdham' Edge*.

480   Stephen Sedley, 'A Singer's Notebook: You've Got to Have Roots', *Sing* 8, No. 4 (July 1965), 4–5.

481   Ibid.

482   Transcript for *A Ballad Hunter Looks at Britain*. BBC Written Archive.

483   Ruth Finnegan, *The Hidden Musicians: Music-Making in an English Town* (Middletown, CT: Wesleyan University Press, 2007), 67–8.

484   Tams also wrote for the magazine *Melody Maker*, and worked for Radio Derby in its earliest days.

485   John Tams, *Millennium Memory Bank* interview (Radio Derby), British Library Sound Archive, C900/03060-61 (Recorded 22 December 1998).

486   Ibid.

487   Laing, *Representations of Working-Class Life*, 163.

488   Ibid.

489   Barron, *Lockout*, 5.

490   Handle, 'Industrial Folk Music', 9.

491   Kenny, *First New Left*, 92. Charles Taylor argued in ULR that socialism could be defined as 'a claim that men can find a solution, that they can build an industrial society without alienation, that they can recreate meaningful social bonds without

tyranny and a reversion to the closed society …. The recovery of participation in cultural life cannot therefore be a simple question of shortening hours so that enough time and energy is left after work, or one simply of proliferating the means to such participation. It involves also re-acquiring the ability to participate.' (Taylor, 'Alienation and Community', *Universities and Left Review* 1, No. 5 (Autumn 1958), 11–12).

492   Svetlana Boym, *Common Places: Mythologies of Everyday Life in Russia* (Cambridge, MA: Harvard University Press, 1994), 284.

493   Frith, 'Youth and Music', 18.

494   Jon Pareles, 'Pete Seeger, Songwriter and Champion of Folk Music, Dies at 94', *New York Times* (28 January 2014).

495   Anthony P. Cohen, *The Symbolic Construction of Community* (London: Tavistock, 1985), 15; 118.

496   Students for a Democratic Society, *Port Huron Statement* (New York: Students for a Democratic Society, the Student Department of the League for Industrial Democracy, 1964).

497   Robert Colls, 'When We Lived in Communities: Working-Class Culture and Its Critics', in eds. Colls and Richard Rodger, *Cities of Ideas: Civil Society and Urban Governance in Britain, 1800–2000* (Aldershot: Ashgate, 2004), 284.

498   Barron, *Lockout*, 10.

499   Ibid., 11–12.

500   Bourke, *Working-Class Cultures*, 137.

501   Ewan MacColl and Peggy Seeger, sleeve notes for *The Elliotts of Birtley*.

502   Ibid.

503   Robert Colls, *The Collier's Rant: Song and Culture in the Industrial Village* (London: Croom Helm, 1977), 17.

504   Colls, 'Born-Again Geordies', 3.

505   Rooney, 'Changing Times', 40.

506   Colls, 'When We Lived in Communities', 307.

Chapter 5

507   Sinfield, *Literature, Politics, and Culture*, 191–2.

508   Black, 'Sheep May Safely Gaze', 29; Savage, 'Sociology, Class and Male Manual Work Cultures', 25.

509   Barnard, *On the Radio*, 29.

510   Hoggart, *Uses of Literacy*, 222–3; 170.

511   Ross McKibbin, *Classes and Cultures: England 1918–1951* (Oxford: Oxford University Press, 1998), 390.

512   Ibid., 391.

513   Brocken, *British Folk Revival*, 40; 44.

514   Bernard Porter, *Britain, Europe, and the World, 1850–1986: Delusions of Grandeur* (London: George Allen & Unwin, 1987), 114. There is a vast literature on Americanization as a global phenomenon. See, for instance: Eds. Reinhold Wagnleitner and Elaine Tyler May, '*Here, There and Everywhere': The Foreign Politics of American Popular Culture* (Hanover and London: University Press of New England, 2000); Reinhold Wagnleitner, *Coca-Colonization and the Cold War:*

The Cultural Mission of the United States in Austria after the Second World War (Durham: The University of North Carolina Press, 1994); Howard L. Malchow, *Special Relations: The Americanization of Britain?* (Stanford, CA: Stanford University Press, 2011); Eds. R. Laurence Moore and Maurizio Vaudagna, *The American Century in Europe* (Ithaca, NY: Cornell University Press, 2003); Donald Sassoon, *The Culture of the Europeans: From 1800 to the Present* (London: Harper Collins, 2006); Victoria De Grazia, *Irresistible Empire: America's Advance Through Twentieth-Century Europe* (Cambridge, MA: The Belknap Press, 2005); Ed. C.W.E. Bigsby, *Superculture: American Popular Culture and Europe* (Bowling Green, OH: Bowling Green University Popular Press, 1975).

515   Malchow, *Special Relations*, 2.
516   Sassoon, *One Hundred Years of Socialism*, 196.
517   Sinfield, *Literature, Politics and Culture*, 156. The EFDSS's Douglas Kennedy, on a visit to New York in 1961, reported via the *New York Times*, that 'there is a thriving interest in American folk music in Britain, where the young generation regards the guitar and banjo as "symbols of liberation."' (Quoted in Robert Shelton, 'British Traditionalist: A White-Haired, Tweedy and Tireless Proponent of English Folk Song', *New York Times* (15 October 1961), XII).
518   Eds. A. L. Lloyd and Ralph Vaughan Williams, *The Penguin Book of English Folk Songs* (Harmondsworth, Middlesex: Penguin, 1959), 7.
519   Raymond Williams, *Britain in the Sixties: Communications* (Harmondsworth, Middlesex: Penguin, 1962), 74–5.
520   Wilfred Pickles, quoted in Ibid., 185.
521   Barnard, *On the Radio*, 27.
522   Ibid.
523   Ibid., 28.
524   Ibid., 29.
525   Ibid., 36.
526   Brocken, *British Folk Revival*, 23.
527   Alan Lomax, 'Skiffle', in ed. Ronald D. Cohen, *Alan Lomax Selected Writings, 1934–1997* (New York: Routledge, 2003), 137.
528   Nuttall, *Bomb Culture*, 42.
529   Colin Harper, *Dazzling Stranger: Bert Jansch and the British Folk and Blues Revival* (London: Bloomsbury, 2007), 32.
530   Transcript for *Ballads and Blues* program 'The Big City', BBC Written Archive, N2/5, Ballads and Blues General Material.
531   Ibid.
532   Media release for *Ballads and Blues*, in Ibid.
533   Ibid.
534   Lloyd, *Folk Song in England*, 396.
535   Pete Frame, *Restless Generation: How Rock Music Changed the Face of 1950s Britain* (London: Rogan House, 2007), 106.
536   Ibid., 106–7.
537   Ibid.
538   Sweers, *Electric Folk*, 214.
539   John Hasted, 'A Singer's Notebook: Woody Guthrie', *Sing* 5, No. 1 (September 1959), 11.
540   Ibid.
541   Ibid.

542 Charles Parker, 'Memo to Head of Features at the BBC', subject 'AMERICAN FOLK STYLE INSTRUMENTALISTS', BBC Written Archive, RCONT1 Peggy Seeger Artist File I, dated 14 July1958 (1956–62).

543 Ibid.

544 Ibid.

545 Ibid.

546 MacColl, 'Preface', sleeve notes for *Two-Way Trip* (1961).

547 Kenneth Blower, 'Mailbag: Vogue', *Melody Maker* (January 1963), 16.

548 Chris Roberts, 'If You Want to Get Ahead, Get an Accent', *Melody Maker* (22 June 1963), 9.

549 McKibbin, *Classes and Cultures*, 511.

550 MacKinnon, *The British Folk Scene*, 27.

551 Ibid., 68.

552 Neil Spencer, 'Ewan MacColl: The Godfather of Folk Who Was Adored – and Feared', The *Guardian* (25 January 2015).

553 Woods, *Folk Revival*, 57; Sweers, *Electric Folk*, 37–8.

554 Lee Marshall, 'Bob Dylan: Newport Folk Festival, July 25, 1965', in ed. Ian Inglis, *Performance and Popular Music: History, Place and Time* (Burlington: Ashgate, 2006), 20.

555 Lydia Fish, 'A Singer's Notebook: Too Much Imitation American', *Sing* 7, No. 4 (January–February 1963), 45. For his part, Bob Dylan – when asked by an English music journalist – argued against the rigidly structured English folk clubs, stating: 'It's the people who ... live by the rules, who cause all the trouble. Life is too small – it's too much one world – to worry about it if a man sings something his grandfather couldn't have sung. If an English singer is happy singing a Southern US ballad, I'd rather see him happy than see him doing something else and being unhappy. I don't like seeing people unhappy. Authenticity? I know authentic folk music when I hear it ... [b]ut what difference does it make?' (Max Jones, Interview with Bob Dylan, *Melody Maker*, (23 May 1964, 12)).

556 Ewan MacColl, *Journeyman: An Autobiography* (Manchester: Manchester University Press, 2009), 278–9.

557 Ibid.

558 Ibid.

559 Ibid., 279.

560 Mike Seeger, 'A Contemporary Folk Music Aesthetic', *Sing Out!* 16, No. 1 (February–March 1966), 61.

561 Dallas, 'Focus on MacColl', 23.

562 Harper, *Dazzling Stranger*, 31.

563 MacColl, 'Preface'.

564 British Library Sound Archive, Revival Singers 24, 1CDR0001662 C102/223 (Recorded 9 May 1967).

565 Anthea Joseph, 'Dovetailing into the Tradition on Tyneside', *Sing* 6, No. 5 (January 1962), 48.

566 Ibid.

567 Ibid.

568 Ibid.

569 MacKinnon, *British Folk Scene*, 28.

570 Peggy Seeger claimed, 'The recent revival of folk music in America, a revival of which I am a product, has included practically every kind of song and instrument,

from Anglo-American ballads (in both their Anglo and their American variants) to jazz, from Yiddish to Spanish music. I sing, for the most part, those songs with a British origin or influence, although there are and have been many factors at work, both consciously and otherwise, changing this music into something distinctively American'. (Peggy Seeger, 'Self Portrait', *Sing* 4, No. 6 (October 1958), 67–8).

571   Brocken, *British Folk Revival*, 37; Bean, *Singing from the Floor*, 103.
572   Robert Colls, *Identity of England* (Oxford: Oxford University Press, 2002), 368.
573   Sydney Carter, 'Going American?', *English Dance and Song* (Special New Year Issue, 1961), 20.
574   Ibid.
575   Ibid.
576   Seeger, 'Johnny Appleseed, Jr', 58.

Chapter 6

577   Marqusee, *Wicked Messenger*, 39.
578   Ibid., 40.
579   The term 'culture industry' is used here to describe the phenomenon of art as commodity.
580   Andrew Hunt, 'How New Was the New Left?' in eds. John MacMillian and Paul Buhle, *The New Left Revisited* (Philadelphia, PA: Temple University Press, 2003), 151.
581   Williams, *Culture and Society*, 74.
582   Hoggart, quoted in Sandbrook, *Never Had It So Good*, 183.
583   Theodor Adorno, 'The Culture Industry Reconsidered', in ed. J. M. Bernstein, *The Culture Industry: Selected Essays on Mass Culture* (London: Routledge, 2001), 85.
584   Andreas Huyssen, *After the Great Divide: Modernism, Mass Culture, Postmodernism* (Bloomington: Indiana University Press, 1986), 7.
585   Theodor Adorno and Max Horkheimer, *Dialectic of Enlightenment* (London: Verso, 1979), 35.
586   Ibid., 121.
587   Ibid., 126.
588   Ibid.
589   Theodor Adorno, 'On the Fetish Character of Music and the Regression of Listening', in ed. Bernstein, *The Culture Industry*, 26.
590   Theodor Adorno, *Aesthetic Theory*, eds. Gretel Adorno and Rolf Tiedemann (London: Routledge, 1984), 297.
591   Adorno, 'On the Fetish Character', 86.
592   Jacques Attali, *Noise: The Political Economy of Music* (Manchester: Manchester University Press, 1985), 3–4.
593   Adorno, 'On the Fetish Character', 27.
594   Sydney Carter, 'Pop Goes the Folk Song', *English Dance and Song* (Special New Year Issue 1961), 3.
595   Carter, 'Going Commercial?' in ibid., 8.
596   Dick Weissman, *Which Side Are You On? An Inside History of the Folk Music Revival in America* (New York: Continuum, 2006), 97.

597 Dominic Behan, *Sing* 8, No. 5 (November 1965), 23. Behan was undoubtedly referring to Dylan here, who by that point had admitted that he had written songs like 'The Times They Are A-Changing' because he knew they would sell.
598 Adorno, 'On the Fetish Character', 31.
599 MacKinnon, *British Folk Scene*, 73.
600 Ed Badeaux, 'The Spectacle Moves On', *Sing Out!* 17, No. 4 (August–September 1967), 10.
601 Ibid.
602 Gruning, *Millennium Folk*, xii.
603 Attali, *Noise*, 68.
604 John Avery Lomax, *Cowboy Songs and Other Frontier Ballads* (New York: Macmillan, 1938), xix.
605 Again, it was the father-son team of John and Alan Lomax that allowed for this revolution in folk collection. Their famous road trip across the Southern United States – during which they 'discovered' Leadbelly – has become the stuff of folklore in its own right.
606 Philip V. Bohlman, *The Study of Folk Music in the Modern World* (Bloomington: Indiana University Press, 1988), 14.
607 Ibid., 125.
608 Frith, *Sociology of Rock*, 10.
609 1960 Berkeley Folk Festival workshop I (30 June 1960) Library of Congress American Folklife Center. AFC 1979/071, AFS 19,450-19, 454, AFS 19,450 LWO 12,960.
610 For instance, in Scorsese's *No Direction Home*, Bob Dylan and Dave Van Ronk tell the story of Dylan's first album, when he recorded Van Ronk's version of 'House of the Rising Sun'. Van Ronk admitted that after Dylan recorded the song, he could no longer perform it because 'after he recorded it, I had to stop singing the song, because people were constantly accusing me of having got the song from Bobby's record.' However, Van Ronk got some measure of revenge when Dylan had to stop performing the song after Eric Burdon and the Animals recorded it. Donald Sassoon also recounted the story: 'In 1962 Dylan recorded "The House of the Rising Sun," a folk song probably originating in seventeenth-century England, first recorded by the black bluesman Texas Alexander in 1928. Then, in 1964, the songs was recorded in Britain by the group the Animals, using electric guitars. After hearing it in England Dylan told a friend in New York: "My God, ya oughtta hear what's going on there. Eric Burdon, the Animals, ya know? Well, he is doing 'House of the Rising Sun' in rock. Rock! It's fuckin' wild! Blew my mind." Thus culture travels.' (Sassoon, *The Culture of the Europeans*, 1348).
611 'Berkeley Folk Festival, Workshop II', Library of Congress American Folklife Center, AFS 19, 451 LWO 12, 960 (1 July 1960).
612 Ibid.
613 Fowke, quoted in Baggelaar and Milton, *Folk Music*, 134.
614 Alan Lomax, 'The Folkniks', *Selected Writings*, 195.
615 Filene, *Romancing the Folk*, 3.
616 Michael Francis Scully, 'American Folk Music Revivalism, 1965–2005', PhD dissertation (University of Texas at Austin, 2005), 38.
617 Brocken, *British Folk Revival*, 10.
618 John Cohen, 'In Defense of City Folk Singers', *Sing Out!* 9, No. 1 (Summer 1959), 32.

619 Marshall McLuhan, *Understanding Media: The Extensions of Man* (New York: Signet, 1964), 19.

620 Ibid.

621 Ed. Richard M. Dorson, *Folklore and Fakelore: Essays toward a Discipline of Folk Studies* (Cambridge, MA: Harvard University Press, 1976), 62.

622 Pickering and Green, 'Towards a Cartography', 1.

623 Karpeles wrote on that occasion that these changes had completely wiped out native cultural traditions: 'The fact is that life in the mountains has been completely revolutionized during the last twenty to twenty-five years and it is no longer the folk song collector's paradise that it once was ... Judged from a material point of view the standard of life is certainly higher but there seems to be a corresponding loss on the artistic and cultural plane.' Some of the more insidious culprits in this process were, Karpeles asserted, the 'electric washing machine and other products of modern progress,' and the radio – 'the arch-enemy ... of folk song.' Maud Karpeles, 'A Return Visit to the Appalachian Mountains', *Journal of the EFDSS* 6, No. 3 (December 1951), 77–8.

624 Pickering and Green, 'Towards a Cartography', 2.

625 Frith, *Sociology of Rock*, 185.

626 Ibid., 186.

627 MacKinnon, *British Folk Scene*, 71.

628 Pete Seeger, *The Incompleat Folksinger*, ed. Joe Metcalf Schwartz (Lincoln: University of Nebraska Press, 1972; 1992), 11.

629 Arlo Guthrie, quoted in Baggelaar and Milton, *Folk Music*, 134.

630 Ken Lindsay, 'Finding's Stealing', *Sing* 6, No. 12 (August 1962), 128.

631 *Ethnic* 1, 3.

632 A. L. Lloyd, 'Who Owns What in Folk Song?', *Sing Out!* 12, No. 2 (February–March 1962), 41.

633 Ibid., 43. At the BBC, hundreds of thousands of memos were exchanged regarding a singer or group's copyright fees for various folk programmes. The files on Ewan MacColl reveal that he was routinely paid copyright fees for his work as a collector and presenter with the broadcaster – both for original broadcasts, and then for subsequent re-broadcasts. For example, he was given a fee of £126 for a repeat of the Radio Ballads programme 'Singing the Fishing' in 1967, for which he had 'collected' the material. In 1974, both MacColl and Peggy Seeger were paid for use of 'source material' from the Radio Ballads programme 'The Big Hewer' to the tune of 200 pounds, as well as another 150 pounds for use of 'additional material, musical arrangements and links'. (Receipt for fees payable as part of repeat broadcast of Singing the Fishing, BBC Written Archives, RCONT18 Copyright – James H. Miller File 2, 1963–67).

634 Sydney Carter, 'A Reel of Recording Tape', *Sing* 5, No. 2 (December 1959), 36.

635 Bill Eitman, 'The Controversy Goes On: Copyrights and Collectors', *Sing Out!* 10, No. 3 (October–November, 1960), 20.

636 Ibid.

637 Ibid., 22.

638 MacColl, 'The Singer and the Audience', 17.

639 John Kirkham, 'Mailbag: Folk or Fake?', *Melody Maker* (12 January 1963), 20.

640 Steve Benbow, 'Folk or Fake?: Hands Off Hall and MacGregor', *Melody Maker* (19 January 1963), 12.

641 Paul Marsden, 'Mailbag: Folk or Fake?', *Melody Maker* (12 January 1963), 20.

642   Sydney Carter, in ibid.

643   Carter, 'Going Commercial?', 8.

644   Berkeley Folk Festival 1960, Workshop I, Library of Congress, American Folklife Center (30 June 1960).

645   Ibid.

646   Ibid.

647   Ibid.

648   The Critics Group was established in the mid-1960s. Sessions were sometimes recorded, with the help of BBC producer Charles Parker. A typical class involved five to six invited folk singers, with MacColl and Seeger running workshops on various aspects of folk song performance and style. For more on the Critics Group, see Bean, *Singing from the Floor*, 111.

649   Critics Group 19, British Library Sound Archive, Ewan MacColl and Peggy Seeger Collection, NP95750R (Recorded September 1972).

650   Ibid.

651   Ibid.

652   Ibid.

653   1960 Berkeley Folk Festival, Workshop II, Library of Congress, American Folklife Center, AFS 19, 451 LWO 12, 960 (1 July 1960). See also Bean, *Singing from the Floor*, 150–5.

654   Woods, *Folk Revival*, 83.

655   Ibid., 90.

656   Armstrong and Pearson, 'Some Reflections', 95.

657   Seeger, 'A Contemporary Folk Esthetic', 61.

658   Mike Aston, 'A Singer's Notebook: A Federation of Clubs', *Sing* 8, No. 1 (1964), 17.

659   Ibid.

660   'Poet Dylan – Bob!' *Melody Maker* (1 August 1964), 15.

661   MacColl, quoted in 'The Folksong Revival: A Symposium', *New York Folklore Quarterly* 19, No. 2 (June 1963).

662   Ibid.

663   Colls, *Identity of England*, 370–1.

664   Ewan MacColl, quoted in Dallas, 'Focus on MacColl', 23.

665   Ibid. It is worth noting that, at least publicly, Dylan had only good things to say about MacColl. In an interview done by *Melody Maker*'s Max Jones in May, 1964, he stated that, while he didn't know 'anything about the folk scene here, nothing at all', he knew 'some of your writers and actors. Who in particular? Ewan MacColl. I like his writing very much.' (*Melody Maker* (23 May 1964), 12).

666   Michael Dewdney-York, quoted in Keegan, 'Money No Object', 14.

667   Dan Atherden, 'Mailbag: Dylan Is Only Using his Freedom', *Melody Maker* (5 February 1966), 16.

668   Jenny Leigh, 'Mailbag: Yes, Dylan's Times They Are a-Changin', *Melody Maker* (28 May 1966), 26.

669   Josh Dunson, *Freedom in the Air: Song Movements of the '60s* (New York: International Publishers, 1965), 75.

670   Ibid., 111.

671   Written following the 1964 Newport Folk Festival – at which Dylan had appeared wearing sunglasses and a leather jacket – Silber cautioned the young singer: It seems as though lots of people are thinking and talking about you these days. I read about you in *Life* and *Newsweek* and *Time* and *The Saturday Evening Post* and

Mademoiselle and *Cavalier* and all such, and I realize that, all of a sudden, you have become a pheenom [sic], a VIP, a celebrity. A lot has happened to you in these past two years, Bob – a lot more than most of us thought possible. I'm writing this letter now because some of what has happened is troubling me … You seem to be in a different kind of bag now, Bob – and I'm worried about it. I saw at Newport how you had somehow lost contact with people. It seemed to me that some of the paraphernalia of fame were getting in your way. You travel with an entourage now – with good buddies who are going to laugh when you need laughing and drink wine with you and insure your privacy – and never challenge you to face everyone else's reality again. (Silber, 'Open Letter to Bob Dylan', *Sing Out!* 14, No. 5 (January 1965)).

672   Ibid.
673   Simon Frith, 'Art vs. Technology: The Strange Case of Popular Music', *Taking Popular Music Seriously*, 79.
674   On the surviving audio, it appears that Dylan responded by saying 'I don't believe you, you're a liar!' before defiantly telling his band to play the following song, 'Like a Rolling Stone', 'fucking loud!'
675   Dylan, quoted in Dir. Martin Scorsese, *No Direction Home: Bob Dylan* (2004).
676   Ibid.
677   Ibid.
678   Ibid.
679   Ibid.
680   'Dylan Brings Own Group', *Melody Maker* (30 April 1966), 4.
681   Max Jones, 'Will the Real Bob Dylan Please Stand Up?', *Melody Maker* (14 May 1966), 3.
682   Vincent Doyle, 'Dublin – Night of the Big Letdown', in ibid.
683   Alan Twelftrees, 'With Bob On Our Side', *Sing* 9, No. 1 (February 1966), 8.
684   Badeaux, 'The Spectacle Moves On', 10.
685   Ibid.
686   Ibid., 11.

Conclusions

687   Gruning, *Millennium Folk*, xvii.
688   Steve Strauss, 'A Romance on Either Side of Dada', in ed. Greil Marcus, *Rock and Roll Will Stand* (Boston, MA: Beacon Press, 1969), 124.
689   Michael Watts, 'The Call and Response of Popular Music: The Impact of American Pop Music in Europe', in Bigsby, *Superculture*, 131.

Bibliography

ARCHIVE COLLECTIONS

WASHINGTON, DC: LIBRARY OF CONGRESS (AMERICAN FOLKLIFE CENTER, ARCHIVE OF FOLK CULTURE)

Berkeley Folk Festival 1960 AFC 1979/071 AFS 19,450-19,454

- AFS 19,450 LWO 12,960 Workshop I (30 June 1960, 2 pm)
- Peggy Seeger, Ewan MacColl.
- AFS 19,451 LWO 12,960 Workshop II (1 July 1960, 9:30 am)
- Peggy Seeger, Ewan MacColl.
- AFS 19,452 LWO 12,960 Workshop III (1 July 1960 2 pm).
- AFS 19,453 LWO 12,960 Workshop III (1 July 1960 2 pm) and Workshop IV (2 July 1960 12 pm).

Newport Folk Festival 1963/1966 AFC 1999/001
NPR Broadcast – 'Fifty Years of Folk Festivals'. AFS 19355 A & B
Richard Reuss Folk Music Ephemera Collection. AFC 1983: 005. Boxes 1–15

WASHINGTON, DC: SMITHSONIAN INSTITUTION (THE FOLKWAYS COLLECTION)

Folkways Collection Podcast

- 'Music and the Winds of Change: The Women's Movement'. Broadcast 25 July 2006.
- 'Subterranean Homesick Blues Part I'. Broadcast 25 July 2006.

GATESHEAD AND NEWCASTLE, CO. DURHAM: FOLK ARCHIVE RESOURCE NORTH EAST, NEWCASTLE UNIVERSITY SPECIAL COLLECTIONS

Sid Chaplin Papers

- 'A Note on Jack Elliott.' SC 1/5/7.
- 'A Pattern of Durham Villages.' SC 1/2/14.

CAVERSHAM, READING, UK: BBC WRITTEN ARCHIVE

As I Roved Out

- R46/26/1 'AS I ROVED OUT' File 1A, 1953–54.
- R46/26/2 'As I Roved Out' File 1B, 1955.
- R46/598/1 'As I Roved Out' File 2, 1956.

Folk Music

- R19/2, 140/1 Folk Music.
- R34/1322 Policy – International Broadcasting Arrangements – Folk Music 1966–72.
- R46/658/1 REC GEN Folk Music 1952–59.

Lloyd, A.L.

- RCONT12 A. L. Lloyd Artist File III – 1963–67 (WAC box 463).
- RCONT12 Albert Lancaster Lloyd Contributors-Artist File V – 1968–72.
- RCONT18 A. L. Lloyd Copyright File IV – 1963–69.

Lomax, Alan

- R46/309/2 Alan Lomax File II – 1947–51.
- R46/701/2 Alan Lomax File V – 1956–60.
- R46/701/3 Alan Lomax – 1961–64.

MacColl, Ewan

- RCONT1 Miller, James H. (Ewan MacColl) Artist File I – 1935–62.
- RCONT1 Miller, James H. (Ewan MacColl) Copyright File I – 1937–62.
- RCONT18 Copyright James H. Miller (Ewan MacColl) File II – 1963–67.
- RCONT18 Copyright James H Miller (Ewan MacColl) File III – 1968–69.
- RCONT20 Ewan MacColl.

Seeger, Peggy

- RCONT1 Peggy Seeger Artist File I – 1956–62.
- RCONT15 Peggy Seeger Artist File IV – 1973–82.
- RCONT20 Peggy Seeger.

LONDON, UK: THE BRITISH LIBRARY SOUND ARCHIVE

A.L. Lloyd Collection

- Industrial Song I & II. 1CDR0002719.
- Songs of Durham Miners/Fresh Thoughts on Industrial Song. 1CDR0002717 (includes live recordings from the Red Lion Public House, in Birtley, co. Durham dated 8.19.1963).

- The Bridge Inn, Newcastle (Live Recording dated 3.15.1971). 1CDR0002723.
- The Grey Cock Public House, Birmingham (Live Recording dated 3.9.1971). 1CDR0002722.

Ewan MacColl and Peggy Seeger Collection

- Critics Group 19 and 20 (Recorded 23.9.1964). 1CDR0001662 C102/223.
- Critics Group 46 (1) (Recorded 28.9.1965). C102/313/1.
- Critics Group 46 (2) and 47 (Recorded 28.9.1965). C102/314.
- Critics Group 90 (Recorded 28.9.1965). 1CDR0002162 C102/318.
- Critics Group 92 (Recorded 14.9.1966). 1CDR0002161 C102/320.
- Hannah Short and Brussel Smith (Recorded 23.10.1961). C102/25 1CDR0001294-1300.
- Recollections on Creation of Radio Ballads BBC Recording, 'Singing the English' with Charles Parker. (Recorded 1961–62). 1CDR0001754-1755 S1 BD2-BD7 NSA.
- *Revival Singers 9*. 1CDR0001625 C102/208.
- *Revival Singers 10*. 1CDR0001625 C102/209.
- *Revival Singers 10*. 1CDR0001755 C102/358.
- *Revival Singers 24*. 1CDR0001662 C102/223.
- *Revival Singers 24*. 1CDR0001670 C102/247.
- *Singing the English 2*. 1CDR0001705 C102/309.
- *The Elliotts of Birtley* Tapes 1, 2 and 3. 1CDR0001296 C102/29-31.
- *The Elliotts of Birtley* Tape 5. 1CDR0001298 C102/33.
- *The Elliotts of Birtley* Tape 6. 1CDR0001298 C102/34.
- *The Elliotts of Birtley* Tape 7. 1CDR0001298 C102/35.
- *The Elliotts of Birtley* Tape 8. 1CDR0001299 C102/36.
- *The Elliotts of Birtley* Tape 10. 1CDR0001300 C102/38.

Topic Records Archive

- Anti-Racism Concert, Birmingham (Recorded Live 4.16.1963). 1CDR0004901.
- Leon Rosselson and Stan Kelly. 1CDR0004225.
- Peggy Seeger. 1CDR0004222.
- *Songwriters* (Proposed LP, never released. Recorded 1965). 1CDR0005515.
- Stan Kelly Radio Programme. 1CDR0002108.

BBC Radio Programmes

- *Folk Song Cellar* 1-11. 1LP0151812-1822 (1966).
- *Folk Song Cellar* 14-26. 1LP0151936-1948 (1966).
- *Folk Song Cellar* 27-39. 1LP0152215-2227 (1967).
- *Oral History of Recorded Sound*. Ewan MacColl Interview (June, 1985). C90/76/03 C1.
- *The Song Carriers*, 1-3. 1CDR0002705 C200/231.
- *The Song Carriers*, 11-12. 1CDR0002710 C200/233.

Millennium Memory Bank Collection

- Interview with John Tams. (22 December 1998, BBC Radio Derby) C900/03060-61.
- Interview with Cliff Hall. (27 January 1999, BBC Radio Kent) C900/07564 C1.

COMMERCIAL RECORDINGS

Elliott Family. *The Elliotts of Birtley: A Musical Portrait of a Durham Mining Family*.
Folkways Records (FW3565, 1962).
Elliott, Jack. *Jack Elliott of Birtley: The Songs and Stories of a Durham Miner*. Leader
(Leader Sound, 1969).
MacColl, Ewan, and Peggy Seeger. *Two-Way Trip*. Folkways Records (FW8755, 1961).
Ochs, Phil. *There but for Fortune*. Elektra (1965).
Seeger, Peggy. *Different Therefore Equal*. Folkways Records (FW08561, 1979).
Various Artists. *Deep Lancashire: Songs and Ballads of the Industrial North-West*. Topic
Records (12T188, 1968).
Various Artists. *'Owdham' Edge: Popular Song and Verse from Lancashire*. Topic Records
(12T204, 1970).
Various Artists. *The Iron Muse*. Topic Records (12T86, 1963).

FILM SOURCES

Lerner, Murray. *Festival*. Film. Directed by Murray Lerner. 1967.
Lerner, Murray. *The Other Side of the Mirror: Bob Dylan at the Newport Folk Festival,
1963–1965*. Film. Directed by Murray Lerner. 2007.
Pennebaker, D. A. *Dont Look Back*. Film. Directed by D.A. Pennebaker. 1967.
Scorsese, Martin. *No Direction Home: Bob Dylan*. Film. Directed by Martin Scorsese. 2004.

PRINTED PRIMARY SOURCES

Abrams, Mark. *The Teenage Consumer*. London: London Press Exchange, 1959.
Adorno, Theodor. *Aesthetic Theory*. Gretel Adorno and Rolf Tiedemann, eds. London:
Routledge, 1984.
Adorno, Theodor, Walter Benjamin et al., *Aesthetics and Politics: They Key Texts of the
Classic Debate within German Marxism*. London: Verso, 2007.
Adorno, Theodor. 'On the Fetish Character of Music and the Regression of Listening'. In
The Culture Industry: Selected Essays on Mass Culture. J. M. Bernstein, ed. London:
Routledge, 2001: 26–52.
Adorno, Theodor. *The Culture Industry: Selected Essays on Mass Culture*. J. M. Bernstein,
ed. London: Routledge, 2001.
Adorno, Theodor, and Max Horkheimer. *Dialectic of Enlightenment*. London: Verso, 1979.
Anon. 'Dylan Brings Own Group'. *Melody Maker* (30 April 1966): 4.
Anon. 'Elliot Family Present a Tribute to Jack'. *Ashington Post* (17 July 1969): n.p.
Anon. 'Folk? No Boom Here, Says Dusty Springfield'. *Melody Maker* (14 September 1963): 18.
Anon. 'For Miners – One Burning Question'. *Newcastle Journal* (22 August 1968): 2.
Anon. 'Miners Storm to Success'. *Newcastle Journal* (1 October 1968): 5.
Anon. 'Poet Dylan – Bob!: Review of The Times They Are a-Changin'. *Melody Maker*
(1 August 1964): 15.
Anon. 'Record of Miner's Life'. *Newcastle Journal* (17 July 1969): n.p.
Anon. 'Sunny South Africa'. *Sing* 8, No. 4 (July 1965): 7.

Armstrong, Frankie, and Brian Pearson. 'Some Reflections on the English Folk Revival'. *History Workshop: A Journal of Socialist Historians* 7 (Spring 1979): 95–100.

Aston, Mike. 'A Singer's Notebook: A Federation of Clubs'. *Sing* 8, No. 1 (1964): 17.

Atherden, Dan. 'Mailbag: Dylan Is Only Using His Freedom'. *Melody Maker* (5 February 1966): 16.

Badeaux, Ed. 'The Spectacle Moves On'. *Sing Out!* 17, No. 4 (August–September 1967): 10–14.

Benbow, Steven. 'Focus on Folk: If the Beatles Turned to Folk ...'. *Melody Maker* (11 January 1964): 11.

Benbow, Steven. 'Folk or Fake?: Hands of Hall and MacGregor'. *Melody Maker* (19 January 1963): 12.

Benjamin, Walter. *The Work of Art in the Age of Its Technological Reproducibility and Other Writings on Media*. Cambridge, MA: The Belknap Press, 2008.

Blower, Kenneth. 'Mailbag: Vogue'. *Melody Maker* (January 1963): 16.

Bradbury, Malcolm. *All Dressed Up and Nowhere to Go: The Poor Man's Guide to the Affluent Society*. London: Max Parrish, 1962.

Bridson, D.G. *Prospero and Ariel: The Rise and Fall of Radio, A Personal Recollection*. London: Victor Gollancz Ltd., 1971.

Brunner, John. 'The H-Bomb's Thunder'. In *New English Broadsides: Songs of Our Time from the English Folk Scene*. New York: Oak Publications, 1967: 18.

Campbell, Alex. 'No More War'. *Sing* 8, No. 4 (July 1965): 11.

Campbell, Ian. 'The Sun Is Burning in the Sky'. In *New English Broadsides: Songs of Our Time from the English Folk Scene*. New York: Oak Publications, 1967: 17.

Carter, Sydney. 'A Reel of Recording Tape'. *Sing* 5, No. 2 (December 1959): 36.

Carter, Sydney. 'Faith, Doubt and Folksong'. *Sing* 8, No. 3 (April 1965): 8.

Carter, Sydney. 'Going American? (Interview with Ewan MacColl and Peggy Seeger)'. *English Dance and Song*. Special Issue (1961): 19–20.

Carter, Sydney. 'Going Commercial? (Interview with Steven Benbow)'. *English Dance and Song*. Special Issue (1961): 8–11.

Carter, Sydney. 'Pop Goes the Folk Song'. *English Dance and Song*. Special Issue (1961): 3.

Chambers, Iain. 'A Strategy for Living: Black Music and White Subcultures'. In *Resistance through Rituals: Youth Subcultures in Postwar Britain*. Stuart Hall and Tony Jefferson, eds. London: Unwin-Hyman, 1976: 157–166.

Chaplin, Sid. 'The "Tyneside Sound"'. *The Guardian* (16 November 1963): 14.

Child, Francis James, ed. *The English and Scottish Popular Ballads*. Boston, MA: Houghton Mifflin, 1898 [1882]. Vols. 1–5.

Clarke, John, Stuart Hall, Tony Jefferson and Brian Roberts. 'Subcultures, Cultures and Class: A Theoretical Overview'. In *Resistance through Rituals: Youth Subcultures in Postwar Britain*. Stuart Hall and Tony Jefferson, eds. London: Unwin Hyman, 1976: 9–74.

Cohen, John. 'In Defence of City Folksingers: A Reply to Alan Lomax'. *Sing Out!* 9, No. 1 (Summer 1959): 32–34.

Comfort, Alex. 'Rain in the Forest'. *Sing* 8, No. 4 (July 1965): 10.

Dallas, Karl. 'Focus on MacColl: The MM Folk Correspondent, Karl Dallas, Talks to Ewan MacColl'. *Melody Maker* (September 1965): 23.

Dallas, Karl. 'Seeger Is Here'. *Sing* 6, No. 3 (November 1961): 23.

Dallas, Karl. 'The Notting Hill Murder'. *Sing* 5, No. 1 (September 1959): 15.

Dallas, Karl. 'The Roots of Tradition'. In *The Electric Muse: The Story of Folk into Rock*. Dave Laing, Robin Denselow, Karl Dallas and Robert Shelton, eds. London: Methuen, 1975: 83–136.

Davis, Beryl. *Folk Songs from Spin*. Cheshire: Spin Publications, n.d.

Davis, Beryl. *Folk Songs from Spin 2*. Cheshire: Spin Publications, 1969.

Davis, Beryl. *Folk Songs from Spin 3*. Cheshire: Spin Publications, 1974.

Denselow, Robin. 'Folk-Rock in Britain'. In *The Electric Muse: The Story of Folk into Rock*. Dave Laing, Robin Denselow, Karl Dallas and Robert Shelton, eds. London: Methuen, 1975: 137–176.

Douglass, Dave. 'The Durham Pitman'. In *Miners, Quarrymen and Saltworkers*. History Workshop Series. Raphael Samuel, ed. London: Routledge & Kegan Paul, 1977: 205–296.

Doyle, Vincent. 'Dublin – Night of the Big Letdown'. *Melody Maker* (14 May 1966): 3.

Dunson, Josh. *Freedom in the Air: Song Movements of the '60s*. New York: International Publishers, 1965.

Dunson, Josh. 'The British Revival'. *Sing Out!* 16, No. 3 (July 1966): 44.

Eckersley, Peter. 'Folk-Song without Folk'. *The Guardian* (13 November 1961).

Eitman, Bill. 'The Controversy Goes On: Copyrights and Collectors'. *Sing Out!* 10, No. 3 (October–November 1960): 20–22.

Frayn, Michael. 'Festival'. In *Age of Austerity, 1945–1951*. Michael Sissons and Philip French, eds. London: Hodder and Stoughton, 1963: 319–338.

Friesen, Gordon. 'Songs of Our Time from the Pages of Broadside Magazine'. In *The American Folk Scene: Dimensions of the Folksong Revival*. David A. de Turk and A. Poulin, eds. New York: Dell Publishing Co., 1967: 130–139.

Galbraith, John Kenneth. *The Affluent Society*. London: Hamish Hamilton, 1958.

Glazer, Tom, ed. *Songs of Peace, Freedom, and Protest*. New York: David McKay Company, 1970.

Goldthorpe, John, et al., *The Affluent Worker in the Class Structure*. Cambridge: Cambridge University Press, 1969.

Gosling, Ray. *Sum Total*. London: Faber and Faber, 1962.

Hall, Reg. 'Editorial'. *Ethnic* 1, No. 3 (Summer 1959): 3.

Hall, Reg. 'The Fifties: 1947–1963'. *Root and Branch* 2 (1999): 4.

Hall, Stuart. 'A Sense of Classlessness'. *Universities and Left Review* 1, No. 5 (Autumn 1958): 26–31.

Hall, Stuart. 'Black Diaspora Artists in Britain: Three "Moments" in Postwar History'. *History Workshop Journal* 61 (Spring 2006): 1–24.

Hall, Stuart. 'Editorial'. *New Left Review* 1, No. 1 (January–February 1960): 1–3.

Hall, Stuart, and Tony Jefferson, eds. *Resistance through Rituals: Youth Subcultures in Postwar Britain*. London: Unwin Hyman, 1976.

Hall, Stuart. 'ULR Club at Notting Hill'. *New Left Review* 1, No. 1 (January–February 1960): 71–72.

Handle, Johnny. 'Farewell to the Monty'. *Sing* 6 (January 1962): 49.

Handle, Johnny. 'Industrial Folk Music and Regional Music Hall in the North East I'. *English Dance and Song* (August 1965): 106–107.

Handle, Johnny. 'Industrial Folk Music and Regional Music Hall in the North East II'. *English Dance and Song* (October 1965): 138–141.

Handle, Johnny. 'Industrial Folk Music and Regional Music Hall in the North East III'. *English Dance and Song* (New Year 1966): 6–9.

Hasted, John. 'A Singer's Notebook: Woody Guthrie'. *Sing* 5, No. 1 (September 1959): 11.

Hinton, Sam. 'The Singer of Folk Songs and His Conscience'. *Sing Out!* 7, No. 1 (Spring 1957): 24–26.

Hoggart, Richard. *The Uses of Literacy: Aspects of Working-Class Life, with Special Reference to Publications and Entertainments*. London: Chatto and Windus, 1957.

Holdsworth, Bill. 'Songs of the People'. *New Left Review* 1, No. 1 (January–February 1960): 48–49.

Hughes, John. 'The Nation's Coal'. *New Left Review* 1, No. 2 (March–April 1960): 50–51.

Jameson, Fredric. 'Reflections in Conclusion'. In *Aesthetics and Politics: The Key Texts of Classic Debate within German Marxism*. London: Verso, 2007: 196–213.

Jamieson, Michael. 'Despair that Drove the Miners to Blackpool'. *Newcastle Journal* (1 October 1968).

Jenkins, Peter. 'Bevan's Fight with the B.M.A'. In *Age of Austerity, 1945–1951*. Michael Sissons and Philip French, eds. London: Hodder and Stoughton, 1963: 233–254.

Jones, Max. 'Interview with Bob Dylan'. *Melody Maker* (23 May 1964): 12.

Jones, Max. 'Will the Real Bob Dylan Please Stand Up?' *Melody Maker* (14 May 1966): 3.

Joseph, Anthea. 'A Singer's Notebook: Dovetailing into the Tradition on Tyneside'. *Sing* 6, No. 5 (January 1962): 148.

Joseph, Nathan, and Eric Winter, eds. *New English Broadsides: Songs of Our Time from the English Folk Scene*. New York: Oak Publications, 1967.

Joshi, Shirley. 'Poverty and the Immigrant Worker'. In *Poverty in the Affluent Society: Four Talks on Aspects of Poverty Given at the S.M.A. Weekend School*. Richmond: Dimbleby & Sons Limited, April 1968: 6–8.

Kaneen, John, and David Callister. 'Editorial'. *Folk Review* 1, No. 1 (December 1963): 1.

Kaneen, John, and David Callister. 'Radio Ballads Axed'. *Folk Review* 1, No. 1 (December 1963): 27.

Karpeles, Maud. 'A Return Visit to the Appalachian Mountains'. *Journal of the English Folk Dance and Song Society* 6, No. 3 (December 1951): 77–82.

Karpeles, Maud. *Cecil Sharp: His Life and Work*. London: Routledge and Kegan Paul, 1967.

Karpeles, Maud, ed. *English Folk Songs from the Southern Appalachians, Collected by Cecil J. Sharp, Comprising Two Hundred and Seventy-Three Songs and Ballads with Nine Hundred and Sixty-Eight Tunes, Including Thirty-Nine Tunes Contributed by Olive Dame Campbell*. 2 Vols. London: Oxford University Press, 1932.

Keegan, Victor. 'Money No Object at Festival of Pure Folk'. *The Guardian* (17 July 1965): 14.

Kirkham, John. 'Mailbag: Folk or Fake?'. *Melody Maker* (12 January 1963): 20.

Laing, Dave, with Karl Dallas, Robert Denselow and Robert Shelton. *The Electric Muse: The Story of Folk into Rock*. London: Methuen, 1975.

Laing, Dave, and Richard Newman. *Thirty Years of the Cambridge Folk Festival*. Ely: Music Maker, 1994.

Lamb, Derek. 'The British Music Hall'. *Sing Out!* 15, No. 4 (September 1965): 34.

Latimer, Hugh. 'Skiffle Intelligentsia'. *The Observer* (16 June 1957): 21.

Leigh, Jenny. 'Mailbag: Yes, Dylan's Times They Are a-Changin'. *Melody Maker* (28 May 1966): 26.

Lindsay, Ken. 'Finding's Stealing'. *Sing* 6, No. 12 (August 1962): 128.

Lloyd, A. L. *Come All Ye Bold Miners: Ballads and Songs of the Coalfields*. 2nd ed. London: Lawrence and Wishart, 1978.

Lloyd, A. L. *Folk Song in England*. London: Lawrence and Wishart in Association with the Workers' Music Association, 1967.

Lloyd, A. L. 'Review: Songs for the Sixties'. *Sing* 6 (1962): 82–83.

Lloyd, A. L. *Singing Englishmen: A Feature Programme of Workers' Songs in British Life, Specially Compiled for the Festival of Britain, 1951*. London: Workers' Music Association, 1951.

Lloyd, A. L. 'So You're Interested in Folk Music?' *Sing Out!* 9, No. 3 (Winter 1959–60): 38–42.

Lloyd, A. L. 'The English Folk Song Revival'. *Sing Out!* 12, No. 2 (April–May 1962): 34–37.

Lloyd, A. L, and Ralph Vaughan Williams, eds. *The Penguin Book of English Folk Songs.* Harmondsworth, Middlesex: Penguin, 1959.

Lloyd, A. L. *The Singing Englishman: An Introduction to Folk Song.* London: Workers' Music Association, 1944.

Lloyd, A. L. 'Who Owns What in Folk Song?' *Sing Out!* 12, No. 1 (February–March 1962): 41, 43.

Lomax, Alan. *Folk Song Style and Culture.* Washington, DC: American Association for the Advancement of Science, 1968.

Lomax, Alan. *The Land Where the Blues Began.* London: Methuen, 1993.

MacColl, Ewan. 'Ballad of Ho Chi Minh'. *Sing* 1, No. 3 (1954): 57.

MacColl, Ewan. *Journeyman: An Autobiography.* Manchester: Manchester University Press, 2009.

MacColl, Ewan, ed. *The Shuttle and Cage: Industrial Folk Ballads.* London: Workers' Music Association, 1954.

MacColl, Ewan. 'The Singer and the Audience'. *Sing Out!* 14, No. 4 (September 1964): 16–20.

MacColl, Ewan. 'Why I Am Opening a New Club'. *Sing* 5, No. 4 (August 1961): 65.

MacRae, Donald. 'Letter to the Editor'. *Newcastle Journal* (24 September 1968).

Makepeace, John. 'Treats from Tyneside'. *Sing* 7, No. 1 (September 1962): 11.

Mann, John. 'A Singer's Notebook: Forest Folk at Southampton'. *Sing* 6, No. 8 (April 1962): 85.

Marks, Neil Alan. 'Reliving the "Golden Years" of Folk Music'. *New York Times* (2 November 1980): D23.

Marsden, Paul. 'Mailbag: Folk or Fake?'. *Melody Maker* (12 January 1963): 20

McLuhan, Marshall. *Understanding Media: The Extensions of Man.* New York: Signet, 1964.

McCreary, Edward A. *The Americanization of Europe: The Impact of Americans and American Business on the Uncommon Market.* Garden City, NY: Doubleday, 1964.

Meissner, Hanna H, ed. *Poverty in the Affluent Society.* New York: Harper & Row, 1966.

Miliband, Ralph. 'The Sickness of Labourism'. *New Left Review* 1, No. 1 (January–February 1960): 5–9.

Mills, C. Wright. 'Letter to the New Left'. *New Left Review* 1, No. 5 (September–October 1960): 18–23.

National Youth Campaign for Nuclear Disarmament. *1961 Aldermaston March Leaflet.* London: Columbia Printers, 1961.

Northern Arts Association, *The Constitution for the North Eastern Association for the Arts.* Newcastle: Northern Arts Association, 1962.

Northern Arts Association. *Notes of Guidance on the Formation of a Regional Arts Association.* Newcastle: Northern Arts Association, 1968.

Nuttall, Jeff. *Bomb Culture.* London: MacGibbon & Kee, 1968.

Phine, Ken. 'For the Record'. *Sing* 6, No. 1 (September 1961): 8.

Phine, Ken. 'For the Record: Thin Time for Folk-Disc Fans'. *Sing* 6, No. 6 (February 1962): 64.

Purdon, Jock. *Songs of the Durham Coalfield.* Chester-le-Street: Pit Lamp Press, 1977.

Redgrave, Vanessa. 'Hanging on a Tree'. *Sing* 8, No. 1 (1964): 6.

Roberts, Alan, and Earl Robinson. 'Black and White'. *Sing* 5, No. 1 (September 1959): 19.

Roberts, Chris. 'If You Want to Get Ahead, Get an Accent'. *Melody Maker* (22 June 1963): 9.

Roberts, Chris. 'Suddenly – It's Folk!: Special Report from New York'. *Melody Maker* (24 August 1963): 13.

Rooney, Ron. 'Changing Times'. In *But the World Goes on the Same: Changing Times in Durham Pit Villages*. Terry Austrin et al., eds. Whitley Bay: Erdesdun, 1979: 36–41.

Rosselson, Leon. 'Battle Hymn of the New Socialist Party'. In *New English Broadsides: Songs of Our Time from the English Folk Scene*. Nathan Joseph and Eric Winter, eds. New York: Oak Publications, 1967: 70.

Sedley, Stephen. 'A Singer's Notebook: You've Got to Have Roots'. *Sing* 8, No. 4 (July 1965): 4–5.

Sedley, Stephen. 'The Folk Laureates'. *The Observer* (5 July 1964): 29.

Seeger, Mike. 'A Contemporary Folk Esthetic'. *Sing Out!* 16, No. 1 (February–March 1966): 59–61.

Seeger, Mike. 'Self Portrait'. *Sing* 4, No. 6 (October 1958): 67–68.

Seeger, Peggy, and Ewan MacColl. 'Jimmy Wilson'. *Sing* 5, No. 1 (September 1959): 18.

Seeger, Pete. 'From Aldermaston to London – They Walked and Sang for Peace'. *Sing Out!* 10, No. 4 (December–January 1960–61): 14–18.

Seeger, Pete. 'Johnny Appleseed, Jr.' *Sing Out!* 12, No. 1 (February–March 1962): 58–59.

Seeger, Pete. *The Incompleat Folksinger*. Joe Metcalf Schwartz, ed. Lincoln: University of Nebraska Press, 1972; 1992.

Sharp, Cecil. *English Folk Songs: Some Conclusions*. 4th ed. East Ardsley, Yorkshire: EP Publishing, 1965.

Shelton, Robert. 'Britain's Folk Scene: "Skiffle Craze" to Clubs in Pubs"'. *New York Times* (6 March 1966): X23.

Shelton, Robert. 'British Traditionalist: A White-Haired, Tweedy and Tireless Proponent of English Folk Song'. *New York Times* (15 October 1961): XII.

Shelton, Robert. 'Britons Enliven Fete at Newport'. *New York Times* (25 July 1965): 68.

Shelton, Robert. 'Folkways on Record'. *Sing* 5, No. 4 (August 1961): 69–70.

Silber, Irwin. 'Ewan MacColl – Folksinger of the Industrial Age'. *Sing Out!* 9, No. 3 (Winter 1959–60): 7–9.

Silber, Irwin. 'Open Letter to Bob Dylan'. *Sing Out!* 14, No. 5 (November 1964).

Silber, Irwin. 'Peggy Seeger – The Voice of America in Folksong'. *Sing Out!* 12, No. 3 (Summer 1962): 4–8.

Silber, Irwin. 'The Size of the Revival'. In 'The Folk Music Revival: A Symposium'. *New York Folklore Quarterly* 19, No. 3 (June 1963): 109.

Students for a Democratic Society. *Port Huron Statement*. New York: Students for a Democratic Society, the Student Department of the League for Industrial Democracy, 1964.

Taylor, Charles. 'Alienation and Community'. *Universities and Left Review* 1, No. 5 (Autumn 1958): 11–12.

Thompson, E. P. *The Making of the English Working Class*. London: Gollancz, 1965.

Towner, G. D. 'Letter to the Editor'. *The Observer* (22 September 1963): 38.

Topic Records. *Topic Songbook: Words and Melodies of Old and New Favourites*. Festival Special. London: Worker's Music Association, 1951.

Twelftrees, Alan. 'With Bob on Our Side'. *Sing* 9, No. 1 (February 1966): 8.

Wickenden, James. *Colour in Britain: Issued under the Auspices of the Institute of Race Relations*. London: Oxford University Press, 1958.

Williams, Raymond. *Britain in the Sixties: Communications*. Harmondsworth, Middlesex: Penguin, 1962.

Williams, Raymond. *Culture and Society*. London: The Hogarth Press, 1987.

Winter, Eric. 'Advertisement for Birtley Folk Club'. *Sing* 7, No. 1 (September 1962): 6.

Winter, Eric. 'Appeal for funding'. *Sing* 1, No. 6 (March–April 1955): 115.

Winter, Eric. 'Ballads and Bravery'. *Manchester Guardian* (16 October 1958): 7.

Winter, Eric. 'Dublin – By Dominic'. *Sing* 6, No. 4 (December 1961): 32.

Winter, Eric. 'DISCUSSION: A Record Year'. *Sing* 5, No. 1 (September 1959): 13.

Winter, Eric. 'DISCUSSION: Larner and Teacher'. *Sing* 6 (January 1962): 50.

Winter, Eric. 'DISCUSSION: Scotland the Brave'. *Sing* 5, No. 2 (December 1959): 39.

Winter, Eric. 'Focus on Folk: TV Trip for New York Folknik'. *Melody Maker* (19 January 1963): 12.

Winter, Eric. 'Focus on Folk'. *Melody Maker* (16 March 1963).

Winter, Eric. 'Focus on Folk'. *Melody Maker* (6 July 1963): 16.

Winter, Eric. 'Focus on Folk'. *Melody Maker* (31 August 1963): 16.

Winter, Eric. 'Seeger on Trial'. *Sing* 5, No. 4 (August 1961): 63.

Winter, Eric. 'Sing Mission Statement'. *Sing* 1, No. 1 (May–June 1954): 1.

Winter, Eric. 'Tees-Tyne Tops and Trads'. *Sing* 7, No. 4 (January–February 1963): 39.

Winter, Eric. 'Unaccompanied Singers: A Singer's Notebook'. *Sing* 6, No. 4 (December 1961): 34.

Woodley, Bruce. 'Seeker Bruce on the New York Scene'. *Melody Maker* (29 January 1966): 9.

Workers' Music Association, The *Pocket Song Book*. London: Lawrence and Wishart, 1948.

Yates, Michael. 'Review: Jack Elliott'. *Folk Music Journal* 2 (1970): 68.

Zweig, Ferdynand. *The Worker in an Affluent Society: Family Life and Industry*. London: Heinemann, 1961.

SECONDARY SOURCES

Allen, John, Doreen Massey and Allen Cochrane. *Rethinking the Region*. New York: Routledge, 1998.

Anderson, Benedict. *Imagined Communities: Reflections on the Origin and Spread of Nationalism*. London: Verso, 1983.

Arthur, Dave. *Bert: The Life and Times of A. L. Lloyd*. London: Pluto Press, in association with the EFDSS, 2012.

Attali, Jacques. *Noise: The Political Economy of Music*. Manchester: Manchester University Press, 1985.

Austrin, Terry, et al., eds. *But the World Goes on the Same: Changing Times in Durham Pit Villages*. Whitley Bay: Erdesdun, 1979.

Baggelaar, Kristin, and Donald Milton. *Folk Music: More than a Song*. New York: Thomas Y. Crowell Company, 1979.

Barnard, Stephen. *On the Radio: Music Radio in Britain*. Milton Keynes: Open University Press, 1989.

Baron, Robert, and Nicholas R. Spitzer, eds. *Public Folklore*. Washington: Smithsonian Institution Press, 1992.

Barron, Hester. *The 1926 Miners' Lockout: Meanings of Community in the Durham Coalfield*. Oxford: Oxford University Press, 2010.

Bean, J. P. *Singing from the Floor: A History of British Folk Clubs*. London: Faber & Faber, 2014.

Becker, Jane S. *Selling Tradition: Appalachia and the Construction of an American Folk, 1930–1940*. Chapel Hill: University of North Carolina Press, 1998.

Bendix, Regina. *In Search of Authenticity: The Formation of Folklore Studies*. Madison: University of Wisconsin Press, 1997.

Beynon, Huw, and Terry Austrin. *Masters and Servants: Class and Patronage in the Making of a Labour Organisation. The Durham Miners and the English Political Tradition*. London: Rivers Oram Press, 1994.

Bigsby, C.W. E. *Superculture: American Popular Culture and Europe*. Bowling Green, OH: Bowling Green University Popular Press, 1975.

Black, Lawrence, et al., eds. *Consensus or Coercion?: The State, the People and Social Cohesion in Postwar Britain*. Cheltenham: New Clarion Press, 2001.

Black, Lawrence. *Redefining British Politics: Culture, Consumerism and Participation, 1954–70*. Hampshire: Palgrave Macmillan, 2010.

Black, Lawrence. "'Sheep May Safely Gaze": Socialists, Television and the People in Britain, 1949–1964'. In *Consensus or Coercion?: The State, the People and Social Cohesion in Postwar Britain*. Lawrence Black et al., eds. Cheltenham: New Clarion Press, 2001: 28–48.

Black, Lawrence. *The Political Culture of the Left in Affluent Britain, 1951–64: Old Labour, New Britain?* Hampshire: Palgrave Macmillan, 2003.

Bohlman, Philip V. *The Study of Folk Music in the Modern World*. Bloomington: Indiana University Press, 1988.

Bourke, Joanna. *Working-Class Cultures in Britain, 1890–1960: Gender, Class and Ethnicity*. London: Routledge, 1994.

Boyes, Georgina. *The Imagined Village: Culture, Ideology, and the English Folk Revival*. Manchester: Manchester University Press, 1993.

Boym, Svetlana. *Common Places: Mythologies of Everyday Life in Russia*. Cambridge, MA: Harvard University Press, 1994.

Bragg, Billy. *Roots, Radicals and Rockers: How Skiffle Changed the World*. London: Faber & Faber, 2017.

Brake, Michael. *Comparative Youth Culture: The Sociology of Youth Cultures and Youth Subcultures in America, Britain and Canada*. London: Routledge, 1985.

Brocken, Michael. *The British Folk Revival, 1944–2002*. Burlington, VT: Ashgate, 2003.

Bronner, Simon J. *American Folklore Studies: An Intellectual History*. Kansas: University Press of Kansas, 1986.

Brooke, Stephen, ed. *Reform and Reconstruction: Britain after the War, 1945–51*. Documents in Contemporary History Series. Manchester: Manchester University Press, 1995.

Buhle, Paul, and John McMillian, eds. *The New Left Revisited*. Philadelphia, PA: Temple University Press, 2003

Bulmer, Martin, ed. *Mining and Social Change: Durham County in the Twentieth Century*. London: Croom Helm, 1978.

Bulmer, Martin. 'Politics in County Durham: Introduction'. In *Mining and Social Change: Durham County in the Twentieth Century*. Martin Bulmer, ed. London: Croom Helm, 1978: 91–94.

Bulmer, Martin. 'Social Structure and Social Change in the Twentieth-Century'. In *Mining and Social Change: Durham County in the Twentieth Century*. Martin Bulmer, ed. London: Croom Helm, 1978: 15–48.

Bulmer, Martin. 'The Character of Local Politics'. In *Mining and Social Change: Durham County in the Twentieth Century*. Martin Bulmer, ed. London: Croom Helm, 1978: 128–149.

Campbell, Alan, Nina Fishman and John McIlroy, eds. *The Postwar Compromise: British Trade Unions and Industrial Politics 1945–64*. 2nd ed. Monmouth, Wales: The Merlin Press, 2007.

Campbell, Alan, Nina Fishman and John McIlroy. 'The Postwar Compromise: Mapping Industrial Politics, 1945–64'. In *The Postwar Compromise: British Trade Unions and Industrial Politics 1945–64*. Alan Campbell, Nina Fishman and John McIlroy, eds. 2nd ed. Monmouth, Wales: The Merlin Press, 2007: 69–113.

Cantwell, Robert. *When We Were Good: The Folk Revival*. Cambridge, MA: Harvard University Press, 1996.

Cayton, Andrew R. L., and Susan E. Gray, eds. *The Identity of the American Midwest: Essays on Regional History*. Bloomington: Indiana University Press, 2001.

Clarke, Peter, and Clive Trebilcock, eds. *Understanding Decline: Perceptions and Realities of British Economic Performance*. Cambridge: Cambridge University Press, 1997.

Clegg, Hugh Armstrong. *A History of British Trade Unions since 1889. Vol. 3: 1934–1951*. Oxford: Clarendon, 1994.

Cohen, Anthony P., ed. *Symbolising Boundaries: Identity and Diversity in British Cultures*. Manchester: Manchester University Press, 1986.

Cohen, Anthony P. *The Symbolic Construction of Community*. London: Tavistock, 1985.

Cohen, Ronald D., ed. *Alan Lomax Selected Writings, 1934–1997*. New York: Routledge, 2003.

Cohen, Ronald D., ed. *'Wasn't That a Time!' Firsthand Accounts of the Folk Music Revival. American Folk Music and Musicians*, No. 1. Metuchen, NJ: Scarecrow Press, 1995.

Colls, Robert. 'Born-Again Geordies'. In *Geordies: Roots of Regionalism*. Robert Colls and Bill Lancaster, eds. Newcastle-Upon-Tyne: Northumbria University Press, 2005: 1–33.

Colls, Robert, and Bill Lancaster, eds. *Geordies: Roots of Regionalism*. Newcastle-Upon-Tyne: Northumbria University Press, 2005.

Colls, Robert. *Identity of England*. Oxford: Oxford University Press, 2002.

Colls, Robert. *The Collier's Rant: Song and Culture in the Industrial Village*. London: Croom Helm, 1977.

Colls, Robert, ed. 'When We Lived in Communities: Working-Class Culture and Its Critics'. In *Cities of Ideas: Civil Society and Urban Governance in Britain, 1800–2000*. Robert Colls and Richard Rodger, eds. Aldershot: Ashgate, 2004: 283–307.

Conekin, Becky. *The Autobiography of a Nation: The 1951 Festival of Britain*. Manchester: Manchester University Press, 2003.

Daunton, Martin J. *Wealth and Welfare: An Economic and Social History of Britain 1851–1951*. Oxford: Oxford University Press, 2007.

Davis, Fred. *Yearning for Yesterday: A Sociology of Nostalgia*. New York: Free Press, 1979.

De Grazia, Victoria. *Irresistible Empire: America's Advance through Twentieth-Century Europe*. Cambridge, MA: The Belknap Press, 2005.

De Turk, David A., and A. Poulin Jr., eds. *The American Folk Scene: Dimensions of the Folksong Revival*. New York: Dell Publishing Co., 1967.

Dorson, Richard M., ed. *Folklore and Fakelore: Essays toward a Discipline of Folk Studies*. Cambridge, MA: Harvard University Press, 1976.

Dworkin, Dennis. *Cultural Marxism in Postwar Britain: History, the New Left, and the Origins of Cultural Studies*. Durham, NC: Duke University Press, 1997.

Emery, Norman. *Banners of the Durham Coalfield*. Stroud: Sutton Publishing, 1998.

Emery, Norman. *The Coalminers of Durham*. Stroud: Sutton Publishing, 1992.

English, Richard, and Michael Kenny. 'British Decline or the Politics of Declinism?' Review Article. *British Journal of Politics and International Relations* 1, No. 2 (June 1999): 252–266.

Esty, Jed. *A Shrinking Island: Modernism and National Culture in England*. Princeton, NJ: Princeton University Press, 2004.

Eyerman, Ron, and Andrew Jamison. *Music and Social Movements: Mobilizing Traditions in the Twentieth Century*. Cambridge: Cambridge University Press, 1998.

Feldman, David, and Jon Lawrence. 'Introduction: Structures and Transformations in British Historiography'. In *Structures and Transformations in Modern British History: Essays for Gareth Stedman Jones*. David Feldman and Jon Lawrence, eds. Cambridge: Cambridge University Press, 2011: 1–23.

Fielding, Steven, ed. *The Labour Party: 'Socialism' and Society since 1951*. Manchester: Manchester University Press, 1997.

Fielding, Steven. '"To Make Men and Women Better than They Are": Labour and the Building of Socialism'. In *Labour's Promised Land? Culture and Society in Labour Britain 1945–51*. Jim Fryth, ed. London: Lawrence and Wishart, 1995: 16–27.

Filene, Benjamin. *Romancing the Folk: Public Memory & American Roots Music*. Chapel Hill: University of North Carolina Press, 2000.

Finnegan, Ruth H. *The Hidden Musicians: Music-Making in an English Town*. Middletown, CT: Wesleyan University Press, 2007.

Fowler, David. *Youth Culture in Modern Britain, c. 1920–c. 1970: From Ivory Tower to Global Movement – A New History*. Hampshire: Palgrave-Macmillan, 2008.

Frame, Pete. *The Restless Generation: How Rock Music Changed the Face of 1950s Britain*. London: Rogan House, 2007.

Fraser, W. Hamish. *A History of British Trade Unionism 1700–1998*. London: Macmillan, 1999.

Fraser, W. Hamish. *Taking Popular Music Seriously: A Collection of Essays*. Hampshire: Ashgate, 2007.

Fraser, W. Hamish. *The Sociology of Rock*. London: Constable, 1978.

Fraser, W. Hamish. 'Youth and Music'. In *Taking Popular Music Seriously: A Collection of Essays*. Hampshire: Ashgate, 2007: 1–30.

Frith, Simon. *Performing Rites: On the Value of Popular Music*. Cambridge, MA: Harvard University Press, 1996.

Fyrth, Jim, ed. *Labour's Promised Land? Culture and Society in Labour Britain 1945–51*. London: Lawrence and Wishart, 1995.

Garside, W. R. *The Durham Miners 1919–1960*. London: George Allen & Unwin Ltd., 1971.

Gilroy, Paul. *'There Ain't No Black in the Union Jack': The Cultural Politics of Race and Nation*. London: Hutchison, 1987.

Gruning, Thomas R. *Millennium Folk: American Folk Music since the Sixties*. Athens: The University of Georgia Press, 2006.

Habermas, Jürgen. *The Structural Transformation of the Public Sphere: An Inquiry into a Category of Bourgeois Society*. Trans. Thomas Burger. London: Polity Press, 1989.

Harker, Dave. *Fakesong: The Manufacture of British 'Folksong', 1700 to the Present Day*. Maidenhead, UK: Open University Press, 1985.

Harker, Dave. *One for the Money: Politics and Popular Song*. London: Hutchison, 1980.

Harper, Colin. *Dazzling Stranger: Bert Jansch and the British Folk and Blues Revival.* London: Bloomsbury, 2000.

Hobsbawm, Eric. *The Invention of Tradition.* Cambridge: Cambridge University Press, 1992.

Hobsbawm, Eric. *The Jazz Scene.* London: Weidenfeld and Nicolson, 1989.

Howarth, Janet. 'Classes and Cultures in England after 1951: The Case of Working-Class Women'. In *Classes, Cultures, and Politics: Essays on British History for Ross McKibbin.* Oxford: Oxford University Press, 2011: 85–101.

Howell, David. '"Shut Your Gob!": Trade Unions and the Labour Party, 1945–64'. In *The Postwar Compromise: British Trade Unions and Industrial Politics 1945–64.* Alan Campbell, Nina Fishman and John McIlroy, eds. 2nd ed. Monmouth, Wales: The Merlin Press, 2007: 117–144.

Hunt, Andrew. 'How New Was the New Left?' In *The New Left Revisited.* John McMillian and Paul Buhle, eds. Philadelphia, PA: Temple University Press, 2003: 139–155.

Huyssen, Andreas. *After the Great Divide: Modernism, Mass Culture, Postmodernism.* Bloomington: Indiana University Press, 1986.

Inglis, Ian, ed. *Performance and Popular Music: History, Place and Time.* Burlington, VT: Ashgate, 2006.

Irwin, Colin. 'Aldermaston – Birth of the British Protest Song'. *The Guardian* (10 August 2008).

Jones, Gareth Stedman. *Languages of Class: Studies in English Working Class History, 1832–1982.* Cambridge: Cambridge University Press, 1983.

Judt, Tony. *Postwar: A History of Europe since 1945.* New York: Penguin, 2005.

Kenny, Michael. *The First New Left: British Intellectuals after Stalin.* London: Lawrence and Wishart, 1995.

Kernot, Charles. *British Coal: A Prospecting for Privatization.* Cambridge: Woodhead Publishing Ltd., 1993.

Kumar, Krishan. *The Making of English National Identity.* Cambridge: Cambridge University Press, 2003.

Laing, Stuart. *Representations of Working-Class Life 1957–1964.* London: Macmillan, 1986.

Laybourn, Keith. *The Rise of Labour: The British Labour Party 1890–1979.* London: Edward Arnold, 1988.

Lin, Chun. *The British New Left.* Edinburgh: Edinburgh University Press, 1993.

MacKinnon, Niall. *The British Folk Scene: Musical Performance and Social Identity.* Buckingham: Open University Press, 1994.

Malchow, Howard L. *Special Relations: The Americanization of Britain?.* Stanford, CA: Stanford University Press, 2011.

Marqusee, Mike. *Wicked Messenger: Bob Dylan and the 1960s.* New York: Seven Stories Press, 2005.

Marshall, Lee. 'Bob Dylan: Newport Folk Festival, July 25, 1965'. In *Performance and Popular Music: History, Place and Time.* Ian Inglis, ed. Burlington, VT: Ashgate, 2006: 16–27.

Marwick, Arthur. 'Images of the Working Class since 1930'. In *The Working Class in Modern British History: Essays in Honour of Henry Pelling.* Jay Winter, ed. Cambridge: Cambridge University Press, 1983: 215–231.

McIlroy, John, Nina Fishman and Alan Campbell, eds. *British Trade Unions and Industrial Politics. Vol. 2: The High Tide of Trade Unionism, 1964–79.* Aldershot: Ashgate, 1999.

McKay, George. *Circular Breathing: The Cultural Politics of Jazz in Postwar Britain*. Chapel Hill: Duke University Press, 2006.

McKibbin, Ross. *Classes and Cultures: England 1918–1951*. Oxford: Oxford University Press, 1998.

McKibbin, Ross. *Parties and People: England 1914–1951*. Oxford: Oxford University Press, 2010.

Mitchell, Gillian. *The North American Folk Music Revival: Nation and Identity in the United States and Canada, 1945–1980*. Burlington, VT: Ashgate, 2007.

Morgan, Kenneth O. *Labour in Power 1945–1951*. Oxford: Oxford University Press, 1984.

Nairn, Tom. *The Break-Up of Britain: Crisis and Neo-Nationalism*. London: New Left Books, 1981.

Panitch, Leo, and Colin Leys. *The End of Parliamentary Socialism: From New Left to New Labour*. 2nd ed. London: Verso, 2001.

Pareles, Jon. 'Pete Seeger, Songwriter and Champion of Folk Music, Dies at 94'. *New York Times* (28 January 2014). http://www.nytimes.com/2014/01/29/arts/music/pete-seeger-songwriter-and-champion-of-folk-music-dies-at-94.html. [Accessed 28 January 2014].

Paul, Kathleen. *Whitewashing Britain: Race and Citizenship in the Postwar Era*. Ithaca, NY: Cornell University Press, 1997.

Peterson, Richard A. *Creating Country Music: Fabricating Authenticity*. Chicago: The University of Chicago Press, 1997.

Pickering, Michael, and Tony Green, eds. *Everyday Culture, Popular Song and the Vernacular Milieu*. Milton Keynes: Open University Press, 1987.

Pickering, Michael, and Tony Green. 'Towards a Cartography of the Vernacular Milieu'. In *Everyday Culture: Popular Song and the Vernacular Milieu*. Michael Pickering and Tony Green, eds. Milton Keynes: Open University Press, 1987: 1–38.

Porter, Bernard. *Britain, Europe, and the World, 1850–1986: Delusions of Grandeur*. 2nd ed. London: George Allen & Unwin, 1987.

Pugh, Martin. *Speak for Britain! A New History of the Labour Party*. London: The Bodley Head, 2010.

Reid, Alastair J. 'The Dialectics of Liberation: The Old Left, the New Left and the Counter-Culture'. In *Structures and Transformations in Modern British History: Essays for Gareth Stedman Jones*. David Feldman and Jon Lawrence, eds. Cambridge: Cambridge University Press, 2011: 261–280.

Reuss, Richard A., and JoAnne C. Reuss. *American Folk Music and Left-Wing Politics, 1927–1957*. American Folk Music and Musicians Series, No. 4. Lanham, NJ: Scarecrow Press, 2000.

Robinson, Emily. 'Radical Nostalgia, Progressive Patriotism and Labour's English Problem'. *Political Studies Review* 14, No. 3 (2016): 378–387.

Samuel, Raphael, ed. *Miners, Quarrymen and Saltworkers*. History Workshop Series. London: Routledge & Kegan Paul, 1977.

Sandbrook, Dominic. *Never Had It So Good: A History of Britain from Suez to the Beatles*. London: Abacus, 2006.

Sassoon, Donald. *One Hundred Years of Socialism: The West European Left in the Twentieth Century*. New York: The New Press, 1996.

Savage, Mike. 'Sociology, Class and Male Manual Work Cultures'. In *British Trade Unions and Industrial Politics. Vol. 2: The High Tide of Trade Unionism, 1964–79*. John McIlroy, Nina Fishman and Alan Campbell, eds. Aldershot: Ashgate, 1999: 23–42.

Schwarz, Bill. "'The Only White Man in There": The Re-Racialisation of England, 1956–1968'. *Race and Class* 38, No. 1 (1996): 65–78.

Shaw, Eric. *The Labour Party since 1945: Old Labour, New Labour*. Oxford: Blackwell, 1996.

Sinfield, Alan. *Literature, Politics, and Culture in Postwar Britain*. Berkeley: University of California Press, 1989.

Sinfield, Alan. 'The Government, the People and the Festival'. In *Labour's Promised Land? Culture and Society in Labour Britain 1945–51*. Jim Fyrth, ed. London: Lawrence and Wishart, 1995: 181–196.

Sissons, Michael, and Philip French, eds. *Age of Austerity, 1945–1951*. London: Hodder and Stoughton, 1963.

Spencer, Neil. 'Ewan MacColl: Godfather of Folk Who Was Adored – and Feared'. The *Guardian* (25 January 2015).

Stedman Jones, Gareth. *Languages of Class: Studies in English Working Class History, 1832–1982*. Cambridge: Cambridge University Press, 1983.

Stekert, Ellen. 'Cents and Nonsense in the Urban Folksong Movement: 1930–1966'. In *Folklore and Society: Essays in Honour of Benj. A. Botkin*. Bruce Jackson, ed. Hatboro, PA: Folklore Associates, 1966: 153–168.

Sutcliffe, Anthony. *An Economic and Social History of Western Europe since 1945*. London: Longman, 1996.

Sweers, Britta. *Electric Folk: The Changing Face of English Traditional Music*. New York: Oxford University Press, 2003.

Taylor, Richard. *Against the Bomb: The British Peace Movement 1958–1965*. Oxford: Clarendon Press, 1988.

Thorpe, Andrew. *A History of the British Labour Party*. 2nd ed. New York: Palgrave, 2001.

Wagnleitner, Reinhold. *Coca-Colonization and the Cold War: The Cultural Mission of the United States in Austria after the Second World War*. Trans. Diana M. Wolf. Chapel Hill: The University of North Carolina Press, 1994.

Wagnleitner, Reinhold, and Elaine Tyler May, eds. *'Here, There, and Everywhere': The Foreign Politics of American Popular Culture*. Hanover: University Press of New England, 2000.

Waller, P. J. 'Democracy and Dialect, Speech and Class'. In *Politics and Social Change in Modern Britain: Essays Presented to A. F. Thompson*. P. J. Waller, ed. New York: St. Martin's Press, 1987: 1–33.

Waller, P. J, ed. *Politics and Social Change in Modern Britain: Essays Presented to A. F. Thompson*. New York: St. Martin's Press, 1987.

Waters, Chris. *British Socialists and the Politics of Popular Culture, 1884–1914*. Manchester: Manchester University Press, 1990.

Watts, Michael. 'The Call and Response of Popular Music: The Impact of American Pop Music in Europe'. In *Superculture: American Popular Culture and Europe*. C.W. E. Bigsby, ed. Bowling Green, OH: Bowling Green University Popular Press, 1975: 123–139.

Webster, Wendy. *Englishness and Empire 1939–1965*. Oxford: Oxford University Press, 2005.

Weissman, Dick. *Which Side Are You On? An Inside History of the Folk Music Revival in America*. New York: Continuum, 2006.

Winter, Jay, ed. *The Working Class in Modern British History: Essays in Honour of Henry Pelling*. Cambridge: Cambridge University Press, 1983.

Woods, Fred. *Folk Revival: The Rediscovery of a National Music*. Poole: Blandford, 1979.

Index

Abrams, Mark 64–5
    the teenage consumer 64–5
accent 84, 87, 88, 102, 104
    American influence on 102, 104
    as marker of authenticity 87, 88, 102
Adorno, Theodor 112–14
    the culture industry 113–14
    and Max Horkheimer, *Dialectic of
        Enlightenment* 112–13
    on popular music 112–13
    theories on mass Culture 113
Americanization 14, 23, 97–100
    and cultural conservatism 14, 98
    in Europe 99–100
    influence on folk music 23, 97–100
Attlee, Clement 44, 46, 70, 98
    first Labour majority 46
    nationalization of coal 70 (*see also*
        nationalization of coal)
    welfare state 44, 46

Baez, Joan 25, 28, 31, 52, 54–5, 124, 135
    n.10
Behan, Dominic 22, 23, 52, 114, 121
    on commercial folk music 114
Birmingham Anti-Racism Concert 59
Bridson, Douglas Geoffrey (D. G.) 27, 33,
    58
    on *My People and Your People* 58
    promotion of folk music on the BBC 33
British Broadcasting Corporation (BBC)
    27, 32–9, 45, 57, 58, 70, 76, 90–1,
    96, 100, 103–4, 116, 131, 142
    alleged Donovan censorship 142 n.160
    American music 100, 104
    Audience Research Department 34
    A Ballad Hunter Looks at Britain 36
    collaboration with A. L. Lloyd 35, 45,
        70, 76 (*see also* Lloyd, A. L.)
    collaboration with Alan Lomax 35–6,
        90 (*see also* Lomax, Alan)

    collaboration with Ewan MacColl
        36, 45, 58, 103 (*see also* MacColl,
        Ewan)
    As I Roved Out 34–5, 116
    Folk Song Cellar 91
    and industrial workers' music 45, 70
    Millennium Memory Bank 57, 90
    My People and Your People 58
    Peggy Seeger Visa 103 (*see also* Seeger,
        Peggy)
    promotion of folk music 27, 32–9, 116
    Radio Ballads 37
    regional programming 91, 96, 131
    The Song Carriers 38
    Songs of the Durham Miners 70, 76

Cambridge Folk Festival 40–1
Campaign for Nuclear Disarmament
    (CND) 44, 51–3
    Aldermaston march 53
    anti-American feeling 53
    development of topical songwriting in
        Britain 51–4
    the New Left 52, 54, 146 n.284
    songs about 53
Carter, Sydney 59, 88, 90, 108, 114,
    119–20, 122
    on accents 88
    on commercialism in folk music 114,
        122
    interview with Ewan MacColl 108
    "A Reel of Recording Tape" 119–20
Centre 42 project 42, 50–1, 71
Child, Francis James 6, 8, 132
class 2, 4, 5, 8, 9, 13, 14, 15, 16, 17, 44, 45,
    46–7, 48–9, 50, 51, 55–6, 60, 61,
    62–5, 66, 67–9, 71, 75, 77–8, 80–2,
    84, 88, 91, 93, 94, 97, 108, 112, 129,
    130, 132. *See also* Hoggart, Richard;
    Zweig, Ferdynand, the affulent
    worker

in context of postwar 'affluence' 15, 47, 50, 61, 62–4, 66
and culture 37, 44, 48, 51, 60, 65, 67, 91, 112
in English society 61, 66, 129, 130, 132
and folk music 2, 8, 9, 14, 16, 17, 44, 51, 61, 65, 67–9, 71, 77–8, 80–2, 84, 88, 94, 108, 112, 129
and Leftist politics and sociology 15, 44, 45, 46–7, 48–9, 50, 65, 67, 75, 93, 94, 97
and race 55–6
and Skiffle 13
in the work of Cecil Sharp 9 (*see also* Sharp, Cecil)
coal mining 7, 11, 15, 20, 37, 46, 61–2, 68, 69, 70–82
after nationalization 55, 61–2, 70–82
as part of Tyneside culture 20, 61–2
the Pit Elegy 61–2, 70, 79–82
romanticization of 76–8
as a subject of folk music 7, 11, 37, 61–2, 68, 69, 76–82
tensions with the Labour Party 70–5
Cold War, the 44–5, 132. *See also* Campaign for Nuclear Disarmament (CND); Vietnam War, the
anti-Communist feeling in Britain 44–5
Colls, Robert 70, 83, 86, 92, 93, 94, 95, 124
on Durham and the Northeast 83, 86, 92, 93, 94
on Dylan and MacColl 124
on importance and decline of the coal industry 70, 95
on regionalism in England 83
consumer culture 2, 14, 46, 50, 61, 62–3, 64, 66, 67, 81, 86, 97, 111–12, 115, 132. *See also* Abrams, Mark; Hoggart, Richard; Zweig, Ferdynand
the 'affluent worker' 66
and fears of Americanization 14, 67, 97, 132
and folk music 111–12, 115
growth after the Second World War 2, 46, 61, 62
influence on class 62–3, 86

leftist views on 50, 63, 67
the teenage consumer 64
copyright 15, 118–20, 160 n.634
arguments over 118–20
and the BBC 160 n.634
complications for folk music 118–20
"A Reel of Recording Tape" 119–20

Dallas, Karl (aka "Fred") 2, 5, 7, 21, 53, 58, 106, 124
on Ewan MacColl 106
on growth of folk clubs 21
Durham (County) 7, 9, 37, 38, 69, 70, 71, 72–5, 76–81, 82, 83, 88, 92, 93–4, 96, 132
local character 94
mining 9, 37, 69, 70, 72–5, 78, 82, 93 (*see also* coal mining; nationalization of coal)
musical traditions and folk songs 37, 69, 70, 71, 76–81, 88, 92, 94, 132 (*see also* Elliott, Jack)
regional identity 83, 93–4, 96, 132
Dylan, Bob 15, 24, 25, 33, 41, 52, 54, 55, 103, 104, 124, 125–7, 128, 131, 133
betrayal of folk music 125–7, 131
emergence as a celebrity 24, 25, 52, 124, 128
Ewan MacColl on 104, 124
on fear of nuclear war 54
1966 tour 125–7

Elliott, Jack 7, 20, 31, 37, 38, 76, 77–8, 79, 82, 88, 94, 102
authenticity 77, 88, 94, 102
family 7, 20, 37, 38, 77
"Farewell to Cotia" 76, 79, 82
relationship with Ewan MacColl 77–8, 94
Songs and Stories of a Durham Miner 77
The Elliotts of Birtley: A Musical Portrait of a Durham Mining Family 77–8, 94. *See also* Elliott, Jack
English Folk Dance and Song Society (EFDSS) 8, 9, 23–5, 40–1, 45, 71, 77, 96. *See also* Folk Song Society (FSS)

development of 9
English Dance and Song 25
Folk Music Journal 77
organization of Keele festival 40–1
Ethnic 26, 27, 40, 119
on copyright 119
establishment of 27

Festival of Britain 4, 49–50, 67, 71, 87
the 'anthropological turn' 87
Come All Ye Bold Miners 71
Labour ideology 49–50, 67
Festival of Labour 4, 49, 67
folk club 18–24, 39, 40, 41, 56, 68–9, 76,
94, 98, 104–7, 109, 122, 123
growth of revival folk clubs 18–24
as indicator of revival's health 39
MacColl on his new club 22
and MacColl's policy 98, 104–7, 109
(*see also* MacColl, Ewan)
in the Northeast 76, 94
social composition of 56, 68–9
Folk Review 27–8, 37
Folk Song Society (FSS) 2, 8, 84. *See also*
English Folk Dance and Song
Society (EFDSS)
Frankfurt School 112–13, 115

Gaitskell, Hugh 47–8
grassroots 6–7, 17–19, 24, 44, 51, 59, 123,
128, 130, 132–4
as antithesis to mass culture 7, 18, 128,
133
as central tenet of English revival 7,
17–19, 44, 51, 123, 130, 132–4
folk club culture 19
Guardian, the 1, 40, 50, 68, 88
association with the Left 50
on folk festivals 40
on the folk revival 1, 68
on regionalism of folk music 88
Guthrie, Woody 32–3, 52, 99, 101–3, 104,
105, 106, 119, 124–7
influence on Bob Dylan 125–7
influence on British folk 32–3, 99,
101–3

Hall, Stuart 47, 49, 56–7, 59, 63–4
the New Left 47, 49

the *New Left Review* 47, 49
on persistence of class divisions 63–4
on racism in Britain 56–7, 59
Handle, Johnny 29, 68, 76, 78, 80, 81, 82,
88, 92, 107. *See also* High Level
Ranters, the
class appropriation 81, 88
"Farewell to the Monty" 80
on Northeast music 29, 68, 76, 78, 92
High Level Ranters, the 19, 31, 37, 80, 91,
107. *See also* Handle, Johnny
"Farewell to the Monty" 80
MacColl folk club policy 107
Newcastle Folk Club 19
on *Radio Ballads* 37
Hobsbawm, Eric 12, 14, 61, 95
invention of tradition 12, 95
on postwar capitalism 61
on Skiffle 14
Hoggart, Richard 14, 17, 65–7, 93, 95,
97–8, 109, 112
cultural conservatism 14, 97–8
on dangers of Americanization 67,
97–8, 109
The Uses of Literacy 93
on working-class culture 17, 65–7, 93,
95, 112

International Folk Music Council (IFMC)
10, 39–40
collaboration with the BBC 39–40
(*see also* British Broadcasting
Corporation)
definition of folk song 10
The Iron Muse 57
and redefinition of English folk music
57

jazz 2, 6, 13–14, 19, 24, 38, 53, 63, 98,
101–2, 107, 112, 132
Adorno on 112
as American musical import 13–14, 38,
99, 102, 132
as precursor to folk revival 6, 13–14,
19, 24, 38, 99, 101–2, 107
Joshi, Shirley 56
on racism in postwar Britain 56

Kennedy, Peter 30, 34, 36, 45

Labour Party, the 3, 4, 13, 15, 44, 45, 46,
　　47, 48, 50, 51, 52, 62, 63, 70, 72,
　　74–5, 81, 129
　　Centre 42 project 50
　　the Festival of Britain 50
　　the Festival of Labour 4
　　first majority and Welfare State 46,
　　　　62, 72
　　focus on working class and 'English
　　　　Problem' 13, 44, 45–7, 51, 63
　　history of 4
　　leadership of Hugh Gaitskell 48
　　nationalization of industry 15, 70, 72,
　　　　74–5, 81, 131
　　tensions with the New Left 3, 47, 129
Leader, Bill 31
　　Leader Sound 31, 77
Lloyd, Albert Lancaster (A. L.) 4, 5, 9, 19,
　　22–3, 28, 30–1, 40, 41, 44–5, 50,
　　65, 69–70, 71–2, 73, 76–7, 78, 80,
　　101, 102, 103, 104, 105, 119, 131,
　　132
　　Centre 42 project 50
　　on commercialization of folk music
　　　　119
　　Folk Song in England 4, 70
　　on growth of folk movement 19, 40
　　on industrial workers' songs 4, 9, 44–5,
　　　　65, 69–70, 72, 76–7, 80–1, 132
　　influence on the English folk revival 5,
　　　　6, 71–2, 76, 80, 88, 102, 131–2
　　as performer 22–3
　　relationship with the BBC 28, 35–6,
　　　　104 (*see also* British Broadcasting
　　　　Corporation)
　　relationship with the WMA 30–1,
　　　　81 (*see also* Worker's Music
　　　　Association)
　　Songs of the Durham Miners 76
Lomax, Alan 6, 30, 35, 36, 45, 90, 99, 100,
　　101, 104, 116–17
　　Ballads and Blues 100
　　A Ballad Hunter Looks at Britain 35,
　　　　90, 100
　　influence on folk revival 6, 35–6, 45,
　　　　90, 99, 101
　　on mass produced folk music 116–17
　　promotion of American folk music
　　　　100

relationship with the BBC 30, 35,
　　100, 101, 104 (*see also* British
　　Broadcasting Corporation)
Lomax, John 115, 120–1
　　relationship with Leadbelly 120–1
　　technology and folk song collection
　　　　115

MacColl, Ewan 7, 20, 21–2, 23, 33, 36,
　　40, 44, 52, 54, 58, 77, 96, 101, 103,
　　105–9, 121, 124, 131
　　anti-Americanism 23, 124
　　"Ballad of Ho Chi Minh" 54
　　"The Ballad of Joe Stalin" 44
　　Ballads and Blues 101
　　Ballads and Blues Club 20
　　on Bob Dylan 124 (*see also* Dylan,
　　　　Bob)
　　collaboration with BBC and Alan
　　　　Lomax 36, 101 (*see also* British
　　　　Broadcasting Corporation)
　　as collector 77, 96, 131
　　and the Elliott family 20 (*see also*
　　　　Elliott, Jack)
　　establishment of Singers Club 21–2, 23
　　on the folk boom 7
　　influence on folk revival 20, 33, 77, 102
　　on mass production of folk music 121
　　My People and Your People 58
　　nationalist folk club policy 105–9
　　Radio Ballads 37
　　relationship with Peggy Seeger 103 (*see
　　　　also* Seeger, Peggy)
　　The Song Carriers 38
mass culture 14, 15, 27, 37, 50–1, 65, 67,
　　86–7, 95, 111–15, 117–21, 123,
　　125–6, 128, 129
　　American influence 14, 98, 123
　　Bob Dylan 125–6, 128 (*see also* Dylan,
　　　　Bob)
　　celebrity and folk culture 113, 125
　　the culture industry 113, 128 (*see also*
　　　　Adorno, Theodor)
McLuhan, Marshall 117
　　and Leftist ideology 65, 67
　　tension with folk music 50–1, 86–7,
　　　　111–15, 117–21, 128
Melody Maker 7, 18, 19, 24–5, 31, 39, 52,
　　104, 121–2, 124–6

on accents 104 (*see also* accent)

on Bob Dylan 124–6 (*see also* Dylan, Bob)

on growth in number of folk clubs 19

on the influence of American folk revival 39, 52, 104

on performance of class in folk music 121–2 (*see also* class)

role in reporting on folk revival in England 24–5

Morris, William 8, 49

on art and Socialism 8

influence on the New Left 49

National Coal Board (NCB) 62, 71–2

participation in the Festival of Britain 71–2 (*see also* Festival of Britain)

nationalization of coal 4, 15, 16, 61, 62, 70–5, 78, 82, 130, 131, 152 n.430

Clause IV 72

ideological importance of 78

Labour Party ideology 70–5 (*see also* Labour Party)

mine closures 61, 70–5, 82, 130 (*see also* coal mining)

miners' opinions of 61, 70–5, 78, 82, 131 (*see also* coal mining)

New Left, the 3, 4, 14, 43, 46, 47, 48–9, 50, 51, 52, 53, 54, 55, 60, 67, 82, 83, 93, 117, 132, 133

importance of culture to 50, 67

and media 117, 133

and music 14, 43, 46, 48–9, 51, 52, 53, 54, 55, 132, 133

relationship with Labour Party 47–8

relationship with *New Left Review* 43, 47–8, 49 (*see also* New Left Review)

in the US 4, 43, 54, 55, 93

youth culture 4, 47, 48–9, 52, 54, 60, 132

New Left Review, the (*NLR*) 37, 43, 48, 49

on folk music ("Songs of the People") 37, 43

on importance of culture 49

tensions with Gaitskell Labour Party 48

New York Times, the 11, 40, 92

on the American folk revival 11

on the English folk revival 40

Pete Seeger Obituary 92 (*See* Seeger, Pete)

Northeast (region) 4, 15, 29, 31, 62, 70–2, 75–8, 83, 85, 88–9, 91–3, 94–6, 131, 132

association with coal mining 62, 70, 72, 75–8, 94–6, 132 (*see also* coal mining; nationalization of coal)

folk 'scene' in 29, 72, 75–8, 83, 88–9, 91–3

as location of renewed interest in folk collecting 4, 15, 29, 62, 70–2, 75–8, 83, 85, 88–9, 91–3, 94–6 (*see also* The Iron Muse; Lloyd, A. L.)

as political symbol 15, 62, 70, 83, 91–3, 96, 131

Topic Records interest in 31, 88–9

Parker, Charles 38, 103. *See also* British Broadcasting Corporation (BBC)

intervention on behalf of Peggy Seeger 103 (*see also* Seeger, Peggy)

The Song Carriers 38

Purdon, Jock 79, 82

on closure of Harraton Colliery ("Cotia") 79

on pit closures and the 'end of an era' 82

regional identity 15, 19–20, 83–7, 90, 93–5, 129, 131

as part of Folk Revival 15, 83–7, 90, 93–5, 129, 131

Somerset 84–5, 87, 94, 132

Tyneside 14, 19–20, 76–7, 79, 88, 107

Rosselson, Leon 48, 53

"Battle Hymn of the New Socialist Party" 48

"Dear John Profumo" 53

Seeger, Peggy 11, 20, 23, 58–9, 68, 69, 82, 94, 103, 105–6, 108, 116

on class and folk music 68–9, 82 (*see also* class)

Elliotts of Birtley 20, 94 (*see also* Elliott, Jack)

on the idea of a folk "idiom" 11

on national traditions and 'the policy' 105–6, 108

on Notting Hill Riot and racism in Britain 58–9

on oral transmission 116
relationship and collaboration with
    Ewan MacColl 58, 69, 103 (*see also*
    MacColl, Ewan)
UK Visa issues 103 (*see also* British
    Broadcasting Corporation;
    Kennedy, Peter)
Seeger, Pete 9, 11, 21, 25, 27, 31, 33, 44–5,
    52, 53, 92, 99, 106, 108, 118
    Albert Hall concert 21
    on Aldermaston 53 (*see also* Campaign
        for Nuclear Disarmament)
    blacklisting 44–5
    on the development of topical
        songwriting in Britain 52, 108
    featured in magazine advertisements
        31
    folk music definition 9
    on importance of community 92
    relationship with the BBC 27 (*see also*
        British Broadcasting Corporation)
    on the role of technology and the
        collector in folk music 118
Sharp, Cecil 2, 4, 8, 11, 35, 39, 40, 83, 85,
    95, 104, 131, 132
    Cecil Sharp House 23, 39, 40 (*see
        also* English Folk Dance and Song
        Society)
    early collection of folk music and the
        FSS 2, 4, 8, 83, 95, 132 (*see also* Folk
        Song Society)
    influence on postwar folk revival and
        reputation 11, 95, 131, 132
    interest in Appalachians 35, 85, 104
    socialism 2, 8
    work with Maud Karpeles 85
Sing 7, 19, 20, 21, 22, 23, 25–6, 27, 29, 30,
    31, 32, 37, 40, 53, 54, 58–9, 77, 83,
    88, 89, 102–3, 105, 108, 119, 127
    on American influence 102–3, 105,
        108
    on Bob Dylan 127
    development and mission 25–6
    financial difficulty 29
    on folk festivals 40
    on folk singers' roots 89
    on the growth of folk clubs 23
    on Northeast folk music 88
    on plagiarism 119

on racism in Britain 58–9
Sing Out! 25, 26, 29, 31, 32, 52, 68, 108,
    119–20, 125
    on copyright 119–20
    distribution in England 32
    Ewan MacColl interview with Irwin
        Silber 68
    influence on English folk publications
        25, 26, 58
    "Open Letter to Bob Dylan" 125
skiffle 2, 6, 13–14, 19–20, 53, 58, 99, 106
    American influence 99, 106
    history of 13–14
    influence on folk revival 19–20
sociology 12, 65, 67, 87, 93
    and the 'anthropological turn' 87
    connection to the folk revival 65
    importance to the New Left 65, 67
    nostalgia 12
    working class culture 65, 67, 93
Spin 26, 28–9
    circulation and readership 29
    establishment of 28–9
Spinners, The 20, 23, 25, 31, 56, 57, 91
    on race and the colour bar 57
Springfield, Dusty 25
    on the folk boom 25

technology 84, 113, 115, 116, 118, 125,
    129, 131, 133
    and the culture industry 113 (*see also*
        Adorno, Theodor)
    and folk music collection 115, 117
    importance to distribution of folk
        music 131, 133
    and oral tradition 84, 115, 116, 118,
        131
topical songwriting 10, 14, 51, 52, 54,
    55–60, 132. *See also* Campaign for
    Nuclear Disarmament; Vietnam
    War, the
Topic Records 30, 31, 88, 131
    financial difficulty 31
    as premier folk label 30
    promotion of regional material 88, 131
    relationship with Bill Leader 31 (*see
        also* Leader, Bill)
    relationship with the WMA 30 (*see
        also* Worker's Music Association)

tradition 4, 8, 9, 10–11, 12–13, 14, 19–20,
27–9, 33–6, 38, 40–1, 45, 52, 57,
60, 67, 70–1, 72, 76, 78, 79, 81, 83,
84–5, 87, 88–92, 94, 95, 99, 100–4,
106–8, 111, 115–16, 122, 128, 130,
131–2
  Ewan MacColl on 11, 22, 38, 106–7,
  122 (*see also* MacColl, Ewan)
folk music 4, 8, 9, 10–11, 12, 18, 19–20,
21, 27–9, 33–6, 38, 40–1, 45, 52,
57, 60, 67, 70–2, 76, 78, 79, 81, 83,
84–5, 87, 88–92, 94, 95, 99, 100–4,
106–8, 115–16, 122, 128, 131–2
invention of 12, 46, 130, 131–2
national identity 8, 14, 21, 45, 60, 84,
95, 99, 100–4, 106–8
nostalgia 12–13, 49, 99
oral transmission 8, 10, 115–16, 128
regional identity 20, 36, 72, 76, 78, 79,
88–92, 94, 95
relationship with authenticity 11, 14,
111
role of Cecil Sharp in defining 9, 84–5

Vietnam War, the 43, 44, 54, 60, 146 n.284
political organizations formed in
response to 146 n.284
songs about 54

Williams, Raymond 47, 49, 67, 92, 109,
112
on community 92
'cultural Marxism' 49, 109, 112
Culture and Society 67
Winter, Eric 21, 24, 25, 26, 28, 32, 37,
39–40, 152 n.422
on 'The Ballad of John Axon' 37
on growth of folk movement in
England 26, 39–40
on Pete Seeger 32
on the political leanings of *Sing*
magazine 26
on relationship with American folk
music 25
review of *Now is the Time for Fishing*
152 n.422
on tensions within the folk movement
21
Worker's Music Association (WMA) 26,
30–1, 45
establishment of 45
relationship with Topic Records 30–1

Zweig, Ferdynand 65–6, 73
the 'affluent worker' 65–6